© Max Lamirande, 2024
Published by Max Lamirande
Edited by Kevin Plaisance, MD
Edited by Eric Roser

© 2024 Saguenay, Quebec, Canada

All rights reserved. No part of this book may be reproduced or modified in any form, including photocopying, recording, or by any information storage and retrieval system, without permission in writing from the publisher.

Cover image copyrights:
Alamy - F2AH3X – Standard Licence
Order reference: OY98902485

Cover image copyrights:
Alamy - BHN99M Standard license
Order reference: OY98902471

Dear Reader,

Welcome to the third installment of the WW1 Alternate Series. I am writing to you from Bryce Canyon, another beautiful American spot. U.S. National Parks are something else entirely. I am on a writing and hiking trip. First, I did Zion, and now Bryce; tomorrow driving to Valley of Fire and will finish with Red Rock Canyon near Vegas.

As we get into 1915, the major changes I have made to the real historical timeline make it a totally different story. The Italians are now part of the Central Powers, Paris is occupied, the Russians are not doing so bad, are on the offensive, and much more.

Things were already interesting, now they will be even more. The front in the West is now a stalemate from Italy to Germany, but that does not mean we are not going to have any action.

We'll also get to experience the first Zeppelin raids on London, the first poison gas attack somewhere in Poland, and the Romanian offensive into Transylvania.

The Greeks will enter into play with an interesting bit of info I found in my research about their navy. We'll get to see Rommel in action just like in the real historical timeline, and many more. Ah! Don't forget naval battles: we'll see if von Spee can escape Togo's clutches, or else the British intercept him in the Eastern Pacific. Perhaps the Austro-Hungarians will even use their own fleet and try to break the Allied blockade of the Adriatic; we will see.

One thing is certain, you will again have a lot of action to process, and I promise you won't want to put down your book once again.

Also, THANK YOU for reading my work, and thank you for taking the time to review my books.

PROLOGUE

Taranto Enclave
Apulia, French 14th Division January 14th, 1915

The bullets zipped by Armand and Philippe as they walked nervously, rifles in hand, on the uneven ground. The sun was bright in the sky, but the two men couldn't see it as they were lost in the battle's maelstrom and the dark cloud of smoke enveloping the no man's land.

The sound of the passing bullets naturally urged them to drop to the ground and hide, but they knew their NCO wouldn't permit it. Behind them, their yelling Sergeant urged them forward. The ground shook hard from the falling artillery, threatening to unhinge their sanity. Then, there was smoke everywhere, to the point where it was a little difficult to find their way across the heavy dark pall and the dust thrown up in the air by the enemy guns and the fighting.

The French 14th Division was attacking the Italian trench systems north of Taranto in southern Italy. The unit had landed there back in the first part of November, along with about 80,000 Allied soldiers during Operation Ares. The first objective of the attack had been the destruction and the capture of the Italian fleet. This had been executed successfully, but they had stayed there, the generals above them deciding to try and break the Italian defenses to conquer the area and try to knock Rome out of the war.

But so far, things were not working out as planned. The Italians had been pretty good at building up a trench line defense, and now the result was that the Allies were banging their heads repeatedly in one futile attack after the other. To the generals and admirals (battleships supported their attack by shelling the shoreline when it was in range), it seemed they progressed, as from one week to the next, they succeeded in taking a trench, a few yards of ground. But for men like Armand and Philippe, the entire endeavor was pure folly.

For they were the ones doing the fighting and the dying with their comrades. Every time they stepped out of the trench on the makeshift wooden ladder, they were met with a wall of bullet fire and exploding shells. Once in a while, some of the guys stormed an enemy trench, and they rejoiced.

But it didn't seem like this would be the case today. Italian shell fire was a lot heavier than usual, and Armand saw men in front of him literally disintegrate in a powerful, blinding explosion. The rumor mill had it that the Germans had sent shells and supplies to their new allies, along with fresh troops. If this was the case, it didn't bode well for the Allied enclave but, more to the point, for Armand and Philippe.

All around, the ordinance was falling; it was so heavy that it became difficult to stay on their feet. Armand was pretty sure it was his time to die, and he just droned ahead. But then Phillipe, who had an uncanny ability to keep a cool head even in this vortex of fire and death, yelled at him. *"Bonnier, for Christ's sake. I've been yelling at you for a while now. The Sarge is dead! No one's forcing us forward!"* Armand turned and, between two blasts (he was again miraculously untouched), saw that he was the only guy standing around. Everyone else either was dead or was out of sight, taking cover as best they could. *"Come on, Bonnier,"* urged Cren again. *"Don't you die on me now!"* And then, his sluggish brain started to register that his friend was right. There was no need to stay up and attack; no one watched over them anymore.

His brain finally snapped back to reality, and he looked for a hiding place. About ten feet from him lay a still smoking shell crater, and he jumped into it.

The shelling and the banging continued for some time, and Armand clutched his rifle to his chest while he stayed glued with his back on the ground. Then, eventually (he'd lost track of time), the explosions, ground shaking, and the overbearing noises abated. *"Come on, Bonnier, the Dago's have stopped firing, and there's still enough smoke for their fucking machine gunners to miss us"* Armand rolled to the side, lifted himself up, and started walking back across the maze of craters, dead bodies, blood and body parts, all the way back to their starting trench. What a mess it was.

25th Brigade Royal Field Artillery
113th RFA Battery, January 20th, 1915

Private gunner Archibald Tottenkam was thoughtful as his gun was unlimbered from its horse carriage in the darkness. He wondered when the battle would be joined once more for him and his men. Looking toward the northern horizon, he saw ominous flashes followed by loud sounds like distant thunder. The 113th RFA Royal Field Artillery Gun Battery had been ordered to move north and closer to the frontline because the higher-ups wanted to start pounding the Italian rear areas to disrupt their supplies. No amount of shelling on the trenches had dislodged any of them thus far, and so a change of strategy was warranted, the Captain said. He'd also been told by his own superior, Lieutenant-Colonel A. L. Schreiber, who commanded the 25th Brigade, of which Archie's battery unit was a part of.

Archie was the son of a factory worker in London, like many of his comrade soldiers in the British Army. He, like everyone in his neighborhood, was destined for hard labor and a life of sweating in the dreary factories of the English capital. He'd seen his dad's worn face as he came home from work every day and had decided that this was not for him, and thus, one day, he had listened to one of the British Army recruiters who came by their church every Sunday and decided to join. *"You will see the world and travel,"* the man had told him. *"You will have exciting adventures,"* he'd added. All of it was true, but perhaps a little too much to Archie's tastes. He'd already seen enough "adventure" and war to last him a lifetime.

The 18-pounder team he was part of worked hard and quickly, and when they were done, they slept right by their gun, as ordered by Lance-Bombardier Stimms. The grass still held the warmth of the day (winter in Southern Italy was quite mild), and they felt good resting before what they anticipated would be a rough artillery gun exchange with the Italians. He dreamt of glory and women, and of blood and gore.

The distant sounds of thunder suddenly grew closer as if they appeared by magic. Archie and the men from the other lined-up guns in the battery sprang to alert. Muffled explosions were heard near the 113th's positions, and the experienced men like Archie immediately sensed something familiar and dangerous. They were sensing the rare possibility of a night-time encounter with the enemy that they'd seen countless times during the terrible fall campaign in France.

The other men in the battery (the four other guns around Archie's) also started to get excited. The genuine sounds of artillery were not cinematic but an omen of something unknown and terrible. The men of the Regiment were especially frightened because the fire seemed to come from all sides. It didn't seem obvious where the Italians fired from, even if intellectually, they knew they did so from the north.

Archie's heart pounded like crazy, like every other time when he knew an enemy artillery barrage was coming. *"Do we fire now?"* asked one of the loaders, private William Bitten, to no one in particular. Then, he addressed Stimms. *"Lance-Bombardier, are we firing?"* The man's voice was shaky, riddled with fear. It was still dark, and no one had the slightest clue where they were. *"Shut up, Bitten,"* grumbled Lance-Bombardier Stimms. The man was not a friendly NCO. *"We aren't being shot at yet. The Italians must be distant since regimental command unloaded us here."* Bitten was still worried. "You can't really tell. Look at those explosions in the distance." *"Bitten, last warning,"* countered Stimms. *"The next time you'll get hit by rifle butt."* That shut the kid up.

Then, the order came to fire, and all of their nervousness dissipated. Their training took over, and the men went about getting the multitude of 18-pounder guns ready to fire. Half a minute after the firing order was passed, the British guns belched their artillery rounds at the pre-determined distances the soldiers had been told to prepare. In artillery warfare, it was common to set up pre-determined firing areas, so it was easy for spotters and reconnaissance to give very specific firing coordinates to the artillerymen. The night disappeared as the gun muzzles blasted away in the sky. Archie's view switched from night to day for over ten seconds as the flashes from the cannons vanquished the darkness in a succession of bangs and blasts of fireballs. They continued to fire their shells northward and kept it up for another twenty minutes. Apparently, the coordinates they were firing at had been decided by aerial spotting. Archie thought it strange, but he remembered those aircraft flying above their position earlier during the day as they moved their weapon north. Then, the stop-firing order was passed down.

The men rapidly went from frantic loading and firing to looking at the distant sky, where their last few shell explosions blossomed. Then, the sound of distant thunder created by their attack faded away, and they were left with the heavy cordite smell and lingering smoke that soon whispered itself into a fog.

The sunrise a couple of hours later quickly became a bright, crisp winter day and the men were able to have some breakfast first from the bread distributed by a couple of ordinance guys. Then, the regimental cooks rapidly went to work making more consistent food for the men. As soon as Archie and his comrades were seated in front of their mess kits, they heard a low and throbbing rumble that quickly grew in the distance, coming from the north.

They scrambled for cover, and about ten seconds later, enemy shells began to whistle through the air. Several of the officers, including Lance-Bombardier Stimms, yelled for the men to take cover. In the exposed plain (they were in the middle of a farm field), it meant flattening themselves to the ground or in one of the shallowly dug trenches near the 18-pounders. Powerful explosions erupted everywhere. Millions of hissing and treacherously whistling shell splinters flew all around, and the largest fragments cleanly cut through the line of wooden crates lined up near their positions. It felt like a storm of debris was suddenly engulfing the area Archie and his comrades were in.

Then the whistling sound stopped, and the explosions abated. Archie stood up but quite shakily. He just stood there, marveling at the power of multiple explosions. He understood that when he fired, he was delivering the same terrible results to the poor sods on the other side, and he wondered why the hell they all could not agree on a peace so that they could go home to their families.

The men eventually recovered their senses and finished their breakfast when the battery's senior officer came down and ordered Stimms to get the men prepared. They had new coordinates for the guns to fire on and had received a full complement of shells. Thus, they would splatter the bastards who had tried to destroy them.

Berlin Imperial Palace
Rommel and the Kaiser, January 14th

Newly minted Captain Erwin Rommel was walked into the palace. As he did, he looked at the bright and luxurious decorations, statues, paintings, and the expensive lacquered wood floor. He marveled at the design of the place. Having considered a career as an engineer before joining the Imperial Army, he could appreciate all the work done to make this place what it was.

The man walking with him was one of the palace officials gravitating around the Kaiser and responsible for his schedule. Being nice enough, Rommel found the man stiff and unsmiling, which was fine. He was used to that in the military.

Rommel was a dynamic man and was chomping at the bit to get back to the fighting. As Captain, he had a new posting in Italy, and he very much looked forward to getting to his unit and fighting the French some more.

They walked up to a large wooden, intricately carved double door flanked by two ceremonial palace guards. The two men opened them, and they gave way to his destination, the Kaiser's study.

The room was surprisingly humble for an Emperor, revealing three high windows opening to the palace gardens (giving a nice view of everything, since they took all of the back wall space), a nice rug, and a few maps, including a globe of the Earth. Above the small wooden desk full of paperwork hung a portrait of Frederick III, the 99-day Emperor and Wilhelm's father. The man had only reigned for a short period before dying, hence his nickname.

The Kaiser was standing in the middle of the room, all smiles. He was dressed in his all-white German Navy uniform, adorned with medals. *"Here is the hero that stormed a British battleship,"* started Wilhelm, opening both his arms in a welcome gesture. "Thank you, Gottard," he said to the palace official. The man, excused, bowed slightly and exited the room. The double doors closed.

"Your Majesty," said Rommel. "You bestow too much honor on me with your presence; I am only but a simple soldier."

"Stop being too modest, Captain. What you did is nothing short of extraordinary, and I wanted to see for myself the man who pulled off this amazing feat," countered the Kaiser.

"Come sit; I want to hear everything about you, the assault on Hibernia, and your next posting. As Emperor, I have to talk to and understand my brave soldiers," continued the German leader.

Rommel blushed and followed his Emperor to the two couches at the back of the room, where teas and pastries were awaiting them on a small stool. He decided that it wouldn't be so bad to befriend the master of Germany.

Luftschiffbau Zeppelin company
Friedrichshafen, Southern Germany, January 15th, 1914

The old General-become-inventor Count Ferdinand von Zeppelin walked right beside the giant sliding door as one of his impressive-looking inventions slid silently out of the large, 400-foot-long by 70-foot-high hangar. The building was massive, complete with support buildings on the side (machine shops and other facilities for the building to manufacture the airship inside a big space).

The 310-foot-long LZ35 airship with a 117-foot control car attached to its underbelly (the section where the crew and the engines were located below the inflated structure) was a true marvel of engineering. The thing was called a Zeppelin, having received the name of its builder, Count Ferdinand. Commanded by Hauptmann Konrad Masius, LZ35 was an M Class Zeppelin, the latest in a long version of models the Count had perfected over the years since the start of his company in 1896.

For the old man who now needed a cane to walk, the machine taking slowly to the sky as it completed its slow exit from the hangar was the pinnacle of his achievement. The Zeppelin Company had always struggled to get any type of governmental funding, but since the war began, there was no shortage of money thrown at him in order to make more and more Zeppelins. The Count couldn't complain since it was finally his chance to make it big. The Army and even the Navy couldn't get enough.

The small town of Friedrichshafen was booming with construction. In the background, over seven more gigantic hangars were being built in order to ramp up the production of the large flying machines. The city itself was nestled on the shores of Lake Constance, and it was a beautiful, quiet place. But now, the war had come to it, and it was busy like the townspeople had never seen before. There were even talk of building airplanes in the area.

"Every time I see one fly out, I am amazed by their grace and beauty, Sir," said his general manager and business partner, Adolf Udet. "Indeed, I feel the same as well, Adolf," answered the Count.

Zeppelin LZ35 was bound for Gontrode base, forty kilometers northwest of Brussels, at an airfield built by the German occupation forces at the end of 1914. The base, initially made only for fighters, had been recently expanded with several support airship hangars to house a Zeppelin airfield.

It was about to make history with the first aerial bombing mission over London.

Istanbul (Constantinople)
Sirkeci train station, near Topkapi Palace January 18th, 1915

The Sirkeci train station was Istanbul's European terminus and was also where the famous Orient Express passenger train stopped, while passengers had to disembark to get on a new train on the other side of the Strait of the Bosphorus. Built in the late 19th century, it was a modern station and was considered one of the most beautiful in the world. Designed by a Prussian architect, it was a perfect mix of European modernity mingled with Ottoman architecture.

The three most powerful Pachas (title of a Turkish officer of high rank) of the Ottoman Empire were on the dock, awaiting the large train on its stop. Beside them was a full-ranked German General, also waiting alongside the three Turkish officials

Enver Pacha was the War Minister and de-facto Turkish Commander-in-Chief of the Army. The Sultan was the official one but held no power since the coup d'etat of 1913 that saw the Committee for Union and Progress rise to power. The other two Pachas were Talaat Pacha, the Interior Minister, heading the civilian affairs of the government, and Cemal Pacha, the Minister of the Navy.

The three men controlled the Grand Vizir, who was supposed to be the head of the Ottoman state and responsible for executing Sultan Mehmed V's will. Enver, who had studied in Germany, could freely communicate in the German language and had thus been one of the prime movers in the Germano-Turkish treaty of alliance the year before.

The fourth official was a German General called Otto Liman von Sanders. The man was the head of the German military mission to the Ottoman Empire to help the Turks modernize their army. He had arrived in 1913 and had been working ever since on getting the Turks on even ground with European armies, which was no small task. Many Europeans had tried before him, with varying degrees of success. But he was getting somewhere, and the Turks weren't as bad as they had been only a few years before during the Balkan Wars.

The train screeched to a halt in a flurry of billowing smoke, and then the dozens of wagon's side doors started to open, with German NCOs beginning to yell their orders for the men to exit the train and get into formation. *"It is as you promised, General von Sanders,"* said Enver with a smile. *"Indeed, Your Excellency,"* answered the German officer. *"Many more trains like this should arrive in the next few days, and the 87th Imperial Division should be complete with a few gun units, as we discussed. Also the promised arms shipments of Mauser rifles and Maxim machine guns should be forthcoming as well. Once we are done, we should be able to push the Russians away."*

Since the fall of Serbia, Germany could send a large number of troops to help their flailing Ottoman ally by rail because they now had a land connection. Before that the only thing they had been able to move to Turkey had been Admiral Souchon's ships. These men were the first of the so-called "Asia Korps," a group of German soldiers designated to fight in the Ottoman Empire. They were finally getting around to do it with the troops freed by the victory in the West.

Enver Pacha was desperate to cover for the disaster in the Caucasus and had been busy burying the evidence of the losses with disinformation. Thus, the arrival of the German troops was a step in that direction, and he was internally proud of himself. He'd worked hard for this, having traveled to Berlin in December 1914 to meet with the Kaiser and proffer his request for support. These new soldiers were earmarked to move to the East and to fight the limited Russian offensive that was underway since the terrible Sarikamish defeat in the late fall of 1914. If it could be stopped, reasoned Enver, then the rest would be forgotten.

The soldiers started to line up in two single files on the docks. An officer walked to the three Pachas and von Sanders, saluting. *"General von Sanders,"* said the man (he was a Colonel). *"The first troops are ready for your review." "Very well, Colonel,"* answered the German General.

The four men and the newly arrived officers thus walked between the men standing at the ready, rifles on their shoulders. Enver inwardly smiled at the thought that these pristine German soldiers would make everything right.

4th Imperial Russian Army
Siege of Przemysl Part 1, January 20th, 1915

Private soldier Dmitri Fedorov shivered uncontrollably from the damned cold seeping into the very fiber of his being. As a Russian, he was used to it, but his discomfort was so extreme that it was hard to take his mind off it. The 16th Imperial Division was in the same trench, give or take about forty feet from where they'd advanced since the start of the Siege of Przemysl. The only good thing about the dreaded winter was that lice and other vermin were either frozen solid or dead. Thus, the scratching was not as bad as it was during the summer heat, at least. For a moment, he wondered which he hated the most. Was it the vermin, or the cold?

Fedorov, a factory worker from Moscow, had been mobilized like many of his fellow countrymen for the war. He'd gone to battle with enthusiasm, but he now laughed at the person he once had been. It was beyond stupid to be excited to go fight in this godforsaken war. He looked to his right, where Sergeant Radetzki lay, his face as unreadable as before. If the man was uncomfortable, but he didn't show it, and had never heard him complain about it.

He wondered if this would one day end. It was hard to believe the war was only entering its sixth month. From his perspective and the one of most of his comrades, they had already had enough and should be heading for home by now. Enough dead friends, terribly gory scenes, stupid officers and their orders... He had gone through it all and couldn't believe it was going to continue for the immediate future.

And yet, Imperial Russia was winning. The frontline ran from the Baltic to Galicia, and they had Austria-Hungary on the ropes. They even had the Germans on the backfoot in front of Koenigsberg, again, according to official news. Now the Romanians, according to the news, had joined in and were attacking in force south of the 16th Division's position in Transylvania. He hoped that they could win a decisive battle in Przemysl, as there were, apparently, over 100,000 enemy soldiers still trapped in the fortress (the estimates spoke of 20,000 enemy casualties since the start of the siege). This meant that if they took the city, they would eliminate a full Austro-Hungarian Army and potentially have them sue for peace.

They had been assaulting and or besieging the city-fortress for over three months now, and Fedorov and his comrades were desperate to finish this battle. From their meager, snow-covered trenches and field fortifications, they saw the columns of smoke climbing to the sky from the many chimneys in Przemysl. God, did he want a fire to warm his bones.

Words came down the line, giving orders to the lieutenants in charge of the platoon, and soon, those lieutenants gave their instructions to the NCOs like Radetzki. The man instantly started barking orders at them to get ready. *"Let's go, you maggots; get ready; we're attacking again,"* he continued, kicking some of the soldiers who took time to move up from their prone positions. Dimitri's mind preferred to pretend that nothing was amiss, but the fears and the expectations coming before every battle soon overcame his senses. He stood up, facing the ladder that would bring him over the lip of the trench and into Hell itself. He looked right at the frozen bit of ground facing him and tried to stay sane with a couple of deep breaths. What awaited him in no man's land was a storm of bullets, artillery shell explosions, and death. He quickly made a prayer and asked his dead grandfather to keep him alive.

All around him, he could hear the other sergeants yelling at their men and the ruckus going along with hundreds of men standing up and getting ready for yet another assault. Radetzki gathered them up in small groups, and one by one, he spoke to them. *"Men,"* he grunted. *"Get ready. When the whistles blow, it will be time."* Loud whistling sounds of artillery blazed above them – Russian shells, thank God – and soon after that, they started to hear the rumble in the direction of Przemysl. The fortress was pounded once more, and Dimitri wondered how there could still be stuff standing there after all the bombardments the Imperial artillery had slammed it with. Then, the whistles blew, and it was time for the attack. Dimitri climbed the ladder and jumped into mayhem itself.

(...) 10 minutes later (...)

The fortified position just ahead of Fedorov exploded in a fury of fire, earth, and smoke. For a moment, it seemed like the hammer of a Norse god had hit the ground. The blast wave slammed him hard on the ground, and he fell on his back, stunned. He was still groggy moments later from the impact but shook himself out of it rapidly as Sergeant Radetzki gave him a hard kick in the ribs. *"Come on, Private. Snap out of it. We are somewhat busy, and I need every able-bodied soldier."* *"Yyyesss, sir,"* he blurted hesitantly. *"What is it, Private,"* yelled the NCO. *"Are you hurt, bleeding, or is something broken?"* Fedorov looked at the man above him, as he was seemingly unaffected by the bullets whizzing by or the ground shaking and the flashes of exploding artillery all around.

"I... I don't think so, Sergeant. Just a bit stunned, that's all." The NCO looked at him for a moment, crouching down toward him and taking his head into his two hands. *"Listen to me, Fedorov. The fucking Austrians are shitting in their pants right now, and we need to kill all of the bastards so we can get into a warm home and cozy up to a fire and a couple of women. Do you get it?"*

The almost admission that the seemingly invincible and unbeatable Sergeant was tired of the entire endeavor sort of boosted Dimitri's confidence, and he found a new strength to get up. *"Private! I need you with me!"* And then Dimitri finally regained his full senses. *"Yes, Sergeant,"* he said in a decided tone, picking his rifle up from the ground where he had dropped it after the enemy shell hit. Bullets continued to stream all around them, but they seemed to live a charmed life.

They were being pounded by heavy Austro-Hungarian howitzers. The things were obsolete and dated back to the turn of the century, but they still packed a mean punch for soft human bodies. An explosion was an explosion, after all.

It was a barbaric scene of battle and mayhem. Explosions rocked the city and the by-now very damaged fortress. The Austrians had a full battle siege line all along the western ramparts and fortifications, laden with large guns, mortars of all calibers, and thousands of troops. Arcing shells left every other second toward the Russian troops and trenches, exploding in cacophonic blasts. The Russian army also had hundreds of big guns lined up further down the line and in the rear, and those pounded the enemy fortress like there was no tomorrow. The fields ahead, to the sides, and behind Dimitri, were a sea of brown Russian uniforms running toward the enemy-fortified positions. There were also bodies on the ground, blood and smoke. A lot of smoke that was clouding Dimitri's vision. In short, Przemysl was a cauldron of burning fire and smoke.

Both Fedorov and Radetzki ran toward the enemy trenches, seeing that there was already a hand-to-hand fight because many of the Russians had reached the Austro-Hungarian line. Then, it was time to fight, and he slammed his bayonet-tipped rifle into the belly of a wide-eyed Hungarian soldier.

CHAPTER 1
Politics and diplomacy and then some

Rome, Italy, Palazzo Montecitorio
January 15th, 1915

The Palazzo di Montecitorio was where the Italian Prime Minister held office, and it also served as the seat of the Italian Chamber of Deputies. It was thus again the place for a meeting for the Italian leadership to decide on its next moves. Antonio Salandra walked the great marble hall giving way to the large meeting room where the rest of his companions awaited him for a discussion that promised to extend well into the evening. A meal was planned, and he knew that while they wouldn't be talking about fun things (the war wasn't going well for Italy), they would enjoy the meal, the wine, and the grappa for dessert. The "*Grand Hall*," as it was called, was constructed out of pink Italian marble, with bright chandeliers hanging on the ceiling. Several Roman-looking statues adorned the walls, along with plants and several large stairways twisting into other floors either down or up. The Palazzo was a majestic and large building, one fit for the leadership of an entire country.

The last few months had not been as Prime Minister Antonio Salandra imagined it. First and foremost, they were now part of the Central Powers and just that fact in itself was a major change of policy for the country. When the war began in 1914, Italy had been leaning toward joining the Entente Powers. The rest of the story on that subject sort of changed the Italian stance because of the major German success at the Battle of the Marne and the conquest of Paris by the Kaiser's forces.

All the way up to that point, things had been looking good for Italy. It was on its way to joining the winning side, was getting decent concessions from Austria-Hungary and Germany, and was going to get new territories from France and England when the war was won (Nice, Monaco, Corsica, and Malta, amongst others).

But then, disaster had fallen down on Taranto like the thunder of God. The harbor was where the powerful Italian naval fleet had been anchored, and the Allies had attacked it with a mind-boggling number of ships and had even landed troops in the area. The net result was a catastrophe of epic proportion for Italy: its entire fleet was gone, either captured or destroyed by the battleship barrage that was launched by the traitorous Brits in their dastardly attack. It was hard to accept that so many ships were gone. The country had invested heavily in its naval power and had been very proud of it. The effect the major defeat had had on the population and the armed forces was difficult to evaluate fully. On the political side, it was also hard to manage.

The Regina Marina was the instrument with which the Italian leadership had planned its expansion, and to seize the French territories it had been promised by joining the Central Powers. It was also the very reason why the Austro-Hungarians and the Germans had wanted them in the alliance.

On land, the Italian Army was entertaining two fronts, and things were stalemated. The Anglo-French attack in Taranto had ended up in them conquering all of Apulia (the heel of the Italian boot), but the Italian Army was able to stop them from advancing further with solid trench lines.

The second front was on the border between France and Italy. There, the treacherous French had attacked but their offensive floundered on the mountain fortifications that were built in the years prior to the conflict. Both sides had heavily fortified their own area of the frontier, and the region was covered in mountains, making it inhospitable for fighting offensively. The Italian Army had thus stopped the bastards there as well.

Which brought Salandra to today's meeting. Italy had stabilized its frontlines, and things were now finally under control. There was no danger of civilian unrest like there had been a month ago. It was time to look further than just defense. After all, the Entente Powers were not doing so well themselves. The very fact that they attacked Taranto and the Italians by surprise told of their desperation. France, with Paris occupied, was in deep trouble, and there were rumors she would eventually drop out of the conflict, leaving Great Britain alone to fight.

With these thoughts, he entered the meeting room, saluted by two heel-clicking Italian Army soldiers. He ignored them as they opened the double doors in front of him.

The men around the table awaiting him all stood up in greeting. *"Gentlemen,"* he started. *"Sit down, I am not the King,"* he continued smiling. The men assembled on that day were the usual minus Foreign Minister Antonio di San Giuliano, the old diplomat who had retired before Christmas. His replacement was standing to his left. Sidney Sonnino was a shrewd man whom Salandra liked very much because they saw things much the same way. On his right sat Tommaso Tittoni, the former Ambassador to France. He had just been recalled since a state of war existed between the two countries, and he was not welcomed in Bordeaux (the new French temporary capital) anymore. The Chief of the General Staff, General Luigi Cadorna, was there as well; since there was a war on, no one could dodge the military. Then, the group was completed by the Minister of the Italian Navy, Admiral Leone Viale. King Victor Emmanuel III, who should attend these discussions, was absent since he continued to suffer from severe psychiatric problems and thus could not attend.

"How are you doing, my friends," Salandra said to no one in particular. They all responded in their own way over the next few minutes, and the small talk proceeded along until the first plates were brought. A great dinner awaited them, and they started talking business once the prosecco wine was served.

"General Cadorna, why don't you start with a report of the frontlines," said Salandra to the Chief of the General Staff. *"Very well, Mr. Prime Minister,"* answered the General, putting his wine glass on the table. *"There is not much change from last week. The two frontlines are static. We are continuing to be on a defensive stance against the*

French on the Aosta-Ventimiglia-San Remo Line, and things are holding fine. We have repulsed several French attacks. They don't seem to get the message that attacking our mountain fortifications is a bad idea." Most of the assembled leaders smiled while they kept busy eating their meals.

"However, our offensive in Apulia has not yielded the desired results. We have not advanced an inch there, either. The enemy trench line, their battleships, and withering machine-gun fire have so far repulsed all of our assaults, even if we have superior forces attacking them. They are also attacking us on a regular basis." "Why don't we just swamp them with numbers, General," asked Sonnino, the new Foreign Minister. "*The Apulia frontline is very small and confined. We can only put so many troops at the front in order to attack. Even if we would have a million soldiers attacking it, it wouldn't make an iota of a difference, just like at Marathon when the Greeks battled the Persians. It's a bottleneck because of the sea on both sides, and the damned enemy battleships can cover both sides, shortening the area we can attack even more.*" Everyone had stopped eating and looked at Salandra. "*Well,*" started the Prime Minister, "*then I guess the enemy has the same problem and won't break through our lines?*" "Indeed, Mr. Prime Minister," answered Cadorna in a relieved tone. The man had nothing positive to report, after all.

Sonnino continued along the same line of discussions. "*I have the German Ambassador, Hans von Flotow, who has just confirmed to me that the German rifles, machine guns, and shell shipments are already on their way. Also, he has confirmed the Kaiser is sending several of his units to bolster our French frontline. They have a few elite mountain units that should come in handy for us, General.*" Cadorna was happy at the news. "This is excellent news, Mr. Foreign Minister. The shells are in short supply right now and will be very useful. And the German troops will do nicely for the counterattack we are planning across the Alps."

"Are the rumors about Greece and Romania true, Mr. Foreign Minister," said Salandra, changing the subject. *"Indeed, Sir. The Romanians are mobilizing and should soon join the Entente, while the Greeks are rumored to do the opposite. My contacts have told me that Greek King Constantine is about to dismiss his Prime Minister Venizelos."* *"Well, that would be good news. Romania cannot touch us, but the Greeks will take up some of the Franco-British attention in the Mediterranean."* And indeed, they would. The Greeks had a very decent fleet, and if they could work alongside the Austro-Hungarians and the Ottoman Germans in Constantinople, maybe the naval blockade of Italy could be broken. If the Allied fleets were forced to move out of Apulia, then their troops would become out of supply, making victory certain for the Italian Army.

"Minister Viale," continued Salandra in the same vein. *"How is the construction of the new Caracciolo class proceeding along?"* The Italian Fleet was completely destroyed in the dastardly Anglo-French attack, but that didn't mean that Italy hadn't been building more ships when war broke out. *"The initial plan was to have the ships launched in 1916 and 1917, but now that we've put all the funds into them, we should see the first of the class launch out of Genoa this year."*

Italy had been working on a new, radical design of battleships to follow the new *"super-dreadnought"* trend started by the British and followed by many nations. The ships were to be faster and better armed than what Italy had had before the fleet was destroyed. Four battleships were thus in the process of being completed in the La Spezia and Genoa shipyards. The four battleships would come in handy for the battleship-starved Italians. They were named the Francesco Caracciolo (the first to be launched, and that gave the name to the new battleship class), the Marcantonio Colonna, the Cristoforo Colombo, and the Francesco Morosini.

"Thank you, Minister Viale; I think the country will need a fleet before this war is over," said Salandra with an ironic smile. Everyone else around the table took a sip of their wine. The entire Italian nation was outraged at the Franco-British attack, and their leaders would do everything in their power to try and get revenge on the Entente in any way they could.

Royal Palace
Athens, January 17th, 1915

The Greek Royal Palace was located in the heart of Athens and was built in the 19th Century. It was a magnificent Neoclassical building with a façade made of bright yellow bricks. Its interior was lavish like all royal mansions of the day. The palace was where King Constantine stayed from the late fall to the early Summer when he moved his retinue and family to his other palace called Tatoi in the hills overlooking the capital.

King Constantine I of Greece laid back in his chair, thinking about the last visit of his brother-in-law, Kaiser Wilhelm II, in 1913. It had been a simpler time when the two men could just be friends and not worry too much about politics and war. *"Are you still here, Your Majesty,"* said his royal councillor, Andralos Kostapukis, with a smile to try and break him out of his reverie. *"Ah, yes, my dear Andralos. I was just thinking about the German Emperor. It is in line with today's subject, after all,"* countered the King with a small laugh. *"Indeed, sir."*

He stood up and walked to the large window of his study overlooking Syntagma Square (Constitution Square). It was a large green space where Modern Greece was brought into being after an 1843 uprising forcing the King of the time, Otto, to grant a constitution to the people. The leaves on the trees were gone, but the place still looked breathtaking. Winter in Greece wasn't truly cold compared to other European countries, and as such, he could see many of his subjects milling about and walking in the square, sitting on park benches, and just going about their business. The scenery in front of him was magnificent in a sense, and the decision he was about to make might remove some of the comforts these people enjoyed. For Constantine, the decision to go to war wasn't one he was making lightly. That made him sad, but he was now convinced he would not be able to steer clear of the world conflagration currently in progress.

As Kaiser Wilhelm's brother-in-law, Constantine would have been inclined to support Germany right from the start, in August 1914. But his Prime Minister, Eleuthérios Venizelos, and his supporters had wanted to join the Entente. Moreover, members of his inner circle, like one of its most important military commanders, General Ioannis Metaxas, had strong ties to Germany and would have also liked nothing more than to join the Central Powers. The sane decision of the time was to stay neutral (to avoid internal conflict), and it had been the only thing on which he and his Prime Minister had been able to agree. Both men didn't like each other very much, after all. They were always at odds on policy and decisions, and the one about which side to join had not been any different.

But the political landscape had now radically changed. The destruction of the Italian Fleet and the recent conquest of Paris had moved many Entente supporters into the *"support Germany camp,"* especially since the Greeks now felt very vulnerable because they had a fleet of their own. Would this mean that the Franco-British would attack them as well?

General Ioannis Metaxas, who stood just beside him, and who sensed his king's hesitation, spoke up. *"Your Excellency, the Army stands with you over this matter."* The Commander of the Navy, Pavlos Kountouriotis, spoke up as well. *"Your Excellency, I know we have had our differences over the country's international stance, but I am now fully united with your vision."* The man had been one of Venizelos' supporters and was against any intervention with the Central Powers. However, the man had changed his mind when he saw what the Franco-British had done to the Italian Navy, a neutral nation. Having his own fleet, he saw the implied threat the Entente had wanted to deliver. *"Whoever courts the Central Powers will get destroyed."* With the well-known Germanophile tendencies of King Constantine, Kountouriotis saw the writing on the wall. The man was a nationalist first, and he felt that if Greece lost its brand-new fleet, it would be a disaster.

The fleet, born out of the Greco-Turkish disagreement over the possession of the Eastern Aegean Islands (currently under the control of Greece since the last Balkan Wars), was now a very respectable force of two pre-dreadnought battleships, two heavy cruisers, and seven destroyers. The two battleships had just been bought (in 1914) from the United States (vessels of the Mississippi Class, the Mississippi, and the Idaho), while the heavy cruiser had been bought by millionaire Giorgios Averof out of his own money, something truly rare in the annals of naval warfare. The vessels were thus thrust right into the Entente's target sight. The proof had been received a couple of weeks ago on Foreign Minister Georgios Streit's desk. The message, enveloped in flowery words, delivered a stark demand and a warning. *"Hand over your fleet, or we will destroy it."* This had ended any hesitation Koundtouriotis had at the time.

GREEK FLEET IN 1914

Admiral Pavlos Kountouriotis	
CA Giorgios Averof (flagship)	CA Helle
Pre-Dreadnought BB Kilkis former Idaho	7 old DD
Pre-Dreadnought BB Lemnos former Mississippi	

Androlos Kostapukis continued in the same vein as his colleagues. The Foreign Minister of Greece, Georgios Streit, was also at the table in the king's study. *"We just need your signature, my King, and the rest will be done swiftly."*

The King continued to look at the square, taking particular interest in a man, his wife, and their two kids playing near a large tree. *"Are we certain that dismissing Venizelos will not cause any major conflict? As you know, gentlemen, we have been close to armed conflict between the two camps before"* (Royalists vs. Parliamentarians). *"Your excellency,"* countered Metaxas. *"The Army stands with you and the Navy as well now."*

Constantine turned back from the window and moved to the table, sitting down. *"Very well. What about the fact that by joining the*

Central Powers, we are also allying ourselves with our staunchest enemy, the Ottoman Empire?"

The King was asking a good question since the two countries had just fought a couple of wars from 1911 to 1914, and there was a very long history of conflicts and hate between the two. After all, the Turks occupied Greece for centuries before the Greeks were able to shake off their yoke.

Foreign Minister Georgios Streit answered as he'd come prepared with the information. *"Your Excellency, I have been assured by the German ambassador that the Ottomans will stop claiming the Eastern Aegean Islands in exchange for our participation in the war. Also, they are willing to harbor our fleet in the Bosphorus if we choose to accept their help."* Constantine wondered what the Germans had given the Turks in exchange for this major concession, as the abyss of hate was deep between Greece and Turkey. They'd given a lot, indeed. German troops were on the rails, moving to Constantinople via the newly conquered rail line from Austria via Serbia and Bulgaria. Enver Pacha was desperate to cover the disaster in the Caucasus with good news. *"They renounce their claim of the islands?" "Indeed, they do, Your Excellency. And the Ottoman Fleet is already under the command of a German Admiral, Wilhelm Souchon, of whom we have heard the latest exploits recently. This would ensure that the Turks don't do anything foolish with our ships."* The King smiled; that was a major diplomatic win and just another reason for the move.

"Very well," he said, signing the paper officialising that he was dismissing Prime Minister Venizelos from office and replacing him with his trusted advisor, Androlos Kostapukis.

Then he signed another paper, which was the declaration of war note from Greece to France and Great Britain, which was going to be delivered the very next morning to the French and German embassies in Athens. The meeting ended with the Greek leadership agreeing to the Ottoman proposal of sailing their fleet into the Bosphorus to avoid it being destroyed by the Entente fleets.

Greece was going to war.

Baranovichi, Western Belarus, January 17th, 1915
Stavka Command

Baranovichi was an important city in the Russian Empire because it was a critical rail junction. It was also close to the frontlines and made communications with the fighting forces a lot easier than if its supreme commander stayed in Petrograd or St-Petersburg.

It was thus where Supreme Commander in Chief, Grand Duke Nikolai Nikolaevich (the Tsar's own uncle), had set up shop to command over his troops.

The building where the Imperial HQ was housed was near the train station and the center of town. It was a former Romanov provincial mansion repurposed into a military H.Q. at the beginning of the war, in the Fall of 1914. Outside, the wind howled as if crazy banshees were yelling at the world, and the hard-biting snow slammed on the windows.

The Grand Duke sat by a warm and inviting fire with his General Yurii Nikiforovich Danilov (1866-1937), his Quartermaster General, and Chief of Staff, General Yurii Nikiforovich Danilov. Both men were reviewing the situation at the frontlines. Obviously, things were going a little slower with the cold, and the German offensive in Poland was thus slowed down. In Przemysl, their siege of the Austro-Hungarian fortress was also hampered by the terrible cold and the snow. Although the Russian soldiers were used to the cold, some things worked better with some heat. The guns froze overnight, the snow had to be plowed, and it impeded the troops from easily moving around. The constant storms and the icy conditions further slowed down the logistical system, as if that needed to have more problems.

"How is the Tsar, Grand Duke," asked Danilov. *"He is well, General. I have just spoken with him on the phone, and he will be visiting us soon to review operations. As you know,"* the Grand Duke stopped to smile, *"our beloved Tsar would still like to take control of the Army."* The

Russian leader and his Commander-in-Chief had spoken over a telephone line. Although it took time and communication was not always good, it was a good way to speak to the Tsar and to give him fresh news. Sometimes, it was garbled, and, especially when it was windy like this night, the line cut out often.

Danilov removed the rest of the snow from his fur coat and then put it on a hanger near the fire. He shook some, moved by the fire, and put his hands near it to warm them. *"Still cold, General,"* said the Grand Duke. The man had just arrived from the front in Poland. The German offensive there was slowed down, but the Russian forces kept retreating. They had built a new system of trenches, and now it was looking like it would finally hold. *"Yes, sir, but this is nothing compared to what the men have to endure on the frontline." "I imagine,"* said Nikolai Nikolaevich, not really caring about what the rank-and-file endured. The Romanovs, the Russian ruling class (the Tsar's family), were so filthy rich and detached from reality that most could not even imagine what it was like for the poor, or the soldiers, even when they commanded over them like the Grand Duke. It was a true problem, and the gulf between the rich and the poor in Imperial Russia was so immense that it threatened the country with a revolution, like in 1905. In short, the Russians had better win this war to avoid big problems. But at the onset of 1915, these problems were far away, since the Empire was doing very well against the Central Powers.

"So, how are things looking like, General," asked the Grand Duke once Danilov had sat down and gulped down a couple of shots of Vodka. *"Well, as you know, we have more troops than the Germans on the frontline. With the assembled Armies (2nd, 9th, 4th, and 7th), we have over a million and a half men on the line defending what we still control of Poland,"* answered Danilov. He then continued after producing a folder for his superior with the details of what he was explaining. *"The intelligence assessment is that the Germans are attacking us with about 750,000 to a million men since they had been able to transfer a lot of forces from the Western Front following their victory and the resulting trench stalemate there. They might have*

been able to send more, but their Austrian Allies need help," finished Danilow with a wolfish smile. The situation had gone from good there to bad following the important German victory at the Battle of Marienburg, where General Samsonov's 1st Army was completely annihilated. In one bold stroke, the new German commander Hindenburg had removed 380,000 Russian soldiers (88,000 killed or injured and 252,000 captured). Less than 40,000 soldiers managed to escape back to Poland. Since then, the Imperial forces had been on the backfoot everywhere across Eastern Prussia and Poland.

While it looked like the Russian trench and defensive preparations (west of Warsaw) were working, things were a little more serious with Koenigsberg. The advancing Germans were coming to break the Russian encirclement of the city.

"We will have to make a choice about Koenigsberg, Grand Duke. We need to take the city now, or else we will have to fight both the besieged and the relief army, or we retreat to more defensible positions." Nikolai Nikolaevich knew that the Germans were not far from the city they were besieging, and there would come a time when the Russian forces would have to face the German newcomers. *"Mmmm,"* said the Commander-in-Chief, thinking out loud. *"How far are the Germans, now?" "Sir, they are about a week away, and they seem to be taking their time as the weather also affects them." "Okay, let's do one more assault on the city, and if it fails, we retreat. Get the order out. I want the attack to be in the next two days." "Very well, Grand Duke."*

"What about Przemysl, General? The Tsar asks me almost every day when we will take it." "Grand Duke, there we are also ready for the assault. The bad weather has slowed us down but it's about time we launch the attack; the enemy is getting stronger in the Carpathians. The Austro-Hungarians have established a new defensive line in the mountain range, and it appears German troops have also been sent there."

The Przemysl Fortress was defended by 120,000 soldiers under the command of Hermann Kusmanek von Burgneustädten. The Austro-Hungarian troops had been stuck there and encircled during the disastrous fall offensive ordered by their Commander-in-Chief, Conrad von Hotzendorf. By the middle of October 1914, the entire city was ringed with Russian siege trenches. The forces under Russian General Andrei Nikolaevich Selivanov were over 600,000 strong and about to assault.

The Grand Duke grunted. *"It's about time we finish this. Also, order the assault on the fortress. We will soon have bigger fish to fry with the start of the Romanian offensive in Transylvania." "Very well, sir."* General Danilov was in agreement with both decisions. Things had taken a lot more time than anticipated because of the terrible supply situation, but now the Imperial forces were ready to launch.

Things did not look so bad for the Russian Empire on the Eastern Front. Although the Germans were getting a lot stronger, the Imperial forces continued to hold their own. There was a lot of hope for victory in Russia. Austria-Hungary was teetering on the edge of the abyss, and with the Romanian offensive just starting, things were about to get even uglier for them. If Vienna dropped out of the war, the Germans would be in a world of trouble.

Peles Palace
Romania Joins the Entente January 19th, 1915

The new King of Romania, Ferdinand the 1st (he was former King Carol's nephew), signed the document in front of him and took a deep breath. Beside him sat his Prime Minister, Ion Bratianu, and the French Ambassador to Romania, Jean-Camille Blondel. The document was the result of a month of discussions, and the Romanian King was happy that he'd finally chosen his side in the war. Everyone was smiling, but things were not as they seemed to be for the two Romanians.

Both Ferdinand and Bratianu had favored close ties with the Entente and had met on the very matter the day following Ferdinand's accession to power. Bratianu convinced the King to wait for an opportune moment to join the Entente, but the King was young and enthusiastic and much encouraged by the successful Russian offensive against the Austro-Hungarians. For him, now was the time to join the Russians in the fight and invade Transylvania. His idea was rooted in logic. Never before and perhaps never again would the hated Austrians be in such a weakened state. Bratianu's voice of caution to his King was disregarded.

The French, who had a pretty good diplomatic mission in Bucharest and a lot of influence with the new King (Ferdinand was a Francophile), were eager to promise everything the Romanians wanted. Thus, the treaty stipulated that in exchange for Romania attacking Austria-Hungary, Ferdinand would get the territories of Transylvania, Bukovina, and the Banat region. It was easy for Ambassador Blondel to promise those things. None of them belonged to France. They were an integral part of the Austro-Hungarian Empire. Even better for the French, the Romanians would have to conquer it themselves, thus diverting precious Central Power manpower to a new region.

"You have made a very good decision, Your Majesty," said Blondel, also apposing his signature to the document.

(...) Four days later, January 23rd, 1915 (...)

The Romanian invasion started with a bang, as the Austro-Hungarian forces were absent from the region, fighting a battle of survival against the Russians on the Carpathian Front and what they still controlled of Galicia. Their weak border units were thus easily brushed aside. Many things could be said about the Romanian Army, but its fighting men were seasoned veterans, having fought two recent wars (the Balkan Wars). What they lacked in modern equipment and training, they partially compensated for with real battlefield experience.

The Romanian 1st Army, under the command of General Ioan Culcer, invaded from the southwest, while General Alexandru Averescu crossed the border to attack via the southeast. And the biggest force of them all, the Army of the North, invaded from the north along the frontlines the Russians held in Galicia, joining forces with them and greatly bolstering their push further into Austria-Hungary.

The news of the invasion sent electric shocks into Berlin and Rome and panic in Vienna. The Habsburg Monarchy was already fighting for its survival, and German help was only now arriving in too small numbers to the Northern Carpathians in anticipation of the fall of Przemysl, which would then, in turn, liberate many Russian troops to attack further into Austria-Hungary. The only thing going for the Central Powers was the terrible January weather in Transylvania. The Romanian forces thus had to fight the elements to advance. And, like all armies in the Great War, their supplies floundered when they got far enough away from their supply depots, grinding the Romanian invasion to a slog.

At that very moment, Austria teetered on the brink of complete disaster, and things wouldn't get better for the Dual Monarchy with more bad news coming to it in Galicia.

Oberste Heeresleitung (OHL) – Supreme Army Command
Berlin, January 20th, 1915

The OHL was, by definition, a mobile command structure. It moved to Belgium during the Western Offensive and then to Versailles as the front moved south of Paris. With the toning down of operations in the West because of winter, and a general need for both camps to rest and refit their forces, the Supreme Military H.Q. of the Empire moved back to Berlin for the time being, leaving capable deputy commanders in the field.

The top people of the Reich were assembled in one of the ballrooms of the Berlin Imperial Palace. It was too big for the small group of people, but it was being held there since there were renovations underway in other parts of the building. The room itself had a magnificent grey polished marble floor, a very large crystal chandelier, and big hearths on the four walls of the room where big fires burned bright. After all, the stone palace was very cold and humid without them. Most parts had electricity, of course, but there was nothing better than a good fire to get rid of the winter freeze.

A table had been brought to the center of the room by the Kaiser's people, who also moved some furniture in case the OHL people needed it. Assembled for the discussion that early afternoon was Helmut von Moltke, the Chief of the General Staff (and thus head of OHL), the recent victor of the Battle of the Marne. Chancellor Theobald von Bethmann Hollweg sat right next to him, with his always serious face. The Minister of War, Erich von Falkenhayn, was to his left with both the Chief of the Operations Division, Colonel Gehard von Tappen, and the Chief of the Information Division (intelligence), Lieutenant Colonel Richard Hentch. At the head of the table and facing them all was the Kaiser, Wilhelm II. To the ruler's left was Paul von Hindenburg, the recent savior of Eastern Prussia and overall commander of all Eastern Front German forces. To the right was Rear Admiral Roman Berger, the Chief of the Admiral Staff's deputy for this meeting, as Admiral Hugo von Pohl was with the Fleet in Brest and St-

Nazaire, getting the fleet back into shape for the next phases in the naval war.

The meeting had been called in haste because of the Romanian emergency, as they were not supposed to meet until the next week (the OHL met in this capacity on a regular basis), hence explaining the improvised nature of the room they were in.

Kaiser Wilhelm II seemed particularly worried on that day, and he opened the discussion as everyone sat down, following some food they'd just been served by the palace servants. *"I dearly hope the war is not lost, gentlemen, but the Romanian entry into the conflict threatens to unhinge everything..."* The monarch paused and put both his hands on the side of the table in a gesture of nervousness. *"The Romanian forces have already entered Transylvania, and the reports I have read this very morning speak of three large armies invading from the southeast, the southwest, and the north. Some of their troops have even apparently linked with Brussilov's Russian forces in Galicia."*

Most of the military men, still stunned by this sudden development, stayed silent for a few seconds, and Chancellor Bethmann Hollweg took the opportunity to speak. *"Your Majesty, while it is true the Romanians are complicating the picture for our already failing Austro-Hungarian ally, we have the Greeks that have just confirmed they will join the Central Powers. I have just received our copy of the treaty last evening."* At this, Wilhelm took heart, and his face brightened. *"Really? Well, that is some good news in a turmoil of bad ones. My in-law is finally coming to his senses."* Helmut von Moltke spoke up on the matter. *"Indeed, Your Excellency. I don't know if he is coming to his senses or he has seen the true nature of the Entente and is now worried about his own fleet, but I agree with you, this is rather excellent news."*

"Lieutenant-Colonel Hentch," started the very calm Paul von Hindenburg. "What can the Information Division give us in terms of strength and troops assessment? We need to know what we are up against here." Hentch cleared his throat and spoke up since he had come prepared for the meeting.

"General, as of the end of the Balkan Wars, when The Romanian forces were fully mobilized, we are talking of troop numbers in the high 400,000s, perhaps mid-500,000s." "What about their equipment," continued the old Prussian officer. *"They don't have a lot of artillery, and what they have is dated. Furthermore, they have some French Hotchkiss machine guns, but in too few numbers to be considered well-equipped."*

"General von Moltke," Hindenburg continued in the same vein, while the Kaiser took special attention observing the experienced man. He liked him and decided he was a man to watch. *"If you give me an additional 300,000 soldiers and the Austrians pitch in a little, I believe we can stop them with a good defense, while the Bulgarians and now the Greeks could open a second front on Romania's southern border. If we can find troops for that to stiffen the spine of our allies all the better."*

"Colonel Tappen," started to answer von Moltke. *"Where can you find me these men?"* The chief of the Operations Division, also responsible for supply and ordinance, thought for a moment. *"Well. We have dangerously thinned our Western Front and have sent reinforcement to Eastern Prussia and to the Italians, including a month's supply of shells and bullets. We have also moved troops to the Carpathian Front and a division had just arrived in Constantinople. For now, we have scraped the bottom of the barrel; I would defer to either Hindenburg to transfer some of his men, you to give me a direct order to thin out the Western Front even more, or else Minister Falkenhayn to get us the new trainees of 1915 (military class of 1915 that were 18 years old) trained as fast as possible."*

Both Moltke and Hindenburg made sour faces as they did not like the answer but knew Tappen wasn't wrong. Germany had won two clear victories and, because of that, was in a great position (Marne and

Marienburg), but its allies were not doing so well. The Italians had been slammed with the complete destruction of their fleet and a big morale drop, fighting on two fronts against the Franco-British and without enough ammunition to do it. The Ottomans had seen the better part of their modernized army destroyed in the futile Caucasus offensive (Battle of Sarikamish), and then, finally, there were the Austrians.

The Dual Monarchy was teetering on the brink of the abyss, with almost all of Galicia occupied and its main fortress (Przemysl) about to fall to the powerful Russian offensive. It also incurred severe casualties and two major defeats against the Serbs before finally overrunning the country with the help of the Bulgarians, who attacked the Serbs in the back.

Austro-Hungarian losses in troops were so important that any sensible ruler would normally sue for peace. But Emperor Franz-Joseph was a proud man, and his Chief of the General Staff, Conrad von Hotzendorf, was not ready to concede defeat.

In short, the Reich was now struggling because of the weak allies it had to support with troops, ammo, shells, and even machine guns (the Ottomans and Bulgarians were particularly badly equipped). The entire endeavor was unsustainable in the sense that German would have to choose what it wanted to prioritize. Continue without any regard to their allies the Army's offensive in Poland, Eastern Prussia, and France, or stop attacking and reinforce the beleaguered areas and countries.

Strategically, the best decision was to try and keep Austria-Hungary, the Ottoman Empire, and Italy in the war, but it was hard for these proud men to stop attacking especially now that they could smell blood. They knew they had the Russians on the backfoot in Poland and East Prussia and that come spring, there could be a major offensive to break them.

Von Moltke tapped the table with his fingers, thinking. Falkenhayn was keeping silent since there was nothing more to say. The Chief of the General staff spoke up. *"General Hindenburg, what do you think?"*

The old Prussian officer made a face, indicating that what he was about to say wasn't something he liked. *"I think that it is more important to support our failing allies. I can, thus, relent on either attacking Koenigsberg or Poland. If I only continue with one of those two offensives, this will free up the necessary force to move and confront the damned Romanians."*

That was an answer the Kaiser liked. He didn't want to abandon his friend Franz-Joseph, and while he didn't care much about the other two, he was intelligent enough to understand that their contribution to the war effort would be sorely missed if they sued for peace.

"I like General Hindenburg's plan, gentlemen," thus said the German Emperor. *"I also support this idea, gentlemen,"* answered Bethmann Hollweg. "The ambassadors from these countries are crying for our help; thus, having good news for them is going to go a long way in their continued interest to fight this conflict."

Von Moltke relented. *"Very well, gentlemen, Your Excellency,"* he said, nodding at Wilhelm. *"General Hindenburg, will you be able to come up with a workable plan soon?" "Yes, sir,"* answered the old commander.

The Kaiser seemed to be in a better mood because they had discussed a solution to Austria's quandary; he thus decided to change the subject. *"Deputy Berger,"* he started, looking at the naval man who had stayed silent during the first part of the discussion. *"How are my ships doing? Are the repairs going along well?"*

"Your Majesty, the ships are almost ready for operation. Admiral von Pohl assures you that he will soon be able to resume operations and that he has a concrete plan for raiding the British convoy lines. The

Entente cannot patrol the area constantly, and there will be many opportunities for the High Seas Fleet to break out from its protected French harbors and inflict mayhem on the enemy transport ships." "Superb," answered Wilhelm, now excited like a little child. He loved his fleet with a passion. *"Will you be able to send me the operational plans and the specific progress of the repairs so I can look at them later?" "Of course, your majesty."*

The OHL meeting continued for some time, and the German leaders spoke about more specific subjects like when the troops would reach Koenigsberg, the weather, or the supply situation. Falkenhayn completed the discussion with a presentation on industrial production and some future figures of when new divisions, guns and ships would be available for the Reich to use.

New War Office building
Whitehall, London, January 22nd, 1915

The new War Office building had an all-white front face, and it looked very imposing. Starting from the second floor and up, the halls and corridors were furbished with rows of columns. On the rooftop sides were placed stone statues showing Peace and War, Truth and Justice, Fame and Victory.

The Main Entrance, Grand Hall, and staircase were placed in the center of the west front, with the principal rooms on the second floor. The Secretary of State for War (Kitchener) occupied a suite above the main entrance, while the Parliamentary Under Secretary of State occupied the room across from the main staircases. The Chief of the Imperial General Staff had his office in a large room in the center of the southern side. The circular tower rooms at the corners were for other members of the Army Council, and the Army Council room was in the center of the north side. The more important rooms and office suites were decorated with great care, and a few were adorned with oak paneling.

The room that surrounded them and their meeting was intricately decorated with wood paneling, an old but expensive-looking rug, and a chandelier above. In the back of the room sat a fireplace where a large number of burning-bright embers gave heat to the room. A large central table with twelve chairs sat right in the middle, where the British leaders were having their discussion on the situation and their next steps.

First and foremost was the British Prime Minister, Herbert Henry Asquith, flanked by Herbert Kitchener, 1st Earl Kitchener, the Secretary of State for War. Beside them sat Winston Churchill, the First Lord of the Admiralty (head of the Navy), and British Foreign Secretary Sir Edward Grey. Also in attendance was the Chief of the Imperial General Staff, Lieutenant-General Sir Archibald Murray, and the Quartermaster General, Major General Sir John Cowans. More members of the War Office could attend these types of meetings, but they were not required for the discussions today.

The main points that were on the agenda that day were the Romanian and Greek entries into the war. They would talk a lot more about the Greeks than the Romanians because the Brits were attracted to enemy nations with warships like moths to a flame. And Athens fielded a very respectable force with which to be reckoned.

There were also some needed discussions about the Apulia Enclave and the Italian ships that were captured. Finally, the support of the beleaguered French was last but not least, since if France surrendered, the war in the West was over.

Prime Minister Asquith opened the meeting as he should. *"Thank you, gents, for being here for the discussions today. We have some good news and some new challenges to talk about."*

Everyone settled down in their seat. Some of them had steaming teas beside them, while most had folders and papers with notes. "Sir Grey," continued Asquith. *"What is the news out of Romania?"* "Mr. Prime Minister, as of yesterday, the Romanian offensive was three days old. They are attacking with over 500,000 men, and the so far very light Austro-Hungarian defenses are being brushed aside. The Bulgarian reaction is as expected, and they are moving their troops to Romania's southern border. What remains to be seen is what the Germans will do about it. Also, this may be the last straw for the Habsburg Empire. There are already signs of unrest with their troops in the Carpathians, as they are barely holding the Russians, and now another enemy has appeared to their south,"* he paused to look at the Chief of the General Staff: *"Lieutenant-General Murray, is the information confirmed on the push Brusilov's about to make to finish off Przemysl?"* "Indeed, Mr. Foreign Secretary," answered the military man. "The Russians are days from launching their own general attacks. By the Spring, gentlemen, we might have one less enemy to contend with."

Churchill laughed softly. *"And they took all of our promises at face value?" "They did,"* countered Grey with a wolfish smile. The Franco-British had promised whatever the Romanians wanted to hear to get them into the war. How and when they would make good on those promises remained to be seen.

"In any case," Churchill carried on, *"We need to settle this unfortunate affair with the Greeks and seize or destroy their fleet as we did with the Italians. There is a real danger that they move into the Bosphorus, and then we won't be able to get them. With your previous agreement,"* he again looked at the Prime Minister, who nodded, *"I have created a brand-new squadron for the Eastern Mediterranean to watch for any Greek and Ottoman incursions beyond the Aegean and perhaps even raid the area and destroy their fleets." "Very well, Lord Churchill. Which ships have you moved there? We agreed at the last War Office meeting to bring back the heavy units to the Home Waters since we now have a very serious threat right here in the French Atlantic harbors,"* asked Lord Kitchener, the Secretary of State for War. There were a lot of nervous people in the United Kingdom over the matter of what the High Seas Fleet would do next. The most likely option was that they would try and raid convoys, but they could also want to give battle, and the heavy units sent down toward Italy for Operation Ares had been solely missed during the previous German fleet breakout from Wilhelmshaven.

"You don't need to worry. Lord Kitchener, I have moved the two heaviest and most powerful units back to the Home Fleet, the battleships Marlborough and Ajax." He paused to pass along one of the folders he'd brought to the discussion. *"Yes, but what of Dreadnought, Conqueror, and Superb, the battlecruisers and the heavy cruisers,"* continued Kitchener. Both men didn't hate each other, but it couldn't be said they were best of friends. In fact, not many were with the eccentric Churchill. Winston continued speaking as if Kitchener's question had been anticipated. *"What we have left in the Mediterranean Sea should be enough to contend with the Adriatic-*

bottled-up Austro-Hungarians and the combined Ottoman-Greek-German navies in the East. I am not saying we would dominate them, but we have enough strength to face them."* People around the table started to open the folders, except Asquith, who already knew.

"In the East, we have the newly constituted Eastern Mediterranean Squadron, composed of the battleships Dreadnought and Superb, the battlecruiser Indefatigable, pre-dreadnought battleships Albemarle and Duncan, plus two heavy cruisers, two light cruisers, and nine destroyers."

Eastern Mediterranean Squadron		
Vice-Admiral Sackville Hamilton Carden		
BB Dreadnought	Pre-dread BB Almermale (6th battle squ.)	CA Amethyst
BC Indefatigable	Pre-dread BB Duncan (6th battle squ.)	CL Falmouth and Diamond
BB Superb	CA Aboukir	9 DD

He looked around the table and then spoke again. *"Need I remind you that the enemy now has two brand-new dreadnought battleships, the German battlecruiser Goeben, two pre-dreadnought battleships, two heavy cruisers, and eight destroyers. There is no exaggeration here, gentlemen. Vice-Admiral Carden, the commander of the Eastern force, has got his work cut out for him."*

Kitchener persisted. *"Fine, Lord Churchill, this makes sense. But what about the Gibraltar Squadron? Surely, now that the Italian fleet is gone, we can move the ships back to the Home Waters?"* Churchill looked again at the Secretary for War. *"Lord Kitchener, the supply convoys need protection from the Austrian Fleet."*

BRITISH MEDITERRANEAN FLEET (Gibraltar)		
Admiral David Beatty, 1st Earl Beatty		
BC Invincible	Pre-dread BB Russell (6th battle squ.)	9 DD
BB Conqueror	Pre-dread BB Cornwallis (6th battle squ.)	4 CA
BB Neptune	Pre-dread BB Exmouth (6th battle squ.)	

It was a fact that the Habsburg Fleet was not too shabby. It was even strong enough to break the blockade of the Adriatic if it chose to. The First Lord of the Admiralty wasn't done. *"The enemy fleet under the command of Admiral Montecuccoli has three dreadnought battleships, nine pre-dreadnoughts, three heavy cruisers, four light ones, and twelve destroyers. The Austrian Fleet can and will eventually attempt to force the crossing. Hence why I need to keep the three dreadnoughts and three pre-dreadnoughts there."* Churchill was referring to the battleships Conqueror, Neptune, and battlecruiser Invincible, plus the pre-dreadnoughts Russel, Cornwallis, and Exmouth.

Austrian Battle Fleet, Admiral Count Rudolf Montecuccoli		
BB Prinz Eugen,	BB Viribus Unitis	Pre-Dread BB Radetzky
BB Tegethoff	Pre-Dread BB Franz Ferdinand	Pre-Dread BB Babenberg
Pre-Dread BB Zrynly	Pre-Dread BB Arpad	Pre-Dread BB Habsburg
Pre-Dread BB Ferdinand Mac	Pre-Dread BB Friedrich	Pre-Dread BB Karl
3 CA	4 CL	12 DD

Placated on the subject, Lord Kitchener decided to relent. "Very well, Winston. Let's hope you are right on this one." Asquith decided to change the subject; he never liked it when the two went at it like that. Kitchener was not happy with Winston's Mediterranean strategy. If it was only him, he would have already evacuated the men from Apulia. He was constantly reminding them that the strategic goal was reached and that anyway, his troops were stalemated in front of the solid Italian defensive positions.

Asquith had to admit the Secretary for War had a good point and that, at some point he would need to support him over Churchill on this. Everything needed to be put into keeping the French in the war. To this, Churchill was always countering that the Germans were not able to send any major offensive to the West because they had more than their hands full in the East and in supporting their failing Austro-Hungarian ally.

"Let's move on to the other items on the agenda, Gentlemen."

French temporary capital
Bordeau, January 24th, 1915

"And that is the sum of it, Mr. Prime Minister," said the new French Commander-in-Chief, General Foch, finishing his presentation on his new plan. Rene Vialdi looked at the French President, Raymond Pointcarré. *"Mr. President, are you sure it is wise to launch an attack now, as our forces are depleted and our supply situation not optimal?"*

"René," answered the President. *"Desperate times call for desperate measures."* General Foch, along with the main Army commanders, were all in agreement with the plan. In the room with them, there sat the commanders of the four main remaining French armies on the Western Front facing the Germans. Louis Franchet d'Espérey (5th Army). General François Lanzerac (9th Army), General Louis Armies (10th Army) and General Joseph Manoury (6th Army). The rest of the forces weren't all destroyed but were busy fighting in other theaters, like on the Franco-Italian border, or the Apulia Enclave in Southern Italy.

"But, Mr. President," continued Vivaldi. *"We still haven't secured the military supplies we want to buy from the Americans, and if we launch this attack, our reserve will dwindle rapidly. What then?"* The Prime Minister had a point. Northern France was occupied by the Germans and the problem going along with that was the fact it was the industrialized part of the country. In one bold stroke, the Central Powers had cut French industrial production by 60%. Steps were being taken to build new munition assembly ships or else buy the ammo and other needed military supplies abroad (USA and Japan, for example).

The entire discussion was centered around the new plan General Foch proposed. The French had seen the German military movements and knew that the enemy had dangerously thinned out its forces in the areas southeast of Paris and also near Verdun. In this, the Reich military leaders had no choice since they needed to face the major threat in the East with their Austro-Hungarian ally on the verge of falling out of the war. The Italians and the Ottomans also needed support. Added to that, a new dynamic (if old) general was on the offensive to retake the Russian-occupied part of East Prussia and also advanced in Poland. All these endeavors took men, guns, and supplies, and the German Army, while extremely powerful, did not have infinite numbers, nor could it be everywhere at the same time. The idea was thus to attack at the same time as the Romanians and the Russians to tax the German forces to the limit and hope they break somewhere.

While General Foch wanted that breaking point to be in France since everyone in the country hoped for the military to reclaim Paris, a victory in the East would be just as strategically significant. A victory in the East because the French pushed the Germans to their limit in the West could mean either the end of the German offensive in Prussia-Poland or else the demise of Austria-Hungary.

"It's a gamble worth taking, Mr. Prime Minister, since the enemy does not have the necessary assets to launch a counteroffensive. Thus, if we fail, we just stay in place, and that is the end of it," countered Foch.

"I hope to God you are right, General," answered a still unsatisfied Vivaldi. The man had been badly shaken by the defeat at the Battle of the Marne and the subsequent fall of Paris. Pointcarré couldn't blame the guy for feeling that way since, after all, he was also quite low on morale like the rest of the country. But things needed to change, and some risks taken to wrest victory from such a disastrous situation. *"General Foch, Generals,"* he finally said to the assembled military officers. *"You have the go-ahead for the offensive as soon as you think it is feasible." "Thank you, Mr. President."*

Changing the subject to defuse Vialdi, he asked a question. *"Mr. Prime Minister, how are the discussions going between Ambassador Jusserand and the Americans?"* Jean Jules Jusserand was the French Ambassador in Washington D.C. France, just like Britain, was trying to obtain American direct support (American participation in the conflict) or indirect assistance (buying supplies and ammunition from them).

The idea for now, since the U.S. President didn't want to have anything to do with the war, was to buy supplies from the Yankees since they were neutral. The Americans had been inclined to discuss the matter, but the prices they were asking were not very accommodating. And if France had one thing in short supply following the 1914 disaster, it was hard currency.

American businessmen were already doing business in France, like Samuel Remington, the President of Remington Arms Company, which had recently opened a sales office in Bordeaux and secured lucrative contracts for the sale of rifles and ammunition to France and Britain. Recently, the British Government had just ordered one million Enfield rifles from Remington. The American industrial giant was open for business.

The problem didn't lie in the American businessmen, who were always keen to make a buck. It lay with France's limited capability to pay. *"Did Ambassador Jusserand convey our open-mindedness about giving them some of our colonies and or territories in exchange for weapons?"* Vivaldi's face switched from unhappy to normal, as this was a subject for which he was better suited. *"Yes, Ambassador Jusserand had proposed the territories of French Guyana, Martinique, and Guadeloupe to President Wilson and Secretary of State Robert Lansing."* *"And?"* said General Foch, eager for the weapons to start flowing into France. "They are consulting with their Congress and the Senate over the matter sir, and also are asking we lower our request in terms of ammunition, rifles, and artillery guns."

"Very well. So, they haven't said no, that is a good start." "Mr. President, I don't think the nature of American business supporting the same politicians can say no. The only issue there is that they would be the ones buying from their companies and then we would give the *territory. It has to do with budget allocations, and that is a Congressional affair."*

"Well, things are underway," finished Pointcarré. *"Indeed, Mr. President, let's hope it works because, with General Foch's offensive, we might need it sooner rather than later."*

Washington D.C.
White House, Oval Office, January 24th, 1915

Speaking of the devil, both Secretary of State Lansing and U.S. President Woodrow Wilson were meeting together at the same time as their French counterparts across the sea in the Oval Office. It was a cold, snowy, and windy day outside, and the two men tried to concentrate on their task instead of on the howling wind outside. A major snowstorm was slamming the entire Northeastern USA with snowfall, wind, and cold.

Wilson was busy reading the newspaper of the day (it was morning in Washington while it was early afternoon in France). He had it up to his face, and thus Lansing, also reading his own copy of the Washington Post, did the same. Eventually, Wilson dropped the paper to talk to Lansing. "And now the Greeks and the Romanians are in it too," he said. "Indeed, Mr. President. This is crazy; soon, all of Europe will be engulfed in war. Seems like they are only missing Spain, Scandinavia, and Switzerland." "Damn Europeans and their wars. If only we could make them get along together," continued the President. *"No hope there, Mr. President. They are not as lucky as us. America was built on a brand-new template without anyone claiming land or having a history about it except the Brits that we beat to kick them back out north to Canada." "I know, Robert, but there must be a way for the bickering bastards to find some common ground." "Well," countered the Secretary of State in a long, winded breath. "From what I hear from the embassies in Europe, peace will not be possible until one side beats the other to the ground."*

"Damn Germans and their Empire. I ain't certain it would be nice to have the Kaiser so powerful." "No, Mr. President, that man would not be good for America, especially if he beats the British and the French. It won't be long before he starts bickering with us over trivial matters and substance," Robert answered with a fatalistic tone since he knew the German Emperor was close to being a raving madman when it came to affairs of state.

"Robert, we need to find a way to agree with French demands. After all, it serves the interest of the United States of America. Our businessmen will be making a ton of money, we will get new strategic territories in North and South America, and finally, we do our part in helping to defeat this damned Kaiser."

"And let's not forget the pressure men like Remington are putting on us and Congress to open the door for governmental arms sales," added Lansing. *"I agree, Mr. President. So, do we accept their proposals*? It will cost us dearly, and Congress will bitch to give us the money, but any of those men cannot say that buying Louisiana from France or Alaska from the Russians was a bad thing now."* *"Indeed not, Robert,"* countered Wilson. *"Go ahead with the deal."*

General Staff building on Ringstrasse
Vienna, January 24th, 1915

"The Romanian offensive is five days old, General von Hotzendorf," said the old Austrian Emperor Franz-Joseph to the Commander-in-Chief of his armed forces. *"What are you doing about it? The Hungarian Government is in full panic and is starting to talk about us leaving the war altogether."* *"But your Excellency,"* countered the General, *"Don't they understand that if we lose, we will have to give in to the Romanian, Russian, and Serbian demands for territories. This will be the end of the Empire."* *"They don't, Conrad, I know,"* answered the old monarch.

The Austrian parliament had been dismissed by the Emperor at the beginning of the war pertaining to the war emergency, but the Hungarians, the other government of the dual monarchy, continued to convene in Budapest. Parliamentarians were not as amenable to military affairs, and thus, the people in Budapest were starting to look for other solutions.

The problem was not about to resolve itself until von Hotzendorf found the troops to put in the way of the Romanians. The Austro-Hungarian leaders needed to find roughly 300,000 men. Since it was 1915, they had a new class of soldiers they could train (the young people who turned 18 in 1915), which would eventually give them an additional 400,000 soldiers. But for now, they needed men and troops in the next few days, or all of Transylvania would be lost and potentially Hungary with it if this combined with the fall of Przemysl and or a big defeat in the Carpathians.

"We need a win in the Carpathians or even to resist and relieve Przemysl. Yes, that's it; we need to attack the fortress and save them. This would be a great morale booster," said the Emperor as he leaned over the map. Conrad seemed thoughtful for a moment but was open to the Emperor's wishes as he was a man fixated on the offensive.

"Come to think of it, Your Majesty, we have German reinforcements coming our way in the Carpathians to bolster our lines. Maybe I could try and petition General Hindenburg to use them offensively. I am certain that with enough pressure, we can reach and relieve Przemysl."

Franz Joseph seemed relieved to hear his military commander say that it was possible. The old Emperor was looking for anything that would make his Empire survive.

Both Conrad and Franz Joseph were not the only ones present in the meeting today being held at the magnificent all-white stone building that was the Imperial General Staff building. It dated back to 1867, when it was constructed as part of the modernization of the Austrian Army following the disaster at the Battle of Sadowa in 1866, which put an end to the Austro-German war.

The Austrian war minister, General of the Artillery Heinrich von Pitreich, was present, as well as the Foreign Affairs minister, Ludwig von Flotow.

"I still need troops to stop the Romanians, your Majesty," said von Hotzendorf again. *"What about my proposal to give the Greeks the possibility of replacing our occupation forces in Macedonia and other parts of Serbia?"* The question was targeted at Flotow, who was just back from a meeting with the ambassador of Athen's people. *"I confirm that Athens has an interest in replacing us as there are many of these territories, especially Macedonia, that the Greeks have been claiming since before the Balkan Wars. They will do it willingly; we just have to guarantee that their claims will be fulfilled after the war."* *"That's no problem, Foreign Minister Flotow, just give them what they want. We need to move our men out of Serbia so we can use them against the Romanians,"* answered Franz Joseph

"And you know what, Your Majesty," said von Hotzendorf with a mischievous smile. *"Perhaps it would be better to use these men in conjunction with the Bulgarians instead of railing them into Transylvania by the long route. If we take the Austrian troops in Serbia, we can march them to the Romanian border and create a diversionary attack in collaboration with what the Bulgars are already doing."* For once, the old and wily General was having a great idea. Instead of just digging into Transylvania (it was the middle of winter, and the ground was rock solid), the Austrians would attack from the south and the west.

With any luck and combined with the Bulgarian attack already underway and the counteroffensive they would launch in collaboration with the Germans on Przemysl, maybe, just maybe Austria-Hungary had a chance of survival.

CHAPTER 2
The war in the East and the Pacific

Yap Island, German territory of Palau
German Pacific Squadron, January 25th, 1915

Admiral Maximilian von Spee, the commander of the German Pacific Squadron, read the repair and supply reports with satisfaction. The man was alone in his Admiral of the Fleet cabin onboard his flagship, the Battleship Westfalen.

He had just finished reviewing the ongoing repairs to his ships. The Westfalen had stern damage, which could only be truly repaired in a German shipyard, but the two damaged secondary guns had been replaced with the parts available in the fleet. The Kaiserin, his other dreadnought battleship, had its rudder repaired. It had not been simple to do on such an island as Yap, as it didn't have repair facilities. But his men had done the impossible, and the thing was patched up. Kaiserin had also received a shell hit from a Japanese battleship on the number two boiler, and that was also repaired. The deck damage had only been repaired with wooden planking found on the island. The light cruiser Nurnberg had also received planking for its deck, and one of its main guns was unjammed. He closed the folder that held the report with a satisfied grin. His fleet was finally ready to move.

After shaking off his Japanese pursuers in the China Sea, von Spee had feinted to go toward the Caroline Islands by going toward this heading but then had turned back and gone on a north-northwest heading to try and get the enemy off the scent. That was last October; thus, he'd surmised long ago that he had indeed successfully sent the enemy admiral on a wild goose chase to the Caroline Islands. After all, the Carolines were the better-developed area, and it had been the logical place to go.

Yap Island was yet another of the German territories bought from Spain in 1899. The small place had a telegraph and a coaling station. Going to Yap had a few advantages. First he knew that a collier was there and that it was full of coal, and also the telegraph enabled him to send news to the German Admiralty and to the Kaiser that he was still alive and kicking. He'd received some news from Europe as well and had been quite ecstatic at the news that the Army had conquered Paris. But even more exciting was the breakout of the High Seas Fleet, giving him hope that Admiral Hugo von Pohl, its Commander-in-Chief, would find a way to send him help or sortie to get him home safe and sound.

He leaned back in his chair, looking at his very modest cabin. Westfalen had been made for short-distance trips as it was originally designed to fight in the North Sea. Thus, the Admiral of the Fleet cabin was not made for long-term trips. He didn't mind as he'd become accustomed to the great ship that was Westfalen. It was one of the Nassau-Class Dreadnoughts, launched in 1909. It was armed with twelve 280 mm guns and was very decently protected by the most modern armor German could put on it at the time. His other battleship, the Kaiserin, was more modern, but he preferred to have his flag on Westfalen.

German Pacific Squadron	
Admiral von Graf Spee	
BB Westfalen stern damage	CL Emden
BB Kaiserin stern and boiler damage	CL Nurnberg
CA Kaiserin Elisabeth (Austria-Hungary)	CL Leipzing

The stay in Yap was one fraught with nervousness for the Admiral, as there had always been a chance for the marauding Japanese to appear over the horizon. But so far, they had been lucky. So lucky, in fact, that a ship was added to their fleet. It was the Kaiserin Elisabeth, an Austro-Hungarian heavy cruiser, that was en route to Tsingtao at the outbreak of the war. Having heard of the Japanese attack, its captain decided to reroute the ship to Yap and, as such, had been waiting for von Spee's fleet when it got there. With the losses incurred so far in the naval battle against the Imperial Navy, the 150 mm armed heavy cruiser (twelve guns) was a very good addition to the German Pacific Squadron.

Von Spee's ships were now fully repaired and topped with coal, with the collier ship Odenwald (the one that had been awaiting him in Yap) that would accompany the squadron as it still had some coal to distribute.

He decided that the time was ripe to try and make his breakout into the Atlantic via the Cape Horn route. In order to do so, however, he needed to choose a route that would allow him to avoid the Japanese searching for him. It was at this moment that his Chief of Staff, Vice-Admiral Max von Krenk, entered his cabin. *"Sir, I have the charts you requested from the helm and the plotting stations." "Ah, perfect timing, Krenk, I was about to inquire if you had them,"* answered von Spee, smiling.

The Chief of Staff laid the maps on the table. *"As you requested, Admiral, here are the three routes we can take with corresponding distances and coal usage. We also have two colliers, here"* (he pointed at the vicinity of Truk in the Caroline Islands) *"and then another one here near Kwajalein in the Marshall Islands."*

The three routes offered to the German Pacific Squadron each had advantages. The short one – the one going to Truk in the Caroline Islands, had the shortest distance and a collier awaiting at the Truk atoll. The second one, Rabaul in New Guinea, was a less obvious route, and the Truk collier could sail to join them there. But Rabaul was now occupied by Australian forces, and thus von Spee ran the risk of running into the British squadron rumored to be on the hunt for him in the Pacific. After all, these soldiers had come on ships since New Britain was an island. The third route was the less obvious and the boldest one since it ran the highest risk of being intercepted by the Japanese fleet said to be roaming the Caroline and Mariana Islands.

"We cannot go to the Marshalls, Vice Admiral," started von Spee. *"Yes, this might be the less obvious, but there is no coaling station there, and we have a high chance of Japanese interception. We need to choose between Truk and Rabaul."*

"Admiral," answered Krenk. *"I believe that Truk is the best option since we still hold the atoll and there is a collier there. We can get there in a matter of days as well. From Truk, we can re-assess, especially since there is a chance for fresh news of the Japanese and the British whereabouts."*

The next day, the German Pacific Squadron picked up steam and left the vicinity of Yap, bound for Truk. The Admiral had decided that it would be the most obvious route and hoped that it would throw off the Japanese Admiral chasing him.

Friedrich Wilhelm I Fort, January 25th, 1915
1st Grenadier Regiment "Crown Prince" (1st East Prussian)

Captain Mikael Lundbeck, an officer in the 1st Grenadier Regiment (part of the German First Division, 1st Corps, based in Koenigsberg), was looking at his non-commissioned officers as they barked their orders at the men trying to fight off yet another Russian assault. The rifles fired one after another, filling the small redoubt they were in with smoke and the acrid smell of gunpowder. The noise was deafening, and the yelling of the sergeants above it made for an incredible ruckus of noise.

As Captain, he was in charge of a company of men, or of 240 soldiers. Well, had been, since their numbers had dwindled down over week upon week of fighting to around a hundred and fifty. The casualty rate was appalling, but it couldn't be helped. Koenigsberg needed to be defended to the last man. It just couldn't fall to the Russians. The city was the symbol of Germanic power in Eastern Prussia. The symbol of the Teutonic Knights of old and the legends of the brave men who fought to expand Germany to the East.

His job was to direct the fight, not participate. He was trying hard to stay back and make sure the NCOs were doing their jobs properly. The 1st Grenadier Regiment (that his depleted company was part of) was tasked with defending the main German fort in Koenigsberg, Friedrich Wilhelm I (in honor of the former Kaiser). The building was the biggest and strongest in Koenigsberg, and it couldn't fall. If it did, the fight was over.

The overall situation in the fight for Koenigsberg was now critical. The siege was a little over three months old, and the Germans were on the brink of disaster, with over 50% casualties across the board. They were supplied by sea, which had helped in holding since they never lacked food or ammunition, but the number of soldiers was running out. Some of the Kaiserliche Marine ships had anchored offshore and supported them, which helped.

But what they needed was more men, and apparently, there were none available. The Imperial forces were strapped for soldiers as the heavy demand for them across the European theater was exploding. The Reich's allies were failing and the OHL needed to send men to Italy, the Ottoman Empire, and especially Austria-Hungary, on the verge of total collapse. They had thus been told to hold and that a relief army was arriving.

The world around him seemed to shake as if the Hammer of God had slammed against it. The wall in front of Mikael exploded in a fury and a large cloud of dust, the men firing from it obliterated by the blast. It was the second time the wall was destroyed by enemy fire. It had been blasted back in October, but the Imperial Engineers had repaired it as best they could. Mikael fell on his back, coughing hard. He noticed his ears were ringing, and his eyes stung because of the dust. *"Captain, are you all right,"* said one of the soldiers, walking by him to give some assistance. *"Yes, Private,"* he said with some hesitation, *"I am good. Get me Lieutenant Strolker and any sergeant or corporal. I need an assessment of the situation."* *"Yes, Captain,"* answered the soldier.

After he conveyed it to his people, it appeared the situation wasn't so bad. The Russians were retiring to their starting positions. This was weird, he thought as he moved to the destroyed wall since they could have assaulted the fort.

What Mikael didn't know was that General Paul von Hindenburg's Army was only four miles from Koenigsberg, forcing General Rennenkampf to reassess his positions and move his men back into a cohesive army instead of in a ring around the besieged German city. After all, he was only doing what the Stavka told him. One last push on Koenigsberg, and then turn your army and fight the approaching German 8th.

Imperial Japanese Navy battlefleet
Dreadnought battleship Setsu, January 24th, 1915

Japanese Admiral Togo Heihachiro looked at half his fleet departing from the main body and going in a different direction than he was aboard the battleship Setsu, and he grunted. He didn't like splitting his force like that, but he was forced to do it.

Elusive German Admiral von Spee was still at large with his damned German Pacific Squadron, and there were no reported sightings of the bastard. *"Well, Sir, it's the way it goes. May the gods bring your plan luck,"* said Vice-Admiral Jinji Nomura to his commanding officer and Commander-in-Chief of the Japanese fleet. Togo grunted in response, looking out to see as the powerful squadron he'd sent in a different direction was moving away from his own.

The last two months had been frustrating for the legendary Admiral. After taking control of Saipan and Tinian and almost catching the German Pacific Squadron, he'd sailed on the most likely route the enemy commander should have taken, and that was on a direct course toward the Eastern and Central Pacific. But several weeks of scouring the Caroline Islands had not produced any result, nor had any sightings of the German ships been reported to him.

Then, some of his ships had to be sent to the Home Island shipyards for repairs, and he himself was eventually forced to scale back his operation and sail to the Marianas to get more coal as his ships were running low.

As he was now back on the hunt, the German scent had been reacquired. According to his information, the Germans had been in Yap all this time. Togo had cursed at the German Admiral's genius. If there had been one thing that he had not expected, it was that von Spee would take his time and go in a direction that actually made him go deeper into the Pacific instead of trying to make a run for it as quickly as possible.

Now, he had a choice to make. He needed to anticipate his enemy's next move while also trying to root him out of his hiding hole if he chose to stay there. No wonder he hadn't found him in the last two months! The wily German had simply not moved!

The quandary he had was simple. If he sailed with his entire battle fleet and the German was gone, he would again miss him. Since he had a great numerical superiority over his opponent, Togo decided to compromise and split his fleet in two. One half would sail to Yap, and the other would try to intercept the Germans on their most likely route. From his point of view, the only two viable alternatives were through the Caroline Islands and the plethora of atolls the enemy could use to hide its ships in, or else bypass them and go for broke toward Rabaul and New Britain.

The city was occupied by the Australians, and Togo was pretty certain that von Spee knew about it since Yap had a telegraph station. The man had thus certainly been connected to some information, and that was one of the facts he would have fished for first. He surmised that it removed that option for the Kaiserliche Marine commander.

Thus, he'd made his choice and sailed for the heart of the Carolines. Not the East Carolines like the last time, but the West-Central part. There were several natural harbors the Germans would be likely to use and he would send ships to all of them in a broad net to try and catch them.

The two halves of his force would still be powerful enough to face the Germans in a standup fight, but he was worried his pre-dreadnought battleships would be outdistanced by the Germans. True dreadnoughts could reach seven to ten additional knots in speed compared to pre-dreadnoughts. To offset this, he put his two battleships in the first squadron and the battlecruiser Kongo in the second.

This way, he hoped that if von Spee tried to run, he would have the ships to fire on him as he sped away.

Japanese Imperial Fleet Battle Squadron 1 Admiral Heihachiro Togo		
BB Setsu	Pre-dreadnought BB HIZEN	Pre-dreadnought BB MIKASA
BB Kawachi armor belt damage	Pre-dreadnought BB IKI	CA X 25
	Pre-dreadnought BB IWAMI	CL X 6
Pre-dreadnought BC Tsukuma,	Pre-dreadnought BB SAGAMI	DD X 30
Pre-Dreadnought BC Ikoma	Pre-dreadnought BB SUWO	-
Japanese Imperial Fleet Battle Squadron 1 Admiral Yamaya Tanin		
BC Kongo	Pre-dreadnought BB TANGO	
Pre-Dreadnought BC Ibuki	Pre-dreadnought BB ASAHI	-
Pre-Dreadnought BC Kurama	Pre-dreadnought BB SHIKISHIMA	
Pre-dreadnought BB KASHIMA,	7 CA	
Pre-dreadnought BB KATORI	17 DD	

Battle Squadron 2 was under the command of old and reliable Admiral Yamaya Tanin and was the one Togo chose to go to Yap to try and root out the Germans. This was why he opted to keep his two battleships together. If the enemy remained on the small island in the Palau territory, then the pre-dreadnoughts would have no problem engaging. But in the case of a running battle in the Carolines or on the open sea, it was better to have at least two fast dreadnoughts to face the two the Germans had as well.

"Let's hope, as you say, Vice-Admiral Nomura, that luck will be with us for a change," finally said Togo. His throw of the dice was done, and now he would sail and hope for the best.

The raid on Nikolayev Part 1
Admiral Souchon back in action, January 25th, 1915

The Nikolayev shipyard was established in 1897 with the help of a Belgian company (taken over by a Russian company in 1908) and was the naval construction unit responsible for many of the Imperial Russian Navy pre-dreadnought battleships. Following a hiatus in ship construction (the budget was quite tight following the terrible defeat at Tsushima), Russian naval shipbuilding was only just beginning to take things in stride when war broke out in 1914. A new shipbuilding program was put in place and planned to span ten years, proposing a powerful fleet of twenty-six dreadnought battleships, ten heavy cruisers, and close to fifty destroyers. However, it only started in earnest by late 1912.

There seemed to be no rush for the Russian leadership in the 1910s as the Ottoman Fleet (the main enemy) only possessed two aging pre-dreadnoughts, and the Tsarist fleet had four. However, the Turks had two completely new dreadnought battleships ordered and built in Great Britain starting in 1911-1912, creating a sense of urgency for the Russians. The budget for two large dreadnought battleships was rushed from the Tsar to the Douma (national assembly), and the battleships were started in the Nikolayev shipyard in early 1913. In January 1915, they were not yet ready, although it was planned they would launch in the early summer.

The events of the fall of 1914 were disastrous for the Russians in the Black Sea, giving control to the Central Powers. First and foremost, the two Ottoman dreadnoughts were delivered a couple of months before the war started, and an experienced German Admiral sailed into Constantinople with a modern battlecruiser (the Goeben) following a harrowing and epic saga of escape from the British in the Mediterranean.

The result didn't wait to be delivered in spades for the Russians in early September 1914. At the Battle of Cape Sarych, the Germano-

Ottoman fleet sunk all four Russian pre-dreadnoughts, tilting the balance completely into the Central Powers camp in the Black Sea

What followed was four months of total dominance for Admiral Souchon's fleet. A raid on Batum on the Eastern Black Sea, raids on Sebastopol, and complete interdiction of any relevant Russian shipping followed. Every reinforcement soldier and supplies that needed to be delivered to the armies in the Caucasus had to be done by land through rail and the abysmal road system in that area.

And it wasn't over.

Admiral Souchon stood by the viewport on the bridge of former battlecruiser Goeben-now Yavuz Sultan, looking proudly left and right at his assembled fleet. He had two magnificent dreadnoughts to command apart from his own. The battleships Sultan Osman-I Evvel and the Resadiye were powerful ships in their own right. Just one of them would have been enough for the Ottomans to dominate the starved-of-battleships Russian navy. He also had two pre-dreadnought ships (Barbaro Hayreddin and Turgut Reis), two heavy cruisers, and eight destroyers.

Ottoman Navy- Admiral Souchon	
BB Sultán Osmán-ı Evvel	CA Hamidiye
BB Reşadiye	CA Mecidiye
BC Yavuz Sultan Selim (HMS Goeben 8 DD	
Pre Dreadnought BB Barbaros Hayreddin	
Pre Dreadnought BB Turgut Reis.	

A lot of training had gone on in the last two months, since the Ottoman sailors had needed a lot of it. After all, the entire idea behind the plethora of raids he'd led against Russian installations since the fall was to get them ready for more fighting. The strategic value of them was in the experience, not the overall impact on the war.

He knew the reason they did okay at the Battle of Cape Sarych was because the Russian training wasn't really any better and because the

Germano-Ottoman fleet had better ships. Souchon knew that there would come a time when his ships would sortie from the Dardanelles Strait and challenge the British. With the sudden joining of Greece and its two pre-dreadnought battleships, the combined fleet that would result from them sailing into the Bosphorus was something to behold. While it remained to be seen if Athens would order its ships to join him, he still hoped.

And for all these reasons, for all the training, and because he would eventually have other enemies to fight, he and his fleet were sailing toward two very juicy targets.

The Russians, fully aware they were in a bind in the Black Sea, were expediting the construction of two new dreadnought battleships, the Imperatritsa Mariya and the Imperatritsa Ekaterina Velikaya. Since the Battle of Cape Sarych, Souchon had been told that three more keels had been laid for more battleships.

The launching of those two modern vessels soon in 1915 was a major threat to him and the Ottomans, and in an ideal world, they were destroyed, or everything was done to postpone their construction. These ships needed to be destroyed.

"Admiral," said one of his officers near him. *"We are sixty nautical miles from the channel leading to Nikolayev; orders for the fleet, Sir?" "We wait for darkness to get close enough to have our guns in range, and we engage their fixed naval defenses." "Yes, Admiral."*

Souchon was preoccupied by the presence of naval mines and the fixed naval fortifications present at the mouth of the channel. Nikolayev Shipyard was located twenty miles inland, and thus, he would have to get in close, but he couldn't contemplate entering the channel. The entire affair would thus have to be executed from a distance.

In terms of range, Goeben's 28 cm SK L/50 guns could fire at a maximum distance of 40,000 yards. The two British-made Turkish battleships, the BL 13.5-inch Mk VI naval guns, could reach targets 35,000 yards away. At a glance, it seemed that Souchon's ships would be able to easily hit the shipyard.

Now, the problem with that idea was that the effective gun range was, at best, 19,000 yards, and even that was considered an incredibly lucky hit. In fact, to date in the annals of warfare, not one hit over that had ever been scored in any conflict in history.

Hence, even if his ships managed to fire at the shipyards, there was no guarantee they would hit the ships. They did have approximate coordinates and emplacements of the yard since, after all, the shipyards couldn't move and had been there for over twenty years. And that was the gist of the plan. Get in close, fire as many broadsides as possible, and try not to lose too much to the powerful Russian fortifications protecting the entrance of the channel leading to Nikolayev.

"Helm," he started, putting his hands behind his back. *"We go in."*

The Battle of Turtucaia Part 1
Dobruja Region. Romania, January 28th, 1915

The city of Tortucaia was a crossing spot for armies since Roman times. It was one of the places on the border between modern Romania and Bulgaria where the large river was the narrowest, enabling the troops to get across better.

With Romania attacking Austria-Hungary's 1st Army through Transylvania with three armies and pushing really hard, it didn't take long for Vienna and Berlin to ask Tsar Ferdinand the Ist to launch his own offensive against the Romanians to calm down their ardor. Kaiser Wilhelm even pledged to send supplies, troops, and heavy artillery to help the Bulgars.

Bulgaria had entered the war in a weakened state because of its major defeat in the last Balkan War in 1912-1913. Its 200,000-man force, divided into three armies, would have never been enough to attack Romania head-on. But now that well over two-thirds of the Romanian forces were engaged in Transylvania, it had become possible for Tsar Ferdinand to get his revenge.

While Germany and Austria-Hungary had asked for help, the Bulgars had not needed any encouragement but only the opportunity that was presenting itself to them. The hate they entertained for their northern neighbors burned bright in their hearts.

The Romanians had been, after all, the very reason for Bulgaria's defeat in the Second Balkan War, as they stabbed them in the back, taking Sofia without even encountering resistance because Tsar Ferdinand's forces were already fighting the Greeks and the Serbians.

The Tsar himself was thus overlooking the enemy fortress from the southern shore of the Danube on that crisp morning of the 28th of January. Winter wasn't too harsh in the Balkans, and thus, military operations weren't hampered severely by the weather. This enabled the Bulgarian 1st, 2nd, and 3rd Armies (the Bulgars attacked with all their forces since there were no more enemies to fight with Serbia gone and the Greco-Ottomans now allies) to launch a powerful offensive all across the border between the two countries. However, the major push was on Turtucaia.

"As you can see, Your Excellency," said General Toshev, the commander of the Bulgarian 3rd Army, "*the troops have crossed overnight and are now moving to encircle the stronghold.*" "Yes, I can see that, General," answered Ferdinand, looking in the distance with a pair of binoculars. "This is excellent news. What of 1st and 2nd Armies, are they also in the process of attacking?" The General answered with a smile. "*Sir, we have crossed the Romanian border on its entire length, and we hope to seriously threaten the enemy as we continue to advance.*"

"Very well. When are we launching the general assault on the fortress?" "We are about to receive some heavy guns from the Austrians with a few 280mm Skoda mortars. The Germans are also sending their 33rd Infantry Regiment. Once everything is in place, we will launch the attack. I estimate that within two to three days, Tortucaia will be ours."

The Tsar smiled. "Excellent. You know, General Toshev, I wonder what that young King of theirs had in mind in joining the Entente and attacking the Austrians in the back. I understand why the Franco-British wanted him to do it, but we and our allies could have hardly watched without doing anything. They should have stuck with the old King Carol's policies. Anyway," the Tsar said, lowering his binoculars and turning to return to his horse, "*We'll take advantage of that stupidity and get our revenge on the bastards.*"

(...) the strategic situation between the two countries (..)

Romania's strategic situation was not an enviable one, with Bulgaria's three armies launching at it (with the help of the Austro-Germans) while it only had the weak, 75,000-soldier 3rd Army under General Mihail Aslan. The remainder of its 400,000 force was "out-of-position" attacking the Austro-Hungarian's 1st Army in Transylvania.

Within the first day of the Bulgarian attack, it was obvious Romania was in a difficult position, with its weak 75,000-soldier-strong 3rd Army facing the entirety of Tsar Ferdinand I's 200,000 experienced soldiers.

ROMANIA			
400,000 soldiers	Commander		Area of operation
1st Army	General Ioan Culcer	750000	Transylvania
2nd Army	General Alexandru Averescu	100000	Transylvania
3rd Army	General Mihail Aslan	75000	Drobudja, Bulgaro-Romanian border
4th Army	General Constantin Prezan	150 000	Transylvania

BULGARIA			
200,000 soldiers	Commander		Area of operation
1st Army	General Kliment Boyadzhiev	100000	Drobudja, Bulgaro-Romanian border
2nd Army	General Georgi Todorov	50000	Drobudja, Bulgaro-Romanian border
3rd Army	General Toshev	50000	Drobudja, Bulgaro-Romanian border

The raid on Nikolayev Part 2
Admiral Souchon back in action, January 25th, 1915

"Let's fire the first broadside, shall we," said Souchon to his gunnery commander. The Admiral looked at his watch, and he smiled. The pre-arranged time for the combined broadside was set at 1206.

There were two forts protecting the entrance of the Nikolayev Channel. Both were relatively modern since they were built following the Russo-Japanese War in 1907. Fort Ekaterina, the first of them, was bristling with coastal defense guns ranging from the modern 203 mm 50 caliber Pattern 1905 to the ancient smoothbore cannon. Fort Nicolas, on the other side, also had 203 mm 50 caliber Pattern 1905 and 203 mm 45 caliber Pattern 1892. The two coastal fortifications were dangerous to the Germano-Ottoman ships, and thus, they were the first targets of the day.

Regardless of his plan and his intentions, the German Admiral was worried that the coastal guns could hurt his ships. Forts couldn't be sunk and thus could absorb a lot of damage.

The guns of the fleet all opened up at the same time, creating a huge flash in the darkness. The two forts had been quiet as they hadn't seen the Germano-Ottoman fleet approach. Their sleepy sentries and gunners were temporarily blinded by the multiple and powerful flashes. The shells started to slam into the walls and the gun embrasures in great rocking blasts. Souchon looked at his watch with nervousness, counting the seconds for the next salvo. The first few were critical to the mission's success. Plant as many shells as possible in the forts before their gunners returned fire.

Then, the second salvo blossomed all across his lined-up ships, and more explosions rocked the two forts. Then, another minute elapsed, and Souchon saw what he'd dreaded during the planning stage of his operation. The first flashes of the fort's guns retaliating. About twenty of them fired, and the shells started to land in the water, straddling some of his ships. Most, like every first naval salvo, either landed ahead of his ships or flew above. The only reason Souchon's first attack had been so accurate was because the fort didn't move and was easy to spot and they had had time to calculate the coordinates to fire. It was a quiet night; the fleet was at a very short range (3,000 yards), and there were no waves. Thus, the gunners were able to accurately have the range.

The third salvo fired, again blasting out in fireballs of fury and might, slamming once more into the by-now very damaged fortresses. With every shot fired from the powerful dreadnoughts, the water in front of them rippled because of their blasts. All the while, the two pre-dreadnoughts, the destroyers, and the heavy cruisers also poured their fire into the fortresses, albeit at a faster rate than their bigger brothers. The fortified buildings and the area around them were alight with fiery burning infernos.

By the sixth salvo, the remaining Russian guns finally started to score some hits. Two slammed on Turgut Reis, damaging one of its guns and a funnel. A hit was scored on the Sultân Osmân-ı Evvel, which bent the ship's armored forecastle at a weird angle. The great armored ship withstood the hit. Two destroyers were sunk, and finally, Goeben received a shell in one of its engine rooms. From one moment to the next, Souchon was thrown up in the air by the resulting steam boiler explosion, and he smashed into the steel deck, stunned.

None of the gunners aboard the Germano-Ottoman ships needed any orders as they pummelled the forts to oblivion, and the duel lasted another few minutes, by which time the Russian fortifications were silenced.

"Admiral," said one of the bridge Lieutenants, helping him up to stand on his feet. *"What... What has happened?"* *"The ship's been hit, Sir. One of the engine rooms and the boiler are gone. Over fifty sailors are dead, Sir. But the forts are silenced."* Souchon, still stunned, could hear

the sound of the guns and Goeben's own reverberations because it also fired. *"The ships are continuing on with the mission, Sir."*

Several hours later, Souchon woke up once more (with a resounding headache), but this time in the ship's sick bay. His men rapidly brought him up to speed; the forts were destroyed, and they'd fired over ten salvos as he had wanted them at distant Nikolayev before departing. They were now en route back to Constantinople.

The German Admiral wasn't to know until much later, but the entire attack had been a waste. The ten salvoes had been fired all right, and they'd done a lot of damage to the city around Nikolayev and killed over a hundred civilians. But none of the shells came even close to the two construction docks where the Russian dreadnoughts were being built. Souchon and his men would just have to fight the enemy battleships when they were ready to float and fight.

Overall situation – East Prussia, Carpathians-Galicia-Przemysl
The fight and the battles to January 30th, 1915

The Eastern situation was completely contrary (disastrous) to what the Central Powers had in the West (victorious). The situation in France was also fixed into a stalemate, while frontlines in the East moved with the ebb and flow of offensives on both sides.

In January, the Russian juggernaut was rolling over the Austrian forces in Galicia and was now pushing them into the Carpathian Mountains. The city fortress of Przemysl still held, but it was now just a matter of time before it fell. The only thing saving the Central Powers (and especially Austria-Hungary) at that moment was the bad weather that impeded offensive operations across the line.

It was also a problem for the Germans, who had broken through in Poland following their victory at the Battle of Marienburg and advanced toward Koenigsberg with the reinforced 8th Army and the newly constituted 10th Army. The 10th was a mix of troop transfers from the West and newly raised reserves, while the 8th had been fighting the Russian enemy since the beginning of the war. 550,000-soldiers strong and under the command of the duo of victorious generals Hindenburg and Ludendorff, the German forces were poised to push the Russians out of their ancestral territory of Eastern Prussia.

GERMANY
East Prussia

550,000 soldiers	Commander	Soldiers	Area of operation
8th Army	General von Hindenburg and Luddendorf	350,000 soldiers	East Prussia
10th Army		200,000 soldiers	East Prussia

Awaiting them as they encircled Koenigsberg were the Russian forces under the overall command of General Rennenkampf, also victorious at the Battle of Gumbinnen. The General, commanding the Russian 1st and 10th Army, had a total of 750,000 soldiers. Rennenkampf had also just ordered his forces to end the siege of Koenigsberg to concentrate in order to give battle to the approaching Germans and not be attacked while besieging the city.

RUSSIA
Siege of Koenigsberg and East Prussia

750,000 soldiers	Commander	Soldiers	Area of operation
1st Army	General Paul von Rennenkampf	350,000 soldiers	Eastern Prussia, Komigsberg
10th Army	General Vasily Flug	400,000 soldiers	Eastern Prussia, Komigsberg

The fight for Galicia and Transylvania, or more to the point, the fight for the survival of the Austro-Hungarian Empire, was a fight of titanic proportions and over mind-boggling distances.

Following a series of ill-advised offensives by Austro-Hungarian Commander in Chief Conrad von Hotzendorf in Galicia, the Russians under the brilliant General Brusilov had first contained the enemy offensive and then counterattacked. The result had been a complete disaster for the Habsburg armies. Russia then proceeded to occupy all of Galicia and encircled the fortified city of Przemysl, trapping 131,000 soldiers in it.

The fight for the fortress was now entering its third month, but it was about to end as the Russians were pushing with the 500,000 soldiers of the 3rd Army (General Rutsky) and 4th Army (General Evert), and the Austrian defenders were at the end of their resistance.

RUSSIA
Galicia and Prezmysl

1,200,000 soldiers	Commander	Soldiers	Area of operation
3rd Army	General Nikolai Ruzsky	200,000 soldiers	Przemysl
4th Army	General Alexei Evert	300,000 soldiers	Przemysl
5th Army	General Pavel Plehve	300,000 soldiers	Carpathian and galicia
8th Army	General Aleksei Alekseevich Brusilov	250,000 soldiers	Carpathian and galicia
9th Army	General Platon Lechitsky	200,000 soldiers	Carpathian and Galicia

Furthermore, the beleaguered Austrians, now reinforced by their German allies, were in no position to help Przemysl, as their frontline defenses in the Carpathians were hundreds of miles away toward the West. In total, the Russian Empire aligned a staggering 1,200,000 soldiers in the combined Carpathian-Galicia-Przemysl front.

Facing them were 688,000 soldiers of the Austro-Hungarian Army, either holed up in Przemysl (117,000 soldiers) or else arrayed on the Carpathian line of defense. It did not look good for the Austro-Hungarians, as the men in the fortress of Przemysl were all but lost, further worsening the situation.

AUSTRIA-HUNGARY

Galicia-Carpathians-Przemysl			
997,000 soldiers	Commander	Soldiers	Area of operation
1st Army	General Viktor Dankl von Krasnik	210,000 soldiers	Transylvania
4th army	General Moritz von Auffenberg	235,000 soldiers	Carpathian and galicia
3rd Army	General Rudolf Brudermann	95,000 soldiers	Serbia, moving to Bulgaria-Romania
2nd Army (former group Covess)	General Heinrich von Kummer	230,000 soldiers	Carpathian and galicia
Przemysl garrison	General Hermann Kusmanek von Burgneustadten	117,000 soldiers	Encircled in Przemysl

Their German friends had sent them 110,000 additional soldiers in the form of the German 11th Army (General Max von Gallitz). They came with a lot of guns and a full complement of Maxim machine guns, and it was hoped that the powerful forces would be able to reverse the dramatic situation.

GERMANY

Galicia-Carpathians			
110,000 soldiers	Commander	Soldiers	Area of operation
German 11th Army	General Max von Gallwitz	110,000 soldiers	Galicia-Carpathians

The Central Powers problem in the East was further worsened by the newly started Romanian offensive in Transylvania. There, 325,000 Romanians fought the outnumbered forces of General Viktor Dankl von Krasnik's 210,000 soldiers, and nothing was stopping them.

ROMANIA

400,000 soldiers	Commander	Soldiers	Area of operation
1st Army	General Ioan Culcer	750,000 soldiers	Transylvania
2nd Army	General Alexandru Averescu	100,000 soldiers	Transylvania
3rd Army	General Mihail Aslan	15,000 soldiers	Drobudja, Bulgaro-Romanian border
4th Army	General Constantin Prezan	15,000 soldiers	Transylvania

The last hope of the Austrians in Transylvania was the opening of the Bulgarian offensive, bolstered by some Ottoman and German troops on the Romano-Bulgar border and, more specifically, in the Dobruja region. There, a battle of epic proportions was shaping up in the Romanian town of Turtucaia. The Romanians had only kept 75,000 (General Aslan's 3rd Army) of their soldiers to guard their southern border, and they now faced the 200,000 men of the Bulgarian Army (1st, 2nd, and 3rd Armies), helped by the Turkish 3rd Army of Hafiz Hakki Pasha, adding 25,000 soldiers to the offensive totals.

The last theater of operations in the East at that moment in time in 1915 was Eastern Poland, following the German breakthrough there. The German General August von Mackensen was entrusted by Hindenburg to continue to push, but not as hard because his men might be needed to bolster the Carpathian frontline if things didn't improve there.

Poland			
500,000 soldiers	Commander	Soldiers	Area of operation
German 9th Army	General August von Mackensen	380,000 soldiers	East of Warsaw
German 12th Army	General Max von Fabeck	220,000 soldiers	West of Warsaw

Thus, the 550,000 Germans slowed down their attack while they faced Russian General Selivanov's 650,000 soldiers (11th, 12th, 13th armies).

Poland			
650,000 soldiers	Commander	Soldiers	Area of operation
11th Army	General of Infantry Andrey Selivanov	250,000 soldiers	East of Warsaw and Belarus
12th Army	General Aleksey Churin	200,000 soldiers	East of Warsaw and Belarus
13th Army	General Mikhail Vassilievich Alekseyev	200,000 soldiers	East of Warsaw and Belarus

Because they were forced to slow down their advance and also since they were outnumbered, the Germans forces in Poland were on the verge of using a new, terrible weapon to try and pierce the enemy lines with minimum risk and involvement.

In all likeliness, the next few months would decide the fate of not only the Austro-Hungarian Empire but the future of Romania, Koenigsberg and Poland.

4th Imperial Russian Army
Siege of Przemysl Part 2, January 31st, 1915

Private soldier Dimitri Fedorov's boot splashed in the wallowing, slushy ground as the icy, melting substance scattered to both sides of him. The man was running amidst the whistling bullets and the shattering explosions all around.

Sergeant Radetzki was near, yelling to the rest of the squad to run as fast as they could in the large space between the two Austro-Hungarian redoubts. The first one they had taken the day before with a storm of fire and lead, following a lucky artillery shot that opened its side completely to attack. Artillery shells weren't very precise, but if you fired enough of them at a target, eventually, they were bound to hit something. The second redoubt was alive with enemy soldiers and bristled with rifles protruding from its viewport and firing ports.

Dimitri slid on a patch of ice and fell hard in a pool of slushy, iced water. He hit the ground hard, splashing all around, grunting. The entire area was sort of melting, but not because of a thaw. It was the recent artillery bombardment launched by General Alexei Evert to prepare for this attack.

The 3rd and 4th Russian armies, under the overall command of Nikolai Ruzsky, had been besieging the Austro-Hungarian fortress of Przemysl for almost three months now, and it was finally happening. They were storming the enemy forts one by one in the last week.

A rush of cold hit Dimitry as he wallowed helplessly in the slush, slipping a couple of times because there was ice under the watery substance. He crawled out, now completely frozen and shaking. He willed himself up and started running. There was only one remedy for this type of cold. A good fire, and fortunately for him, the major battle underway had so far produced several large ones. Thus, he made his way to one of the large bunkers on fire and just dropped as near as he could from it. The fire was immediately soothing, and he looked around, not seeing the damned Sergeant Radetzki order him forward. He was sort of sheltered from the withering enemy fire as the burning structure blocked the Austrian gunner's view. His skin started tingling in a good way (before, it tingled in a bad way with the skin-burning, soul-wrenching cold), and within another ten minutes, he felt okay to rejoin the battle.

A gust of wintery wind slammed the billowing cloud from the fire right at him, and he coughed hard. Using the cover of the dark cloud, he ran right into it. This enabled him to approach the enemy position undetected.

The enemy soldiers and the two machine guns inside the redoubt were firing continuously at the Russians, but several of them (now, Dimitri saw Radetzki, his back to the base of the redoubt, rifle close to his chest) had reached the Austro-Hungarian fortification.

He finally sprinted to the concrete building amidst blasts and enemy bullet fire, arriving unscathed. There, he was close enough to hear Sergeant Radetzki tell the men to fish what they had left in hand bombs (also called grenades) and throw them into the apertures, viewport, and firing ports. The model the Russians were using was called the M1915 Stender Hand Grenade. It was a half-foot stick with a bulge at the end containing a charge and shrapnel inside. The goal of the weapon was to kill infantry inside the redoubt and then hope to be able to storm it.

He also had a couple left and thus primed them. He threw them into the holes. The moment the Russians started throwing them, yells of panic were heard inside the fortified building. Seconds later, the blasts were heard in a sort of muffled bang because the detonations were inside the redoubt.

"We go around and find the entrance to this thing and fucking storm it," yelled Radetzki to his men. Dimitri followed the Sergeant and the men in front of him as they went around the structure, slipping as they

went on the rubble-strewn ground. On the other side was the same view. Smoke. Debris, but in the far distance, there were no more bunkers of enemy fortifications. It was an empty field and a river in the background. Dimitri felt suddenly excited that they might just take the damned city.

The same scene was repeating itself across the entire city, and the Russians were in the process of destroying or storming the last bunkers and forts of the Przemysl fortress.

They arrived at a large door, and just as he thought they would never be able to open it, the large steel-reinforced thing opened, giving way to Austro-Hungarian soldiers with their hands lifted in the air in surrender.

A lot of yelling and nervousness went on both sides as Fedorov and his comrades pointed their rifles at the slowly walking, unarmed men coming out of the redoubt. The enemy soldiers were pushed to their knees, and then Radetzki ordered half the men to go inside and make sure the thing was done for.

They returned a few minutes later and smiled. The place was empty of living enemies. The scene repeated itself many, many times that day as the Austro-Hungarian resistance just crumbled in place. The 117,000 soldiers of General Hermann Kusmanek von Burgneustädten had fought well and held on for almost three months, giving time to their brothers in the Carpathians to establish a good line of defense and for the Germans to send help.

Bad news
February 1st, Austro-Hungarian 4th Army field headquarters

Conrad von Hotzendorf, the Commander-in-Chief of the Austro-Hungarian forces, looked at the snow-covered scenery before him. The Carpathian Mountains formed a high barrier about sixty-five miles wide with an average elevation of 3000-some feet. The entire area was very limited in roads, and most communication went through the few rail lines built in the mountain passes by the Austrians over the years. He was near the frontline in the Carpathian Mountains, about 100 miles from the military catastrophe that had just unfolded for the Central Powers and, more specifically, for his own country. With lots of rainfall and dampness, the area was foggy and rainy in the fall and covered in snow, like now, in the winter months from November to February. Hotzendorf faced Galicia, the Imperial territory he had lost to the Russians. Galicia was won over by the Empire in the successful and successive partitions of Poland before the Napoleonic Wars in the 18th Century. It was thus an old and important land for the Emperor. For the Austrian commander, the loss was a matter of pride. The news of the fall of Przemysl stung him hard, and he was of the mind to launch an attack once again.

The area they were in possessed no important cities but only small mountain towns and organizing defense and entrenching an army there had not been a simple feat. But they were ready for the enemy onslaught now, thanks to the brave men of the Przemysl fortress. *"Are you certain it is a good idea to attack in the dead of winter, General,"* said German General Max von Gallwitz. The man was the commander of the 110,000-strong newly arrived German 11th Army and the main reason why Conrad thought they should attack. The Kaiser's troops were superbly equipped and trained and recently victorious from France.

The commander of the Austrian 4th Army, General Moritz von Auffenberg, didn't say anything to support his commander, and his silence spoke volumes of his opinion over the matter of attacking against the terrible winter and the numerous Russian forces.

Conrad was a proud man and had the confidence of Emperor Franz Joseph, although only God knew why. The man had presided over three crushing defeats after ordering ill-prepared offensives in Serbia and Russian Galicia in the Fall of 1914. The Emperor was in his eighties, and that was the only plausible explanation. Any sane military man would have already sacked the Austrian Commander-in-Chief.

Von Hotzendorf's idea was that an offensive had to be attempted to retake Galicia to avoid the country being knocked out of the war. He saw the Carpathian Mountains and all the preparations (the armies he had in the sector were relatively well-supplied and rested) as a way for Austria-Hungary to regain prestige. Thus, he pretended not to hear Gallwitz's words.

"General von Auffenberg, our main objective is to liberate Przemysl and then if we can push the enemy hard, to reclaim Lemberg, the capital of Austrian Galicia." Conrad's plan, prepared in December because he knew the Germans were finally coming, was an offensive action on a broad 120-mile forested front by the Austro-Hungarian 4th Army. The idea was to slam hard on Brussilov's extreme left flank. *"Generals, I understand your reservations. However, I believe our troops can do this, and if one thing is certain, it's that the enemy does not expect us to attack."* He turned to face the two men who stood a little in the background to him on the ledge they were on, overlooking the snowy valley below. *"We can surprise them, gentlemen, and win,"* he continued, hitting his left palm with his fist.

The German commander didn't relent right away. *"Perhaps you are right, General,"* answered von Gallwitz. *"But I will confer on this with General Hindenburg to see what he decides."* Before Conrad could speak up, he lifted his hand again. *"We have been sent here, my men and I, on a defensive mission, and the purpose of this line of defense is the preservation of Austria-Hungary. This set of instructions has been given to me as my priority."* He paused to walk on the side of the ledge as a cold wind blew light white snow around in a billowing swirl. Conrad finally spoke up. *"General von Gallwitz, you are in Austrian lands and thus under my command."* The German grunted. *"General von Hotzendorf, I understand what you say, but I will nonetheless confer with my superior in East Prussia."*

The Battle of Koenigsberg Part 1
The German attack, February 2nd, 1915

The stage was set for the battle that would decide the fate of Koenigsberg and with it, all of East Prussia. A Russian victory would mean the fortress would fall and that the Germans would be in grave difficulties, with Berlin even threatened. After all, not so long ago, the Russian Imperial forces had advanced all the way to the Vistula before they were beaten at the Battle of Marienburg. If the Germans won the battle, it would mean trouble for Russia, as it would open the way to more offensives into Lithuania. Combined with the Kaiser's troops advancing in Poland (the front one was now east of Warsaw), it could truly unhinge the Tsar.

On the one side of the fight were General Rennenkampf's forces, the Russian 1st and 10th Army. The General was the victor of the Battle of Gumbinnen and now had a fierce reputation, notwithstanding his inability to storm Koenigsberg since October 1914.

Siege of Koenigsberg and East Prussia			
750,000 soldiers	Commander	Soldiers	Area of operation
1st Army	General Paul von Rennenkampf	350,000 soldiers	Eastern Prussia, Komigsberg
10th Army	General Vasily Flug	400,000 soldiers	Eastern Prussia, Komigsberg

The Russian forces' supply situation had somewhat improved over the months, but it remained that some of the troops were hungry, and the artillery could not fire every day at the fortress. The shell and small arms ammunition shortage problem lay not in the logistical system but in the general lack of ordinance across the Empire. The country was vast but not very industrialized like Germany or France, and thus, it struggled to provide constant and sufficient shell supplies to its armies in the field. Nevertheless, Rennenkampf's troops were numerous (750,000 soldiers), and the troops' morale was high because of the fact that the Empire was on the offensive.

On the other side of the soon-to-be battlefield, the Germans approached Koenigsberg with 550,000 soldiers of the 8th and 10th Armies and led by what would become to be recognized as the best duo of generals of the First World War, Paul von Hindenburg and Erich Ludendorff. The two men were competent, resolute, and well-organized, just like their troops.

East Prussia			
550,000 soldiers	Commander	Soldiers	Area of operation
8th Army	General von Hindenburg and Luddendorf	350,000 soldiers	East Prussia
10th Army		200,000 soldiers	East Prussia

The troops of the Kaiser were, contrary to their Russian opponents, very well supported by a powerful industrialized nation. In fact, the Reich was the top industrial powerhouse in the world, even ahead of the Americans. They produced shells, ammunition, and everything in between at a prodigious rate, and thus, their soldiers were well fed, well-stocked in bullets, and their cannons always had a full complement of shells. This in itself was a factor that would prove decisive to the approaching Germans.

General Rennenkampf had ordered his troops back a few kilometers from Koenigsberg, and they abandoned their intricate siege trenches and installations. The move took over five days to complete, but when he was done, the Russian General and his troops had repositioned to face the incoming Germans and were well-entrenched, if not in permanent and well-built defenses. They had a week to prepare their defenses, and nothing was spared. Even the local population was forcibly put to work.

The battle started in the early hours, with heavy German artillery preparation. The barrage lasted far shorter than Rennenkampf would have thought, however, and that piqued the defender's curiosity. Amidst the receding smoke and haze of the bombardment, the loud grumble and ground shaking of the Russian guns were replaced by the pounding feet of thousands of yelling men. Above, German biplanes flew in reconnaissance, thundering down on them like hawks and firing their machine guns. Hindenburg had decided to try and surprise the Russians with an early attack.

The German losses as they approached the Russian positions were very serious as there was nowhere to hide from the enemy fire since Rennenkampf had positioned his troops on the plain south of Koenigsberg. The Russian fire was like a stream of fire that washed over the poor attacking Germans. And then, the artillery shelling started again, catching Rennenkampf's men in the open as they were out of their trenches somewhat to fire at the enemy. They saw and heard the arriving shells too late, and thus, a serious blow landed on their heads. Then, the German troops truly started sprinting.

The ground continued to shake mightily, the entire area an echoing reverberation reminiscent of the end of the world in one truly shattering sound. It didn't take long for the air to saturate with dust, smells of cordite, and blood. The yells of soldiers from both sides could be heard, as well as the crackling and unending chime of rifle and machine-gun fire.

(...) German frontline (...)

Rifleman Daniel Kranheim ran as hard as he could amidst the shattering explosions and blasts of fire. One particularly large enemy artillery blast wave knocked him to the side, and he fell into a ditch or what looked like a large artillery shell crater. He was stunned for a moment, and his ears rang like a broken doorbell, but otherwise, he was unscathed. He did a cursory inspection and didn't find anything broken or bleeding. He had to do it visually since, for a moment, his body felt completely numb. And then he snapped back to reality. The explosions could be heard again, the ground shook, and rifle fire was flying above the small ditch he had fallen into. He decided to peer his head a little over the ditch, crawling to the top of it.

The scene before him was filled with dust and smoke, and he saw the backs of hundreds of assaulting German soldiers. Here and there, a few of their houses and barns burned fiercely, having been hit by enemy artillery or machine guns. The battle was in a field, but there was also a small village in the middle of the battlefield, and thus, there were scattered buildings. Dead or horribly wounded bodies lay everywhere. He wasn't afraid, he thought for a moment, but he wondered if he could stay in this ditch and not be noticed.

Then the face of his rough Corporal and then of the Sergeant hovered at the forefront of his mind, and he dreaded to think what these two would do to him if they found out he'd tried to hide or slack off. NCOs didn't like cowardice under fire in any army, but it was even worse in the German one since it was punishable by death. His two NCOs were tough bastards, and he had no doubt they would be on him if they found out, and he decided that he preferred to brave the enemy's fire than their ire.

(...) Russian trenches (...)

Private Yvan Krasinski fired his rifle once more at one of the onrushing enemies. The bastards came in waves, and they kept knocking every one of the German bastards down like duckpins. But that didn't stop them from attacking again and again. He looked beside him and saw the other Russian soldiers also firing at the enemy. He was at the junction between his division and another one in the army; thus, he didn't know these guys well. As he looked, one of the men in their group had his head disappear in a spray of blood, hit by an enemy bullet. Not everyone had yet adorned the metal helmet in the Russian Army, both because of skepticism it was effective and also because not enough were issued to the troops. Yvan figured the guy might have died anyway, but at least he would have had a chance of surviving with some protection. He reloaded his rifle and heard several of his comrades yelling. *"In front!"* yelled one of their sergeants, pointing at yet another of the enemy charges. The Germans were almost upon them.

(...) German frontline (...)

Rifleman Daniel Kranheim was getting so close to the enemy trenches and makeshift fortifications that he could see the faces of the soldiers shooting at them. It was a mix of steel-helmeted and cap-wearing soldiers. For a moment, he wondered why a man would go to war only with a headdress. He'd heard it had to do with supply problems in the Russian Army or something like that.

In any case, it didn't matter one bit to him since the bastards were easier to kill. From what he could tell, he was at the junction of two different enemy units since there was a clear distinction between the soldiers on the right (with helmets) and the ones on the left (without).

"Guys," said the dreaded Sergeant. No one answered. They were all crouching in a shallow trench and a few half-demolished buildings. *"What are you waiting for?"* One of the men ventured a question since the enemy fire was very heavy, and they had a good chance of getting killed. Daniel was of the same mind and didn't like to be suicidal. *"What do you mean?"* The Sergeant didn't like the soldier's question. *"I mean, we need to go on the attack again and destroy the enemy,"* he blurted out.

In a general sense, the first German assault had been repulsed. What remained in the field of battle were fiercely burning houses, buildings, and bodies, more dead bodies, and several injured soldiers crying for help on the ground. Small pockets of survivors hid in shell holes or other makeshift cover, like Daniel's little group. General Erich Ludendorff was about to send another wave, and the Sergeant, an old veteran from the fighting in China (the Boxer Rebellion), instinctively knew that more men were coming. *"We wait for the coming wave of fresh reinforcements and we attack again. Get some water and take a breather. We're about to go back into the action."*

(...) Russian trench, 15 meters away (...)

Private Yvan Krasinski didn't like the sudden stillness over the battlefield. They'd repulsed the first enemy assault. Proof of that was hundreds of bodies strewn about in the field facing him, some dead, some burning, and others moving about, seriously hurt. Their small victory had not come without losses, however. Dead soldiers surrounded him and his surviving mates. On the side of the other Russian unit beside him, a few meters down the line, the casualties were just as horrendous.

"What now?" He wondered if the enemy was done, but it appeared unlikely. He'd been told the German Army had at least three times their numbers.

(...) The commanders on both sides - Rennenkampf (...)

General Rennenkampf looked nonchalantly at the Baltic Sea over the horizon and thought it nice that this part of his view seemed unperturbed. To one side, he had the German assault, and then to his right, he had the burning, smoldering, and smoking fortress of Koenigsberg that he'd done his best to destroy during the long siege.

He wondered if the enemy commander was done for the day, but it appeared unlikely. *"What's our shell reserve,"* he said to his Chief of Staff beside him. Both men were on a small promontory about a thousand feet behind their main trench line. *"Sir, we've got about two thousand shells left."* At that, Rennenkampf cursed to the high heavens. Stupid supply officers had told him he would receive much more before the battle, but the things were never delivered.

(...) The commanders on both sides - Ludendorff (...)

"It's time," said General Erich Ludendorff to his field commanders of the German 8th and 10th Army. *"Yes, sir." "Also contact the garrison commander that his part in the plan is also a go for now,"* continued the Commander-in-Chief.

Both Ludendorff and Hindenburg's plan for the liberation of Koenigsberg was in two phases, and now they were starting the second, seven hours after the first one in the morning. The idea was to attack frontally by sending most of its force there and slam the

Russians with a powerful artillery bombardment. Once Rennenkampf's men were fixated and fighting what was in front, the German 18th Corps, some 55,000 strong, would swing south and then north to attack the extreme left flank of the Russian armies. The extreme right flank would also be attacked by a sortie from the Koenigsberg garrison, reinforced the night before by two fresh divisions landed in the harbor under the guise of darkness.

The general idea was not to encircle and destroy the Russians like at Marienburg, as they had too many soldiers in front of Koenigsberg (750,000), but to force Rennenkampf to withdraw and thus retake control of Koenigsberg's immediate area and put an end to the siege once and for all.

The two army commanders left the field HQ Erich Ludendorff was in. The man was acting as a deputy of Paul von Hindenburg, as both men had hatched the attack plan and he was the one supposed to execute while the old General stayed in the main HQ behind the lines.

(...) German frontline (...)

A loud rumble slowly rose from gentle and far away to overwhelming. The ground beneath Daniel first hummed and then shook for real as the entire enemy line of the trench lit up with blasts of fire. Smoke rose to the sky, and a major dust cloud expanded horizontally like a wall. The thing slammed into their positions as well, and for a moment, it was difficult to see as there was heavy dust. Daniel coughed hard. Through it all, he heard the steady voice of his sergeant. *"Keep steady, lads, it's all right. We're only getting dust; imagine what the fucking Russkies are getting."*

He was privy to the incredible power of the German artillery in full action. The Russians' guns had been uncharacteristically shy since they arrived. He remembered that things were a lot livelier and more difficult with the enemy counterbattery fire. It almost seemed like the Russians didn't want to fire. Daniel had no idea, but Rennenkampf was almost out of shells and was keeping enough to have in case of an emergency or to break the German attack.

The second wave of the German attack was coming; they could all hear the thousands of human feet and horse hooves pounding the ground. "Wait, guys; *we need to wait for the attack to approach, or we'll just be shot down.*"

(...) Russian Trench (...)

Yvan was startled to see a German soldier sticking out of the large craters only forty yards in front of him and the trench. He was having trouble getting back to his senses after the incredible shelling of the last ten minutes. Everyone that survived the surprise shelling was at the ready, rifle on the ground and ready to fire. The next enemy wave was coming, and it was time to fight again. An incredibly heavy cordite smell hung in the air while a fog reminiscent of a morning haze hung over the trench and the field in front of him. It was eerie, and he was nervous, especially since he started to see those damned German spiked helmets move toward their trench. The man who rose out of the crater brandished a gun, and he almost laughed as he targeted him and fired. The round hit the man in the belly, and he fell backward and back out of sight into the hole. The rest of the line fired as well, and bullets poured into the exposed Germans running toward them.

(...) German frontline (...)

The Sergeant's body fell back with a thud into the shallow water of the crater with a bullet to the belly dead. The NCO's eyes were bloodshot, and he was mumbling. The man was dying. Not one of the soldiers moved to help him as they were also getting out of the crater and their hiding spot, obeying the dying man's last words. *"Sergeant,"* said Daniel, taking him into his arms and dragging him back to cover. Above them, mayhem was in full swing, and the bullets were flying. The man opened his mouth, then closed it, eyes then wide open, and died. *"I'll avenge you, Sarge,"* said Daniel, with a mounting rage inside of him. He picked up his rifle and walked over the crater and into a vortex of death and fire.

1st German Division, 1st Grenadier Regiment
Sortie, February 2nd, 1914

"Aaaattaaackkkk!!!!" yelled Mikael to his leftover men as they slammed into the enemy forces by the Baltic Sea. He yelled through his lungs because of all the frustration of the last few months, the men that died, and all the hardships he and his unit endured in defending the Fredrich Wilhelm I Fort in Koenigsberg.

The German 1st Division and especially its 1st Grenadier Regiment, which had been defending the most important fort in all of the defensive network, suffered greatly during the Russian siege of the city. Over 60% of the unit was gone due to death or severe injuries. Mikael and his seventy-five men were all that was left of his section. It was mindboggling, and now they finally got to have their revenge.

His Lieutenant, Werner Lotar, was also a survivor, and the man brandished his sword and sidearm, running beside him. Mikael knew that even Colonel Thomas von Kracken was part of the assault, along with two newly landed German divisions the night before.

Their part in the fight was to attack the extreme north of the enemy lines that extended to the Baltic Sea. The overall goal was, of course, to break through, but the Commander-in-Chief, Erich Ludendorff, had told the Colonel that it was not the final goal. Their purpose was to put pressure on the enemy and make him think that he was going to get encircled, which he might if he didn't retreat.

And thus, they attacked across the expanse between Koenigsberg and the Russian lines with all they had left. As he ran, he was rocked from side to side by the enemy explosions, and his comrades fell by the droves as a sea of bullets streamed toward them. Blood splattered everywhere.

Horses ran past him, brought the day before with the two divisions. The men atop them were German Lancers, the elite of the Kaiser's Army, and they galloped toward the enemy trench.

He stopped to fire his sidearm, then started running again. Looking to his side to try and find Lieutenant Lotar, he noticed he wasn't there anymore. He didn't have time to look for him and thus urged his men forward. The Lieutenant was lying fifty yards behind, dead in a pool of expanding blood.

"We're almost there," he yelled, gesturing his people forward with wide arcs of his arm. And his men ran, holding their rifles at their waist. The entire assault disappeared in a cloud of dark, billowing smoke.

The Battle of Koenigsberg Part 2
The German attack, February 2nd, 1915

(...) Russian trenches (...)

Private Yvan Krasinski could hardly believe how tired he was. The last two hours had been one horrendous enemy assault after the other. Most of his mates were now dead, replaced by faceless men from the rear, whatever they could find in the division, clerks, cooks, supply men. They all came from very different lots, but it was what it had to be. General Rennenkampf filled the depleted line with everything he had.

The enemy had launched no less than eight assaults, and now they were attacking from the south, and to the north, the Koenigsberg garrison had sortied out to join in the fight. Yvan rubbed his eyes like when he was a child to try and stay awake. If only this damned army had some tea or other type of stimulants. During the lull, it was not uncommon for exhausted soldiers to just fall asleep where they were. Yvan had done so a couple of times with his rifle at the ready. It only took one moment; both eyes closed, and that was it. He was a goner.

The officers and the NCOs weren't particularly understanding when that happened, and he'd been woken up by more than a few kicks in the ribs for his trouble. *"Haverr, you heardt that,"* said another soldier with his terrible accent from Siberia. The man had an Asian look about him, just another man in the faceless millions of the Tsar's armies. He was one of the new arrivals in the trench. *"Not a peep; stop trying to hear shadows. It's just the wind,"* one of the older hands (another surviving original like Yvan) said nervously. It was not that he completely disregarded the Siberian's words; it had more to do with the fact that he wanted there to be nothing attacking. No one wanted that.

Yvan rubbed his eyes again, slapped his face a couple of times to make sure he was awake, and scanned the ragged battlefield with his rifle-targeting sight. There was a lot of smoke, and a fog now ruled over the battlefield. The fog wasn't born out of water but more or less out of the rough fighting during the last day. Fires still burned here and there, and the entire area had an eerie look to it. Yvan's eyes lingered on a dead enemy soldier lying face down in the mud. For a moment, he thought he'd seen some movement...

(...) German assault line (...)

Private soldier Daniel Kranheim crawled very slowly like he'd been told to do. They were to play dead men and only advance when the bastards weren't looking and only if there was enough smoke or fog. He'd thought he did just that... But one of the enemy soldiers seemed to have spotted him. South and north of him he could see the flashes of battle as the Koenigsberg garrison fought hard in the north and the German 18th did the same in the south. Daniel was lying prone on his side and looked at the men about 60 yards distant with only thinly opened eyes. They'd been told to wait for the artillery bombardment and to start sprinting the moment they started hearing the loud whistling sounds of the shells flying above them. The idea was to fire a rolling barrage that would advance as the Germans attacked. He, like the rest of the guys, could sense that the bastards in front of them were about to break.

Daniel tried to stay as still as possible. As he did so, he noticed the whistling sounds of their artillery shells and mortar rounds arcing over them. Moments later, they landed hodgepodge all across the enemy position, blanketing it in detonations. That was his moment to move. They'd crawled for the last hour; now it was time to sprint. Daniel, like the rest of his comrades, yelled out of his lungs.

The plan was to shell the enemy until they got to within fifty yards. Then, the artillerymen would stop firing in order to avoid hitting their own comrades. He noticed the noise of shells and the number of explosions ahead slackened, and thus, it was time to attack; he was almost over the enemy trench line.

(...) Russian trenches (...)

As the enemy shelling finally stopped, Yvan crawled out of his hole amidst a heavy smell of cordite and even more smoke than before. He coughed a few times but was otherwise unharmed. This hole he'd dug for himself saved his life many times over in the last few hours. The enemy artillery fire had very good accuracy, since they now had a lot of occasions to adjust their aim. The shells now routinely landed either on the side of the trench or in it. Thus, it was good to have a hole to shelter from the flying shrapnel. The place was not 100% shrapnel proof. After all, it was just a hole in the side wall of the trench; a direct hit right beside him would still kill him.

The first thing he did when the shelling stopped, and he was able to put his rifle over the lip of the trench, was look at the spot where he'd seen the suspicious *"dead soldier."*

"Alarm! Enemy assault!" Many voices rose through the maelstrom, and it was again time for fighting. The yelling of the enemy was upon them, and he leveled his bayonet-tipped rifle.

(...) Battle epilogue, February 3rd, 1915 (...)

Russian General Paul von Rennenkampf forcibly rolled up the map, ripping it partially in his rage. *"The damn battle is over, Colonel,"* he finally said to one of the staff officers near him in his field tent. *"But General, we still have the men."* The Commander of the Army took a deep breath in hesitation but soon steeled his resolve. *"We're done. We don't have any more shells; we are under threat of being flanked from the north and the south, and the very reason for being here isn't possible to achieve anymore."*

"Colonel Gadrazin," he finally said. *"We have the men, but they are out of ammo. We have the guns, but they are out of shells. It's*

dangerous to run dry; then the enemy could counterattack us and sweep our army out from under us."

Gadrazin seemed unconvinced. *"Then, let's retire a few miles east and get more supplies,"* he said defiantly. *"For one more time, Colonel,"* countered Rennenkampf in a giant exasperated tone. *"We have already asked for more supplies. Numerous times, and it's been acknowledged that they were coming soon. That means that they are not coming."*

Gadrazin didn't answer and instead glared at the General. He stormed out of the room. After he left, Rennenkampf turned toward his Chief of Staff. *"Retire the troops to defensive positions east for one hundred miles while there's still time to unentangle us from this battle. We are wrapping up our offensive and sending inquiries to Grand Duke Nikolai Nikolaevich for further instructions."* "Yes, sir," said the other man, saluting and turning to leave the room as well. Rennenkampf crossed his arms behind his back and walked to the large window of his billeted house east of Koenigsberg and wondered if the Tsar would recall him.

The Battle of Turtucaia Part 2
Dobruja Region. Romania, February 2nd, 1915

The mingling together of the fighting bodies from both sides flooded the fortress and the field around it. The battle was terrible, with soldiers from both sides dying in droves. But one thing was certain. There were a lot more Bulgarian and Ottoman uniforms.

The Central Power's offensive across the Romanian border was working, as over three-quarters of new King Ferdinand the 1st's army was busy fighting the Austro-Hungarian First Army in Transylvania. Orders had come out to the three attacking armies there to retreat and come back to Romania to fight the invaders, but it was not an easy thing to do to extricate an army from fighting another and also from an area as remote as Transylvania. Some of the troops were starting to trickle back to Bucharest and form into a cohesive force, but it was already too late for the too-thin 75,000 soldier force defending the border.

It was even more disastrous for the 45,000 men bottled up in the all-important fortress of Turtucaia. The place was Romania's safeguard against a major Bulgarian crossing over the Danube and towered over the Dobruja region. But now, it was about to fall to the Central Powers.

With it would go the Romanian defenses across the Danube, and Bucharest would lay open to conquest, leaving Romania defenseless. It was a disaster of epic proportions, and the Romanian armies, busy trying to retreat from Transylvania, couldn't do anything about it.

Their fight was epic, and they gave their all. But when General Mihail Aslan left them and escaped the fortress, their will to fight disappeared along with him.

It was to be the young nation's worst defeat, notwithstanding the terrible defeats at the hands of the Ottomans eons before the Great War.

At sundown on the 2nd of February, the leftover forces of the Romanian garrison surrendered, and with it, sealed the future of Romania.

The war in the Balkans had just taken a quick, unexpected, and terrible turn of events for the Entente powers.

Truk Lagoon, February 3rd-4th, 1915
Caroline Islands, some 1100 miles Northeast of New Guinea

The Caroline Islands are a group of well over 250 coral reef-encircled atolls and islands mixed together in a large area in the Central Pacific. Originally a Spanish territory that Madrid never really gave any attention to (there was no real ground occupation to speak of), it became German in 1899 when the Kaiser, looking for land and prestige in the Pacific, bought the Carolines from the Spaniards, along with several other islands and atolls like New Britain, the Marshals, Marianas, and Palau.

Within these islands lay one of the best natural anchorages in the Pacific called Truk. The name was derived from the native Chuuk but ended up being Truk for Europeans because the Germans could not pronounce the native word properly.

The entire setup of islands and coral reefs mingled together to make one hell of a hiding place for the German Pacific Squadron. The collection of jungle-covered islands was hilly (they were the tip of drowned volcanic peaks), and there was even a large mountain the locals called Tonnachau. After all, Chuuk meant "high mountains" in the language of the collection of small native tribes living on the island.

The barrier reef that surrounded the collection of small islands around Truk was forty miles around, with only five passes to sail in or out of. Inside the barrier, the entire sailable area was forty-three miles by twenty-seven miles in surface area.

For all these reasons, German Admiral Maximilian von Spee had chosen the island as a stop-over for his fleet. It was easy to have watchers on small motorboats or one of his light cruisers watching one of the five entries/exits, and the peaks and hills also could hide his ships from being spotted while they took on more coal or lay there at anchorage.

(...) German Pacific Squadron, early morning (...)

Admiral von Spee's fleet had sailed into Truk on February 1st and immediately dropped anchor between the island harboring Mount Tonnachau and two others in order to be invisible to any approaching ships outside of the lagoon. He'd then put watchers on the islands facing the five entries into Truk to watch for the Japanese fleet. These men were ashore and set up small camps. They would signal the fleet with a network of flag-signaling sailors on other islands. Von Spee's idea was to get notified in silence of the arrival of an enemy fleet.

Meanwhile, his ships took on more coal, emptying collier Odenwald's hold and then taking on more from the last available collier in the Pacific for the Germans, the Brukenheim. The ship had sailed from Rabaul a week before the Australians invaded New Britain and had stayed in Truk, hidden, the entire time. Von Spee knew of the possibility of the Brukenheim being there since it was one of the pre-war arrangements they'd made in case of war with the British and or the Japanese. Truk was thus the fallback position for any ships in the Central Pacific.

"What are your thoughts on the enemy's whereabouts, Captain Ritter," said von Spee to the Captain of the Austro-Hungarian heavy cruiser Kaiserin Elisabeth that had just joined his fleet not long before, as it also tried to escape the predatory clutches of the Entente navies.

When war broke out, the K.u.K. Navy ship had been on a "world tour for peace," and was thus stuck in the open and without friends when the Japanese declared war on the Central Powers. It had found the German fleet by chance and was now, of course, sailing along as the safety of numbers and the coaling von Spee could provide could be found nowhere else by the Austrian heavy cruiser. *"In a sea of enemies, as they say, you'd better find the friends you have."*

"This Admiral Togo chasing us is one clever devil; I am certain he will figure out we are here eventually, Admiral," answered the Austro-Hungarian Captain. The two men were having breakfast in the Admiral of the Fleet cabin onboard von Spee's flagship, the dreadnought battleship Westfalen. Putting his fork on the table (they were having fish as it had been caught that same morning by some of the crew), the German commander seemed thoughtful. "I am pretty sure you are right, Captain. If I were Togo, I would split my fleet, thus doubling my chances of finding my enemy. After all," continued von Spee, picking up his fork again, "He's got enough ships to do that."

Captain Ritter shook his head, then drank a sip of his tea. "Admiral, it's hard to believe we are being chased by the legendary commander who destroyed the Russian Baltic Fleet at Tsushima. This Togo is something to behold." Von Spee seemed thoughtful for a moment. "I know, Captain. I am having trouble coping with this as well," answered the German commander, putting his small tablecloth to his mouth to wipe it clean.

"How long do you think we have before the Japanese show their ugly heads in Truk," countered Ritter with another question. "I have no clue, but it will be soon. The man is far from stupid, and we've eluded him for a long time already," said von Spee.

The Austro-Hungarian's question would soon be answered.

(...) Japanese Imperial Fleet Battle Squadron 1, afternoon (...)

Japanese Admiral Heihachiro Togo moved up to the viewport on the bridge of the Imperial Navy dreadnought battleship Setsu. "Admiral, we are in range of the Truk Atoll," said Captain Yasujiro Nagata, the ship's commander. Togo looked in silence at the collection of lush green islands before him. He also saw the surf breaking on what looked like an immense coral reef barrier. "Damn, how long is that barrier," he said, meant as a question to the plotting officer. The young sailor looked at his map and paperwork and then answered. *"Sir, it is estimated at 40 miles in circumference."*

Togo readjusted his cap and then crossed his arms behind his back, still looking out and trying to spot anything moving. But from the looks of it, the place was just deserted islands. No signs of fire or ship funnels. The faster a coal-fired ship sailed, the more smoke it made; thus if the Germans were in there and steaming hot, he would have seen the smoke columns. But it was also entirely possible that the damned elusive von Spee was simply at anchor and laying low. *"These islands are quite high compared to what we've seen so far, Admiral,"* said Nagata, echoing what his commander was thinking: the place was large, a natural anchorage and with islands high enough in elevation to hide a large fleet. *"Yes, Captain, my thoughts exactly. Plot, how many known entries into this coral barrier?"* The young sailor took some seconds to answer, finding the relevant information his superior asked about. "Five known ones, Admiral. This is from the Spanish survey map of 1885. More may have been found, Sir."

Togo kept thinking, trying to divine what the opposing commander would do. If von Spee was here in Truk, he had lookouts on those islands, and these men would have already started to relay back the information about the arrival of the Japanese fleet to their commander. *"Lookout,"* he then said. *"Yes, sir?"* *"Tell your people to watch for sudden gusts of smoke. I suspect that if the enemy is here, he has spotted us, and it may be that the German Admiral in charge wants to make a run for it. If he does, the smoke of his funnels and boilers will be quite obvious."* "Yes, Sir," answered the lookout officer, relaying the order right after.

Togo turned around and went right to the plotting table to look at the maps. *"Captain Nagata,"* he said, inviting the commander of the Setsu to his side for advice and counsel. The Japanese Admiral put both his palms down on each side of the table, taking a long, hard look at the old Spanish map they had on the ship. It showed a large barrier encompassing well over thirty to forty islands, with known entry points. *"Now, Captain, please help me out here,"* he started. *"Sir,"* answered Nagata willingly. The plotting sailor stood erect beside the Admiral, waiting for orders or a question.

"Now, if the Germans are in there now, it's obvious they're stationary since we can't see any smoke from their funnels." Togo leaned closer to try and again divine the answer he was looking for. *"We obviously don't have enough ships to cover all the exits and hope to box the enemy inside. If we divide our forces into five parts, von Spee will simply barge in on the exit he's chosen and battle his way through."* *"Indeed, Sir,"* answered Nagata while the plotting sailor nodded silently.

"So, if I was von Spee and I got a signal from my spotters on land that they have just seen the enemy fleet off the atoll, what would I do..." Togo readjusted his white cap, with an obvious question mark on his face. The Setsu's Captain ventured an answer. *"Well, sir, the first order of business would be to lay low and hope that we do not enter the atoll."*

Togo continued on Nagata's train of thought. *"Yes, exactly. And I keep my ships ready to raise their steam if we get too close. We cannot spot the Germans from very far unless we are in direct line of sight because of these high cones and jungle-covered islands. Mmm,"* continued Togo with a smile. *"If von Spee is in there, he's going to wait for us to enter and see what direction we take. With the size of this thing, it could take a while for us to spot him."*

"Captain Nagata, please relay orders for four of the fleet's destroyers to head for the other entries into the lagoon and to try and spot the enemy. They are to contact us if that is the case." Japanese ships in 1915 didn't have radio communication on board but had telegraph and Morse code, and this is what Togo referred to when he said to communicate. If a destroyer spotted the German Pacific Squadron, he would know soon enough. *"Yes, Sir,"* answered Nagata. *"And the main*

body of the fleet, Sir?" Togo then smiled. *"The rest of the battle squadron is to enter the atoll. Let's see if our elusive enemy is in there."*

German East Prussian Army HQ
Danzig, Morning of the 4th of February

The German Army Danzig headquarters had all the looks of being temporary. It was installed in the Westerplatte, a large building by the harbor normally used as the city garrison's barracks. And indeed, it was, as none of the two generals in the dynamic Hindenburg-Ludendorff duo intended on staying long behind the front. Their goal was to advance and defeat the Russians, to drive them out of East Prussia, the god-anointed and legendary German-Teutonic Knights lands.

Paul von Hindenburg, a man born out of the old Prussian intelligencia and with a long military career behind him, was the direct contrary to his deputy, Erich Ludendorff, who was a commoner. They thus both came from different backgrounds, and their characters were antipodal. The old Prussian General was calm, stolid, modest, and placid, while his young and fiery German General was arrogant, driven, and ambitious. In normal life, they would probably never have gone for a meal together or been part of the same social circles. Far from it, in fact. But their mismatched personalities actually complemented each other quite well.

One (the older, wiser one) displayed a true depth in measured judgment and had a steadfastness that was hard to fathom. The other, younger and more energetic, was the more brilliant of the two but was prone to rash thinking and could be paralyzed by anxiety. Ludendorff was driven to achieve his goal to the point of craziness, while Hindenburg was the restraining hand that enabled all of it make sense. Together, the two men were a formidable military command powerhouse.

They'd first proven it at the Battle of Marienburg in the fall of 1914 when they salvaged a disastrous situation against the Russians and destroyed the entirety of Russian General Samsonov's 2nd Army, which was at the gates of the Vistula and the Germanic heartlands. Then, Hindenburg's steadfastness had been a driving force in getting the right reinforcements to the beleaguered spots along the entire Eastern theater, applying the right number of troops where they were needed.

More recently, that is, just a few days ago, they'd won another great victory and relieved Koenigsberg. The Russian siege of the fortress was over, and East Prussia was saved. General Rennenkampf's forces were retreating towards Lithuania to regroup while the Germans were left masters of the field.

The two men were meeting in a large room with one wall occupied by a window giving a magnificent view over the harbor. The building of the Westerplatte had been, a few years before the war, a bathing resort, and this had probably been the main reception room.

The center of the room was occupied by a large conference table that Hindenburg had ordered built here when he arrived in Danzig a month and a half before. The two men sat right beside each other, overlooking the many maps laid before them.

"The situation is improving, Sir," said Ludendorff with his right-hand fingers on his chin in a thoughtful manner. "Indeed, General," answered Hindenburg. *"Where are the enemy troops now?"* *"A hundred and twenty miles beyond our own positions. As we have decided, we are not pursuing them for now, our objective being reached while waiting for what will happen on other fronts."*

"I have just spoken to the Kaiser and he sends his congratulations to both of us for the great victory at Koenigsberg. He told me we'll have a medal of some sort," continued the old Prussian officer, smiling at the concept. Ludendorff smiled in return. "Sir, we need to decide

where to station the troops for the rest of the winter," continued the younger officer. The two of them had decided that they would advance as far as the Russians retreated but wouldn't push too much, and instead wait to launch a really nice offensive when the weather got better in the late spring. *"I trust you will find how, where, and when, General. You have my full confidence."* Ludendorff nodded as an answer.

"Any more news from the Romanian front," asked Hindenburg. *"Sir, the Bulgar-Ottoman forces have completely trounced the minimal forces the Romanians had left in place to guard the border. The town of Turtucaia is in their hands, and Bucharest is open to attack. As a consequence,"* he continued, pulling the map of the Balkan sector to both of them on the table, *"this has had an impact on the Transylvanian front and the extreme right flank of the Austro-Hungarian Carpathian front defenses,"* he continued, pointing at the area where the Romanians had been attacking only days before. *"Now, we're getting reports from the K.u.K. headquarters of widely disengaging Romanian units trying to get back into their territory. No doubt,"* Ludendorff smiled, *"the bastards are trying to reposition their forces to face the southern invasion."*

"With these two recent developments," Hindenburg was referring to the victory in Koenigsberg and the breakdown of the Romanian offensive into Transylvania, *"The only thing we need to address now is do we let von Hotzendorf go ahead with his winter offensive in the Carpathian Mountains and tell von Gallwitz to follow his orders?"*

The 11th German Army Commander had sent for orders and instruction following the Austrian Commander-in-Chief's project of attacking the Russians in the middle of winter. Ludendorff thought for a moment since the two of them had spoken about this. Before the fall of Turtucaia, they had been completely against it. Now that the Austro-Hungarian right flank was free, it warranted a new look.

"Sir, I still believe we should wait for the good weather. To attack now is simply too risky, as in the spring we will be in a great position to apply more pressure on the Russians in Galicia now that we have both Koenigsberg and Transylvania safe."

Hindenburg grunted and nodded. *"I am of the same mind, General. Let's send instructions to von Gallwitz to tell Hotzendorf that we are against a winter offensive and that our troops will not participate."* He paused to stand up and look at the harbor, where a couple of ships were slowly unloading their cargoes, all bound for the front.

"We need to get command of the Austro-Hungarian forces in Galicia. This Conrad von Hotzendorf doesn't have a good score card since the war began." "How do you propose we do this, Sir?" Hindenburg turned back to look at Ludendorff. *"For now, it's a pipe dream, and we'll just have to put up with the man for the time being."*

Truk Lagoon, February 3rd, 1915
Caroline Islands, some 1100 miles Northeast of New Guinea

(...) German dreadnought battleship Westfalen (...)

It was in the middle of the afternoon on another beautiful Pacific day on the 3rd of February that Admiral Maximilian von Spee was notified of the sudden appearance of a Japanese fleet at one of the main coral reef entry points of the Truk Atoll. The message was relayed back from island to island via flag signalers and local lookouts (there were about 300 German residents in the Truk area).

While he was not surprised that the enemy had finally showed up, he was not happy about it. All his ships were fully stocked in coal, having enough to easily round Cape Horn at the tip of Chile's coastline and hope for a rescue from the German High Seas Fleet. While at Yap, he'd arranged for Kaiserliche Marine command (through messages with the telegraph station) to have colliers ready in the vicinity of the Falkland Islands to refuel. The last message had told him to hang on and that help was also coming since the German High Seas Fleet now had access to the Atlantic via the French-occupied ports.

That was all fine and well, but he needed to escape the Pacific Ocean first. The Japanese fleet was hot on their heels, and while he had not sniffed a whiff of any British ships hunting for him, he was pretty certain a squadron or several were sailing across the large expanse to try and find him. He'd secretly hoped to continue to dodge the enemy forces, but he guessed that he'd been lucky enough already. The Siege of Tsingtao had been over since October 1914, and thus, he surmised that his fleet's survival to date wasn't a bad feat in itself.

"What to do now..." he said to no one as he was alone in his Admiral of the Fleet cabin. He'd asked to be left to his own self while he thought about a plan. He went through his options once more in his head. Do nothing and stay at anchor. Not ideal. Pick up steam and try

to sail away as quickly as possible. That was one good option. Or else, stay and fight.

The flag signal had said the Japanese fleet was a smaller force than he faced when he escaped from Tsingtao. Two dreadnought battleships, eight pre-dreadnoughts, twenty-five heavy cruisers, ten light ones, and thirty destroyers. He laughed out loud. Even if smaller, it was one hell of a force. He surmised that Togo had probably split his fleet to increase the odds of finding him.

His only chance lay in escaping, he decided. But once he decided to do that, the enemy Admiral would be hot on his heels. The moment he told his ships to fire their coal engines, the funnels would gush dark smoke, and he would be spotted. The good thing about his position near Mount Tonnachau was that, yes, his smoke would be seen, but he wouldn't be in a direct line of sight and, thus, not fired at right away.

And then an idea came up. He might get away with speeding his ships in the middle of the night. The trick was, however, to hope the enemy fleet wouldn't sail for his position right away.

(...) Four hours later, early evening, dreadnought battleship Setsu (...)

"Admiral!" yelled the lookout officer out of excitement. Togo smiled since he knew why the man was like that. *"Yes, Captain Atanama?"* "Admiral, the lookouts have spotted large and dark columns of smoke coming from the other side of the island. *You were right, sir. The enemy was indeed anchored on the other side of Moen Island and using the large mountain to hide behind!"*

And indeed, Togo had been right on the spot with his decision to sail there first. It seemed logical; It was the best place to hide as there was a trio of islands placed in a rough triangular shape that effectively hid any ship anchoring right in the middle of the triangle.

"Now, gentlemen," he said, signaling to Captain Nagata to come close to the plotting table, *"the problem is to guess where von Spee will sail. Thoughts, Captain?" "Sir, if I were him, I would sail in the direction directly opposite to us." "Yes, maybe,"* thought Togo. But that was exactly the type of thinking that had led to those frustrating weeks and then months of searching. They were not facing the typical, run-of-the-mill naval officer. Von Spee was a true naval commander.

"I don't believe that this is what he will do," said the Japanese Admiral. *"I believe he is going to try and roll around the island behind our backs and then make his escape through here,"* he continued, pointing to two large islands with high enough elevation and in a direct line of sail toward the nearest exit from the Atoll. *"In this way, the Germans can avoid being fired at for a while as they make their exit into the open sea."* He put his fingers to his chin in a concentrated gesture. *"How should we counter this, Captain?"*

Nagata thought for a moment. *"Well, sir, the solution is simple. We split our fleet in two. The upside is that we get to fight him for certain, but then we will do so at a much more even ratio. The other fleet would eventually sail around the island, but it would be several minutes before we can actually concentrate our forces against the enemy ships, sir."*

"Agreed. Let's split the fleet," answered Togo with a predatory smile. The move would trigger a battle, but at the same time the casualties on the Japanese side promised to be a lot higher. The German Admiral also had a couple of twists of his own that Togo had not necessarily thought about.

CHAPTER 3
The war in the West

San Remo, Western Italian Alps
Württemberg Mountain Battalion (Württembergische Gebirgs-Bataillon), January 20th, 1915

The Württemberg Mountain Battalion was one of the best units in the German Army. It was comprised of a sizeable number of sports enthusiast volunteers and had received good training in rock climbing and in everything that made its members good mountain troops. As such, it had been moved to the frontlines between Italy and France because all of the fighting was done in the Alps.

Being a unit of volunteers, it was well-stocked with good and motivated soldiers, with several of them having earned medals during the fighting in the fall against the French. Some even came from the Eastern Front and were involved in the Battle of Marienburg or, even before that, the Battle of Gumbinnen.

If one thing was certain, Major Theodore Strosser, the unit commander, had a unit of mavericks and sportsmen on his hands. Thus, Rommel, with his recent action and bravery in the capture and ultimate destruction of the British battleship Hibernia, fit right in.

"Pretty impressive, Captain," said Strosser, leafing through Rommel's transfer papers. All the while, the young officer stood at attention rigid like a steel bar. Both men were in the Württemberg Mountain Battalion's HQ in Sam Remo, Italy, a small coastal town near where the fighting between the French and Italian armies was happening. The Germans had just recently arrived but were already taking their job in stride, with most of the battalion already up facing the enemy mountain fortifications. *"Thank you, Sir,"* answered Rommel. Strosser smiled. *"I was wondering who this Kaiser's favorite was. It appears there is a real reason you have a medal, son."* Strosser lifted his eyes from the paperwork, looking at Rommel. *"Assaulting a British battleship, really?"* *"Not as hard as it looks, Sir."* *"Well, you're the only one that's done it so far in the war, so good job on that,"* answered the Major. The room they were in was by the harbor, and it had white

walls with other people going about working on some errands for the battalion. The major's desk was a shamble of paperwork and over ten old and unwashed teacups. *"How is the Emperor? Is he a nice guy?"* Rommel didn't know what to answer to that one, but the truth. *"He was nice enough to me, Sir,"* he answered. Strosser grunted with amusement. *"Indeed. I think you'll get along well here, Captain. Be ready to go up the mountains by sunrise tomorrow; we're going up with the rest of the new arrivals." "Yes, Sir."*

The next morning, Rommel was on a truck driving the bumpy road up the mountain. As the machine moved, he started hearing a distant thunder, and he smiled. It was soon time to fight and again prove his mettle. He felt he still had a lot to prove and wanted to go up in rank. His father had always told him that the price for ambition is hard work and audacity when it is needed. He'd found that this combination of things (ambition and temerity bordering on the reckless) worked well in the army. It was hard to explain, but he was good at it.

Following his meeting with the Kaiser, he was given leave for a couple of days in Berlin and he took advantage of the time to rest and party some with friends he had in the city. Most had gone to the war, but a few were back because they were injured or on leave; thus, he spent time with them. After those two days, his orders were to report to the train station, where a few soldiers from the unit would be there with him for the ride south to Italy. The train ride took several days but was nice enough, especially when it got to cross southern Germany and the Austrian Alps. The entry into Italy was uneventful and then he eventually made it to San Remo.

The Battalion was currently helping the Italian alpine units in their attempt to storm the Fort du Mont-Ours (Fort of Bear Mountain) that sat right on the border with Italy, overlooking Monaco. The place held a commanding position over the entire region and was built before the war when Italy joined the Triple Entente that became the Central Powers later. Fort du Mont-Ours was even a place garrisoned by

Roman soldiers at one time, following their conquest of Gaul eons ago. Rommel had heard that just about a hundred yards from the French fort lay Roman ruins and a road built there by the leaders of the time as a commemoration for the conquest of Gaul. He hoped he would get to see them.

Everyone knew this was not going to be easy. Already, three Italian assaults had been repulsed with heavy casualties. He couldn't wait to see the lay of the land and to get some action.

He would soon be served.

Somewhere north of Versailles
German frontline, Infanterie-Regiment Graf Schwerin (2nd Army, 4th Division), January 20th, 1915

The resounding blast rocked the earth near him, showering him with dirt that slammed his helmet and his face. *"Reload, you bastards, reload and fire,"* said Sergeant Wilhelm. *"We are, we are,"* Oskar heard his friend Florian Storch mumbling, low enough so the NCO wouldn't hear him.

In front of them was mayhem. Bullets whizzed about, and artillery shells exploded everywhere. The French were attacking yet again, and it was one hell of a fight.

Private Oskar Dantz, a soldier in the German 2nd Army and the 4th Division, was doing his best to pour as much bullet fire as possible into the charging Frenchmen. So far, it seemed to be working, and none of the bastards had reached their trench.

The Infanterie-Regiment Graf Schwerin had been fighting the enemy ever since the German advance had stalled north of Versailles. Oskar didn't know why, but orders had come down from Division, who had received orders from the 2nd Army Commander, who in turn had received orders from the OHL. These orders had been to stop and dig.

And so, that's what they did, and they built an intricate network of trenches and defenses. Oskar wasn't traveling much these days, but he'd heard the frontline extended from Alsace-Lorraine to the Atlantic Ocean and that no one moved, regardless of the offensives launched.

The Germans were relatively quiet in terms of attack since a lot of troops had departed to help with the beleaguered Eastern Front. As he went through the motions of firing his rounds and then reloading, he could not help but think about the last few months that had brought him here.

At first, the offensive from Belgium had been one hell of an adventure with the destruction of the Belgian forts. Then, had come the back-and-forth fighting in Northern France until they got to the Marne and beat the Entente forces. The storming of Paris and then the fight for the French Channel ports followed. He was even part of a maverick mission aboard a battleship with a crazy fellow named Rommel. Even that had ended well, and they were able to take control of the ship before it was destroyed, and thus helping with the final conquest of the city the guns of the Hibernia had been protecting.

After that the Regiment, along with the rest of the German 2nd Army, had advanced south all the way to Versailles, and then they were ordered to dig. It had been one hell of an adventure, and Oskar would trade his current trench life predicament for reliving it again without a second thought.

"What are you fucking doing, Dantz," said Sergeant Wilhelm, kicking him in the leg. *"Reload faster and stop daydreaming!" "Yes, Sergeant. Sorry, Sergeant!"* He fumbled with his clip but was able to put it in the rifle to fire again. The reloading was done through a *"stripper clip"* of five bullets that he entered from the top of the weapon.

He spotted a French soldier running with his rifle at the waist, aimed and fired. His first bullet hit the ground, missing the man. The second one grazed his shoulder, and the Frenchman didn't even seem to notice, even though blood spurted out of his uniform in a small cloud of red. The third round did it, as the man was not even ten yards from the trench. It slammed the soldier in the chest, and the force of the impact slammed him backward in a somersault worthy of an Olympic athlete.

With two bullets left, he looked for a new target, and he found one in a sidearm-brandishing officer who was urging his men forward. He fired but missed on his first shot. He missed again with his second shot, not because his shooting skills were bad, but because an enemy artillery shell had blasted the earth some distance behind him. With the ground shaking so hard, his aim had erred to the side, and he'd missed. The enemy soldiers were very close now, and he fished for another five-bullet clip and opened his bullet chamber by sidestepping the pin. He put the clip inside and turned the pin back in its position.

While he had been reloading, he'd crouched into the trench to avoid being killed because he was busy doing something else other than looking at the enemy. When he put his gun over the lip again, he saw that the French soldiers were almost upon them. There was no time to aim and so many targets that he just rapid-fired the five bullets. "Fix bayonets," yelled Sergeant Wilhelm. He fumbled the blade on the ground, and then it was too late to clip it on his Mauser rifle. He picked it up and resolved to use it as a short saber. Already, the French were jumping into the trench, flooding it with blue uniforms. Oskar lunged at the one that was coming right for him, sidestepping and slashing at the same time, mortally wounding the poor man, who landed hard on the dirt.

The next moment, his back bumped into another Frenchman, and he turned, slashing with his short blade at the same time. He gave the man a horrible cut across the face, and he fell in pain on his knees, clutching his face. He finished him by thrusting his blade into his upper back at the base of the neck.

Then, it seemed there was no enemy right in front of him, enabling Oskar to get a feel for his surroundings. Everywhere he looked, he saw blue uniforms mingled with the German grey, sprays of blood, and bodies lying on the ground. It was one hell of a gory scene, with soldiers from both sides yelling and fighting.

And then, another enemy soldier jumped into the trench, and it was time to do more grisly work. He clutched his bayonet (there was a small hilt to use it like a knife) and swung at the Frenchman with a yell of pure fury.

Port of St-Nazaire, France
German High Seas Fleet, January 20th, 1915

Grand Admiral Hugo von Pohl looked at the magnificent dreadnought battleship Ostfriesland sliding out of the St-Nazaire harbor repair dock and felt excitement that the flagship of the High Seas Fleet was finally repaired. It had only received superficial damage and thus had been put into the dock last. Its sisters had received more damage during the breakout through the Channel. Heligoland had been hit by a mine, and thus, the big hole in the hull had to be repaired as a priority. The Nassau, yet another modern dreadnought battleship, was also hit by a mine, and a big fire had ravaged the ship. The Rheinland had received a shell hit from one of the British dreadnoughts, and its captain had been killed. The bridge was almost entirely replaced, and a new commander was named. The rest of the repairs had been on his pre-dreadnoughts and support ships, and that was about it.

Other ships had been damaged, but critically, and were now sunk. Pohl still shuddered at the last message of the captain of the pre-dreadnought Kaiser Wilhelm II before he rode what was now called the *"death ride of the battleships."* Pohl had no choice in the matter but to sacrifice a few to get the many to escape because the British, between their minefield and their overwhelming number of ships, would have swamped his fleet if he hadn't sacrificed a part of it.

Vice-Admiral Max von Grapow had commanded the 5th Battle Squadron, which included four pre-dreadnought battleships, three destroyers, and three light cruisers. They were all gone now but had given enough time and space for the High Seas Fleet to escape to the French harbors. He still remembered the words of Vice-Admiral Henning von Hotzendorf, his chief of staff, trying to soothe him with his terrible decision. *"Sir,"* had said von Hotzendorf, *"There is no choice; the main body of the fleet needs to survive."* Somehow, the old naval commander's words had not done anything to make him feel better then, and now it remained a very painful memory for the Admiral. The feeling he had was a mix of sadness and guilt that never seemed to wash away, regardless of the time of day or night. He still had nightmares about it almost every time he went to bed.

He steeled his revolve and took a deep breath. It was time. Almost three months after the fleet arrived in Brest and St-Nazaire, he was finally ready to sail again.

The High Sea Fleet Hugo von Pohl

Chif of staff Henning von Holtzendorff

1st Battle Squadron, 1st Division (Vice-Admiral Wilhelm von Lans)

BB Ostfriesland (Flagship)	BB Oldenburg	4 CA
BB Helgoland	BB Thüringen	5 DD

1st Battle Squadron, 2nd Division (Rear-Admiral Friedrich Gädecke)

BB Posen (Flagship)	BB Rheinland Bridge (captain killed) boiler damage crippled	4 CA
BB Nassau		3 DD

2nd Battle Squadron, 3rd Division (Vice-Admiral Reinhard Scheer)

Pre-Dread BB Preussen (Flagship)	Pre-dread BB Hessen	3 CA
Pre-dread BB Deutschland	Pre-dread BB Lothringen,	4 DD

2nd Battle Squadron, 4th Division (Kommodore Franz Mauve)

Pre-dread BB Hannover (Flagship)	Pre-dread BB Schlesien	4 CA
Pre-dread BB Dantzig	Pre-dread BB Prussia	1 DD

3rd Battle Squadron, 5th Division (Rear-Admiral Felix Funke)

BB Grosser Kurfürst	BB König	4 CL
BB Markgraf	BB Kronprinz	1 DD

3rd Battle Squadron, 6th Division (Rear-Admiral Carl Schaumann)

BB Prinzregent Luitpold (Flagship)	BB Sharnhorst	4 CL
BB Kaiser	BB König Albert	1 DD

Battle squadron

quadron, 7th Division (Vice-Admiral Ehrhard Schmidt)

Pre-Dread BB Wittelsbach (Flagship)	-	2 CL
Pre-Dread BB Mecklenburg	Pre-Dread BB Wettin	2 DD

5th Battle Squadron, 8th Division (Rear-Admiral Hermann Alberts)

Pre-Dread BB Braunschweig (Flagship)	Pre-Dread BB Zähringen	1 CL
Pre-Dread BB Elsass		

5th Battle Squadron, 10th Division ((Kommodore Alfred Begas)

Pre-Dread BB Brandenburg waterline and	Pre-Dread BB Kaiser Karl der Grosse	
Pre-Dread BB Kaiser Friedrich III (Flagship)	3 DD	

There were many things on his plate to consider, as the presence of his fleet in French Atlantic harbors opened up a plethora of possibilities.

The most obvious one was to try and raid the British convoys supplying the United Kingdom and help the submarine arm of the Kaiserliche Marine to sink transports and commercial vessels bound for the British Home Islands.

The other was to try and be a little creative to attempt destroying enemy warships if the enemy commander was foolish enough to have them scattered. He didn't think that would be the case if nothing was done, but if he himself split his fleet and sent them on missions, he just might be able to outmaneuver John Jellicoe, the British Commander of the Grand Fleet.

And then, there was this epic developing saga from the brave Admiral Maximilian von Spee, who was trying to extricate his ships from the Pacific. He'd been able to exchange some telegrams with him since the Pacific Squadron stayed for some time at Yap, the German telegraph relay station in the Pacific. During that time they hatched a plan to get him some coal colliers to the Falkland Islands and also a battle squadron. The prestigious implications of von Spee's epic story ending in a grand return to the Reich were too good to pass up. He knew his own status with the Kaiser, as well as in Germany as a whole would be boosted by such a feat. And, plain and simple, he wanted those sailors' home because they were his people, and it would help the morale of the entire nation.

German newspapers were kept apprised of von Spee's saga through British papers and through the information that he had shared with the press. It was one of the most read-about and talked-about adventures in the entire Reich.

"*Admiral,*" said Hotzendorf, his Chief of Staff, as he walked beside him on the dock near where Ostfriesland was sliding graciously into the waters of the harbor. *"Yes, Henning." "The Captains of the fleet are ready for the meeting, Sir." "Ah yes, let's do it."* And at that, he turned his back on the magnificent dreadnought battleship and walked toward the HQ building near the center of the port facilities.

Regardless of his daydreaming, he had a fleet to lead and missions to allocate to his captains.

Grand Fleet's new headquarters
Southampton, Southern England, January 26th. 1915

Another commander was pondering as much on the events of the last few months as the ones to come. It was Admiral John Jellicoe, the Commander-in-Chief of the Royal Navy's Grand Fleet. His ships were now mostly based in Southampton, the great southern British port.

The place had a long and eventful naval history. It was from there that the English forces left for the Battle of Crecy in 1316. Many of the fleet's big battleships were built in its docks. When it was time to ferry the British Expeditionary Force (BEF) to France, it did so from Southampton.

And now it housed the greatest fleet ever fielded by man. The harbor boasted a plethora of deepwater docks ideal for the repairs of dreadnoughts and pre-dreadnoughts alike. It was also located at the head of a body of water that was called the Solent. This was a deep-water channel that stretched past the Isle of Wight. It was thus a deep and sheltered waterway ideal for keeping important ships away from the predatory clutches of German surface ships or submarines.

But its primary quality was its proximity to where the enemy fleet was. The German High Seas Fleet, the only naval force capable of challenging the Grand Fleet, was now based in Brest and St-Nazaire, a little over 200 miles away.

Jellicoe wanted to blockade the two German-occupied French harbors, but it was not possible to do so as it had been during the age of sail. There was too much moving around and coal burning to be effective. Instead, the way to do it was to manage the blockade from a position further away and keep a screen of ships to watch for any enemy sortie into the Atlantic Ocean. While this undeniably gave the Germans the first move, it also meant that Jellicoe's ships could start the pursuit and hunt the enemy down. One variable was always constant. The Kaiserliche Marine ships would have to sail back to the same harbor they started from unless they wanted to try and cross the Channel again, where the Grand Fleet was now positioned to block them effectively. This was in contrast to the Royal Navy, which had ports and coaling stations spanning the entire globe and, thus, could sail out of Southampton and cross the Atlantic and stop in Canada. The Germans had no such luxury; they had their territories, and the rest of the world was either hostile to them or neutral.

"Are you still with me, Admiral Jellicoe," said the First Lord of the Admiralty, Winston Churchill. *"Ah, yes, Sir. I was just thinking about the blockade and what was going to be von Pohl's next move. He's bound to sortie at some point."* Churchill fished another cigar from his front pocket and put it to his mouth. *"Indeed, Admiral. What about..."* he started, puffing with his now-lit cigar, *"an answer to my question?"*

"Well, ah, yes, Sir, but could you repeat the question?" Churchill looked at him for a second, not very pleased that his top Admiral had been sort of not listening to him. *"Again, Admiral. The Greeks declared for the Central Powers almost two weeks ago, and we still have not attacked their fleet, nor have you presented a plan to me over the matter. The attack on the Nikolayev shipyards by the Germano-Ottoman fleet should be enough of a confirmation that the Turks and the Germans are nowhere near the Greek fleet and that we can move against the Hellenic Fleet."* The First Lord paused, taking a long drag of his burning cigar. *"So, Admiral, what is your plan on the matter?"*

Jellicoe wasn't born yesterday and had worked long enough with Winston Churchill to come prepared to such meetings. The man was relentless, bordering on reckless, and would have him barge into Greece's most strongly fortified harbor just to sink two aging pre-dreadnoughts and a couple of heavy cruisers.

Thus, instead, he had come up with a plan but waited for the First Lord to bring it up. The problem of the Greek fleet potentially wanting to sail into the Dardanelles Strait and to safety was an acute one since Jellicoe couldn't order the Eastern Mediterranean Squadron to just sail in circles in the Aegean and wait for the opposing Admiral to make his move.

"As you know, Sir, the Aegean is an enemy-controlled body of water. Between the Turks and the Greeks, all of the islands are under their control, making any foray into the area a danger in terms of the possibility of hitting naval mines or else being fired upon by the numerous naval fortifications on these islands." Churchill picked up the cigar to put it between his fingers and rested his arm on the couch's armrest. "Yes, I know that, Admiral." The naval boss rolled his eyes.

"The fleet is anchored in Alexandria, hundreds of miles away, and wouldn't have time to intervene if the Greeks made a break for it. The distance they would have to sail compared to our ships is a lot shorter." He fished a couple of maps out and also a folder and gave them to Churchill.

The two men were in a large room of a white brick building near the harbor. The place was owned by one of the many British shipbuilding companies (it was one of their administrative offices), and the owner of that company had graciously lent the entire building to the Royal Navy.

Jellicoe continued while Churchill leafed through the papers, munching his cigar all the while. *"If we want to truly bottle up the Aegean, Sir, I propose we invade and take control of Crete. That way, we'll be a lot closer to Athens and in a position to intercept anything the Greco-Ottomans, even if they join forces, would decide to do."* "What about the Greek Fleet?" answered a skeptic Churchill since Jellicoe had answered his question with something else. *"The Greek fleet doesn't matter, Sir, if it's bottled up in the Aegean."*

Looking at Churchill's face, Jellicoe inwardly smiled. He knew he had him. The First Lord of the Admiralty liked adventures, and this Crete invasion had the prospect to be a good one.

The First Zeppelin attack on London
January 23rd, 1915

"Then a war broke out in heaven. Michael and his angels fought with the dragon, and the dragon and its angels fought back."

Book of Revelation, 12:7-17

The large, long, and cigar-shaped airships flew along silently in the air above the British capital in the dark of night. There were some clouds, but the Germans could see the lights of the British capital of London. The machines didn't make a lot of noise, and thus, no one saw them. Because, anyway, they never bothered to look at the sky and think there was a threat. It was just something that never happened.

The two Zeppelins were about to make history. Flying at fifty-two miles an hour and sitting just under a giant structure filled with lighter-than-air hydrogen gas, the airships could transport nine tons of structure and whatever cargo the Germans chose. In this case, they transported bombs. The undercarriage was quite heavy by itself (housing the crew, the engines, and the rest), and there were 3.5 tons left for the bombs themselves.

Hydrogen was highly flammable, and thus, one single fighter could ignite the entire structure with a few well-placed shots. The Zeppelin was consequently well-defended with four machine guns, two in the undercarriage and two firing stations on top of the structure.

The British didn't expect the attack that night since attacking cities from above was not yet something that had dawned on most people. The way to launch bombs was also quite rudimentary, as they were simply dropped from a hole in the undercarriage. Each of the two Zeppelins carried ten bombs each. Upon receiving their orders, the bomb handlers opened the chute and started sliding the bombs through the hole, with great gusts of air slapping their faces and making their hair fly wildly in every direction.

And then weapons of death fell down toward the ground. They slammed on the paved streets and on a few buildings. The next moment, they exploded, startling the sleeping Londoners, who had no idea what was happening. It was a truly traumatic event for the civilians.

A big fire was started when one of the bombs hit a shoe factory, and it would take much of the next morning to put it out. Once they were done, the German airmen closed the hatch, and the big, lumbering Zeppelins slowly turned back toward the Channel and left, leaving the British capital with seven dead and a few demolished buildings. Some of the sharpest military men and some civilians saw the big silhouettes in the sky, and they were recognized as Zeppelins.

In terms of overall damage, the raid was insignificant. But psychologically, it was devastating. From one moment to the next, the British people realized that no amount of ships from the Great Royal Navy nor any soldiers could protect them completely from Germany.

The airmen returned to Germany for a hero's welcome and were immediately mobbed by journalists who covered their story at length for the next few days. It was as much a great morale boost for the Germans as it was a disaster for the British.

The moment was traumatic enough for the Londoners to spark a drive to organize rudimentary air defenses, with machine guns installed on top of the highest buildings and fighter planes protecting the big British cities. Rear-mounted machine guns were starting to be mounted on the back seats of the British biplanes, and that process was sped up by the British leaders, who were as afraid as their citizens were of the terror from the sky.

The war had just taken a new dimension: the air war.

Assault on Bear Mountain Fort (Fort du Mont-Ours)
The Italo-German attack on the Séré de Rivières system, January 22nd, 1915

The Séré de Rivières system was a line of forts and defenses built by France starting in 1882 in response to Italy joining the Triple Alliance (Germany, Austria-Hungary, and Italy) the year before. The impetus for the construction was constantly fueled by the intense political tensions between the two states for the next ten years, only abating in the early 1900s.

The fortifications bore the name of their designer, Architect Raymond Adolphe Séré de Rivière, a Brigadier General in the French Army. By 1914, they could not necessarily stop any of the modern guns from smashing their walls (because the shells were better) but were still used regardless by the French to defend their border.

The small but well-positioned fort was finished in 1898 and controlled the access to the Col des Banquettes. It was part of the ring of forts with Fort Mont-Angel and Fort du Barbonnet on its flanks. It was closer to the border than its two bigger brothers and thus served as their outpost to make sure any enemy attack would be seen and confronted as far forward as possible.

The entire setup was a bunch of angle-of-fire blockhouses and bunkers, with many of them positioned on the main road to block it with withering fire.

The main building of the fort was a large square reinforced structure with two floors fielding gun ports and another double wall further down to strengthen the ensemble against artillery explosions.

The war between the Italians and the French had so far produced no advances on either side. The French had attacked first as part of the entire surprise attack on Taranto (Operation Ares). The Italians, watchful and ready in their own forts and defenses, had resisted and weathered the storm.

The last two months had been more a story of artillery duels than infantry attacks because both sides had been in no position to prosecute an attack. The French offensive having failed, the troops had moved back to their defensive positions. The Italians had needed to mobilize and get ready, as the Entente surprise attack had caught them with their pants down in terms of the general readiness of their armed forces.

Now, the Italian Army was ready to do something about these *"dastardly French"* as they saw them. Their artillery guns had been brought forward beyond San Remo and concentrated near the border, and German troops had been called as reinforcements (like, for example, Rommel's own Württemberg Mountain Battalion). By the end of January, they were ready to go.

Newly arrived Captain Erwin Rommel looked through his pair of binoculars to see the fort the battalion was about to attack along with their Italian comrades. The thing looked more like a pile of rubble now than a proud French fortification. The mix of heavy Germano-Italian guns had pummeled the Bear Mountain Fort to a mound of debris.

But appearances could be deceiving. Below the billowing fog, settling dust, and a pile of rubble (the fort was bombarded constantly), the French stood guard, their gun ports being still quite operational. This was not a theory since Rommel had been told that the last two days had seen an important Italian assault repulsed by the brave French defenders, still very much alive and very much armed.

Another assault was planned by the Italians that very day (it was early, and the sun had just risen), but the German Captain did not believe it would work. What he did believe, however, was that it would be a great diversion for what he had planned.

One of his men had spotted a goat trail heading into the mountains, and after a recon the night before (Rommel had gone with the enterprising Private), he'd seen that the trail led directly to the back of the French fort. He'd thus decided (with the Major's permission) to take the track while the enemy's attention would be fixated on the Italian attack. He hoped to be able to flank the fort and attack the enemy from the rear, or at the very least, infiltrate the place and cause a world of trouble.

"Private Stark," said Rommel. *"Go and get Lieutenant Stammer and tell him I need to know what time the Italians will start their attack."* "Yes, Captain," said the man who had discovered the goat track and that the young captain was already leaning on heavily for advice.

An hour later, he and twenty of his men were ready to go, fully armed and waiting for the start of the Italian attack. Lieutenant Stammer had protested strongly to Rommel that it wasn't his place to lead attacks like that, but he had disregarded his opinion. He was a man of action and, as such, was the one going to make this work.

The artillery bombardment prior to the attack was relentlessly pounding the area where the French fort (or the pile of rubble) stood. For Rommel and the men, what they saw was flashes and heard the sounds reminiscent of a powerful summer thunderstorm, as they were over a ridge and didn't have a direct line of sight to the forts.

The goat track snaked upward at a steep angle and was not made by or for humans. That much was obvious because they often had to crouch to force their way through hard-biting thorny trees. In other instances, they had to climb rocks and keep their balance. On the way there, one of the ten men (there were eleven, including Rommel) sprained his ankle and had to abandon the trek.

Private Theo Stark was in front, but no French soldier was seen, the track completely ignored. Rommel's theory on this was that the track ended at some point before it got to the fort. The only reason the

Germans had spotted it was because they ventured outside the main road in a bid to find new ways to assault the fort.

They finally came to the end of the trail, and from there, they had a great view of the relentless pounding the Bear Mountain Fort was taking. The shells landed in great concussion blasts, followed by spreading fire and scattering rocks and rubble.

"We are going to have to wait for this pounding to stop before we get close. Everyone gets comfy; we're going to be here for a few hours," said Rommel. The men answered by spreading along the ridge in cover positions to avoid being spotted by the enemy. "Stark," continued the Captain. *"You're with me; we'll try and find the best way down."* "Yes, sir." He also ordered one of the men to go back down and get the rest of the company (250 men).

After ten minutes, it was just as Rommel had suspected. There was no track coming down, and thus, the French had no chance of seeing it from their position. The way down was quite steep, so he guessed none of the enemy soldiers had bothered to check that potential blind spot in their defense.

A couple of hours later, the Italo-German artillery barrage stopped, and the sudden silence felt eerie as it echoed away into the mountains, fading as it went. A persistent fog hung over the area, and Rommel decided to move rapidly. During that time, Stark and a couple of other guys had also installed ropes, enabling the entire company to get down rapidly.

They walked cautiously to the more level part of the now blasted-out fort, rifles at the ready. From a distance, they could start hearing the Italian soldiers and probably the German battalion coming up the mountain. *"Watch for an entrance or an opening,"* said Rommel in a hushed voice. The large pile of rubble that had been the fort was reminiscent of an old pile outside an underground mine.

Then, Stark signaled to Rommel that he'd seen something. The rubble was moving about ten yards from their position. Moments later, a steel trapdoor opened, and Frenchmen started pouring out. The moment they did, they were greeted by leveled muskets in their faces, and they could only get their hands up.

Over fifty Frenchmen exited before someone in their camp realized something was amiss, and by then, German soldiers were inside the structure. In the end, it wasn't much of a fight; the French were completely stunned and numbed out of their mind by the bombardment of the last few hours and of the last few days. Their fort was a shambles, and they were completely isolated in front of the remaining line of forts.

As he came within view of the fort, Major Strosser could hear laughs and relieved voices both in Italian and German. One of the men pointed to the top of the peak where a German flag floated, and several German soldiers towered over the rubble.

The Commander of the Württemberg Mountain Battalion smiled broadly and decided that he would like this Rommel guy very much.

Somewhere north of Versailles, after the fight
Infanterie-Regiment Graf Schwerin (2nd Army, 4th Division), January 20th, 1915

"Damn," said Storch to his friend Oskar as they both struggled with the corpse they were moving. "*This is grisly work.*" Both men, like French and Germans alike, were walking the no man's land between the trench lines as a temporary truce had been called for to retrieve the dead and the wounded. It was the humane thing to do. "*Stop bitching, Flo,*" answered Dantz. "*At least you are standing on your feet and are unharmed.*" Storch grumbled but didn't say anything else.

It was not always possible to make this happen, but once in a while, the commanders on both sides were able to agree on it, especially when they were both exhausted and didn't want any more fighting.

Oskar watched as a pair of medics walked by with a stretcher where a young German soldier was lying, gravely wounded as his uniform was completely stained with blood.

He almost bumped into a French soldier who had come to retrieve one of his dead as well. They both turned, startled, and the man smiled at him. He thus smiled back. Not speaking a word of German (and Oskar didn't speak a word of French), the man lifted a finger and fished out a pack of French cigarettes, gesturing something to Oskar. "*What does the animal want,*" said Florian. His friend was no fan of the French, his grandfather having been killed in the 1870-1871 Franco-Prussian war. Dantz pretended not to hear him and continued trying to understand what that Frenchman meant. And then he got it. The French soldier wanted to make a trade. He fished out his own pack of cigarettes and showed it to him. The man smiled, nodding his head, and extended his arm to give him the pack he had. On it, it was written "*Cigarettes de Troupe,*" which seemed army issued. The pack was of plain paper, yellow colored. He gave him his own green Eckstein pack (Eckstein was one of the oldest brands of cigarettes in Germany).

And just like that, Private Soldier Oskar Dantz and Florian Storch discovered that the enemy soldier was just a poor grunt like them, after all. The man had a lighter and proposed to light their smokes, and then he did the same for his own. They all took long drags, and It felt great to be almost normal again, just lounging and having a cigarette.

Even the normally grumpy Florian smiled as he tried it. *"These are not so bad, Oskar,"* he said, gesturing his thanks and his appreciation as best he could to the French soldier while the smoke from his cigarette billowed around him. Soon, a bunch of soldiers from both sides gathered and started exchanging cigarettes and trinkets. They smiled, tried to speak to each other, and joked. Soon, the officers had to intervene to break them up. After all, they had a war to fight when the truce was over, and it was a lot harder to get soldiers to fire at friends.

The moment was truly magical for those men. Just hours before, they had tried to kill each other and would again do so again when they got back to their trenches. But for one fleeting moment, they were back to being ordinary, sensible human beings.

The French offensive in Verdun
Phase one, February 5th to 10th, 1915

If one thing was certain, it was that the German Army and the leaders of the OHL did not expect an attack in the Verdun sector. After all, the French had lost Paris, and that was where the most obvious target for any offensive should be launched. Paris and its general area were, for all intents and purposes, about a third of the country's production and economy.

Furthermore, Verdun was the most fortified area in France, as it was ringed with forts (no less than fifteen) and gun batteries (over ten); thus, it looked like the French would use the place as a defensive stronghold and not a springboard for an offensive.

As things were taking a turn for the better in the East with the Hindenburg offensive in Koenigsberg, the Bulgarians in Romania, and the strengthening of the defenses in the Carpathians and Bulgaria, that positive development was done with the German Army dangerously thinning its frontline in the West.

After all, the Russians attacked with over three million soldiers across the entire eastern frontline, and when the war started, the German 8th Army only had 250,000 men. The Austro-Hungarians could oppose with about a million men, and thus, things could not hold without sending major reinforcements.

Furthermore, the Italians, the Bulgarians, and the Ottomans were also all failing to keep their frontiers whole, and thus more troops were sent there from the Western Front to help them.

From a tactical and strategic stance, it was the thing to do. The Franco-British were apparently defeated, most of industrial France was in German hands, and the troops were urgently needed elsewhere.

However, several fundamental advantages remained for the Entente. First and foremost, they had not completely lost their offensive impetus. Second, the French had worked hard on getting the ammunition, guns, and rifles they needed and bought them from other countries, mainly the United States, with eager gun manufacturers and lots of industrial capability, but also with neutral Spain, which needed hard currency for its broken economy. Negotiations were even underway for the French to sell Guyana and their remaining Caribbean Islands to the United States in exchange for a lot of military supplies.

For the last month and a half, both the British and French armies also accumulated supplies, troops, and guns in the Verdun area for an attack in the sector. While their offensive capabilities were limited by the defeat and the terrible losses of the fall, it was possible to attack in a very concentrated fashion over a small part of the front. When all was said and done, the Entente forces about to launch at the German lines on the eve of the 3rd of February 1915 had accumulated 400,000 men and over a thousand guns, with enough ammo to last firing in a continuous manner for several days, ensuring the infantry assault would have enough support and artillery preparation.

The German forces in Verdun were, well, thin in comparison. Will all the troop removals and the moves to the East or to the other allies of the Reich, in the Verdun sector, considered a "quiet" one, the Army had a paltry 60,000 men where the attack would be launched. And these forces were not considered *"top-of-the-line."*

The Franco-British offensive opened in the wee hours of the morning on the 3rd of February with a bang, with the 1,000 guns firing one hell of an artillery barrage at the German trench line and positions. For five relentless hours, the shells churned, slammed, destroyed, and blasted the ground.

Then, out of the billowing, artillery-created fog came the hundreds of thousands of brave French and British soldiers yelling out of their lungs.

The first attack was repulsed by the multitude of Maxim machine guns, and they died in their thousands. Then, more artillery was fired for another couple of hours, and a second charge was sent. Again, it was repulsed, but the German forces started to feel pretty thin with their mounting casualties and dwindling ammunition.

On the 6th of February (after a long night of more artillery shelling), French General Foch and British General French sent even more men to the German lines, and they finally reached the first trench line and took it in a bloody and gory fight.

Later during the day, the next attack was launched at the second line (most German defensive lines had three to four trench lines as they defended in depth), and again it was taken. By the 7th of February, the OHL had to react and send reinforcements to the beleaguered area. Men who were earmarked to move from Paris and Northern France to the East to continue fueling the Hindenburg-Ludendorff offensive were thus diverted to the Verdun area.

Even that wasn't enough because the German Commander couldn't fathom the possibility of the Allies having accumulated so many troops and so much ordnance for just one offensive.

On the 9th of February, the third line of defense was taken by the Entente, and that was when things really started to look scary for the Germans.

The next day, on the 10th, the last, very thin fourth trench line was stormed, and then the Franco-British were faced with emptiness in front of them. Nothing stopped them from advancing toward Belgium and into the German rear.

The advance was lengthy compared to what had been seen in the last few weeks, by over ten kilometers, and the Germans were faced with a major disaster if nothing was done.

The OHL had already reacted a few days earlier by railing well over 100,000 men to the area to re-establish the front, but these moves were done at the expense of the East, completely stopping the attack in East Prussia and eliminating the possibility of any German support for the Hotzendorf offensive in the Carpathians.

The dynamics of a two-front war were starting to wear down on the German forces, who had to send troops and supplies everywhere to help their allies as well. It was time for Germany to switch to the defensive for the time being, or else risk losing everything.

Oberste Heeresleitung (OHL) – Supreme Army Command
Berlin, February 10th, 1915

Things could change rapidly in war, and the Franco-British offensive on Verdun had again shown this fact. As much as the Koenigsberg or Marienburg victory had changed the landscape in the East, or the Marne victory had done the same in the West, the successful and surprising Entente offensive on Verdun had shattered all of the German OHL High Command's certainties about the state of the war.

They'd thought the war was almost won in the West; the French broke, and the British Army was too few in numbers to go through more problems. After all, they now had millions of Italian soldiers with the Central Powers, controlled Paris, and had their High Seas Fleet poised to strike at the enemy fleets and convoys in the Atlantic.

But the dynamics of a modern two-front war were just starting to be understood. The simple fact was that none of the Entente powers were strong enough to face Germany alone was not enough to factor in if victory was near or not. Defeating France or Russia on one side of the map or the other meant that to achieve overwhelming victory, the German Army also had to send overwhelming forces, thus thinning the other side. There was no win scenario if the Reich concentrated too hard on one side over the other. Then, a balanced approach only worked if you wanted to be defensive since in war (and especially trench warfare), the attacker had to have a three-of-four-to-one ratio and be fairly well stocked in artillery ammunition and guns.

The sad truth for Germany was that while individually, none of the Entente powers could stand up one-on-one against its land forces, they could from diametrically opposed frontlines (east and west).

It was in this mood that the members of the OHL met on that dreary, icy, and rainy day of February as the enemy breakthrough was in full progress. They weren't meeting because the frontline would shatter.

No, they had already moved enough troops to the area to stop the enemy and dig new trench lines. They were meeting to discuss the next step since the Reich could hardly win the war if it stayed in its trenches and waited for the enemy to come at him.

The top people of the Reich were again assembled but this time in one of the formal meeting rooms of the Berlin Palace. The room itself had Italian marble for flooring, a nice blue glass chandelier, and a big hearth where a blazing fire burned bright to keep everyone warm.

The following people had come for the meeting that morning: Helmut von Moltke, the Chief of the General Staff (and thus head of OHL) and the Minister of War, Erich von Falkenhayn. Then there was also the Chief of the Operations Division, Colonel Gehard von Tappen, and the Chief of the Information Division (intelligence), Lieutenant Colonel Richard Hentch.

At the head of the table and facing them all was the Kaiser, Wilhelm II. To the ruler's left was Paul von Hindenburg, the Eastern commander, flanked this time by his faithful acolyte, General Erich von Ludendorff. To the right was Rear Admiral Roman Berger, the Chief of the Admiral Staff's deputy for this meeting, as Admiral Hugo von Pohl was about to sortie with the High Seas Fleet from St-Nazaire in France. The Fleet wouldn't be part of the discussion, but it had a seat at the table and so it was invited.

The Kaiser opened up the discussions this time. *"Gentlemen, thank you for being here at this grave hour. We are facing a major crisis,"* said Wilhelm, with a tinge of panic in his voice. *"Indeed, Your Majesty,"* said Helmut von Moltke, the Head of the OHL, slightly annoyed that his sovereign had spoken before him.

"We need to discuss the country's stance as the recent enemy offensive on Verdun shattered the belief that the Western Powers were tamed for the time being. We are now facing a major crisis, and there are indications the enemy is also massing troops in the Paris

area." Moltke's words seemed to unsettle the Kaiser even more, and Hindenburg made a face because he knew what his Commander-in-Chief was getting at. The top OHL man continued. *"In light of the Army's major obligations on two fronts, the support it has to give the Bulgarians, the Austrians, the Italians, and the Ottomans, I propose we switch to the defensive for now until such a time that we can confidently go back on the offense."*

The Reich was already on the defensive in France, but its offensive stance in the East had forced the Army leadership to thin out the troops and send many of them to help fuel Hindenburg's offensive and shore up the Austro-Hungarian defenses in the Carpathians.

The old General, who was already planning with Ludendorff the invasion of Russia through East Prussia and Lithuania, grumbled out loud. *"When will be able to launch an offensive again, General Moltke,"* said Hindenburg. *"We have the Tsar on the ropes right now."*

If there was one man who didn't like to switch to the defensive, it was Helmut von Moltke, but there was no choice. *"I do not know, General Hindenburg. We have to stop this French offensive first and make sure our allies do not sue for peace. We also have a limited supply of artillery shells and bullets. Our industries are struggling to keep up with weekly consumption, and fighting on two fronts really does not help right now."* In this, Moltke was right, and no argument could counter it. Modern war consumed ammunition and men at a prodigious rate, one that none of the powers had anticipated. The industry of every country at war thus struggled to meet the demands of the fighting armies. Germany has the biggest economy of all, but at the same time fought on two fronts and against four to five times its numbers.

The *"industrialization of warfare"* was in the process of gearing up, but in early 1915, it was not yet up to the standards for modern fighting armies engaged in a long, protracted war of epic proportions spanning the entire globe.

The old General didn't answer anything, deciding to sulk in his corner. Moltke continued. *"Your Majesty, with your approval, we will begin the immediate transfer of 400,000 soldiers from both Hindenburg's forces in East Prussia and General August von Mackensen's troops."*

Kaiser Wilhelm, almost panicked at the thought of losing it all on the Western front, answered right away. "It is just as we decided, General Moltke. Stop the Franco-British and preserve our gains so far."

And that was that. The entire German 10th (200,000 soldiers) Army was being re-transferred to the west (already 60,000 of them were in the Verdun area to block the enemy offensive), and half of the 9th Army (180,000 soldiers). Their mission was to bolster the defensive lines.

While this move would secure the West, it decidedly put an end to any German offensive ideas in the East, giving the Russians in Lithuania under General Rennenkampf a much-needed reprieve and time to reinforce while leaving the initiative for Russian Brusilov to continue his attacks on Austria-Hungary now that Przemysl had fallen.

The keener minds around the table started to see what the rest of the war would look like for Germany.

Allied Field HQ, France
Fort Douaumont January 24th, 1915

The structure of Fort Douaumont was built like a hexagon, as all modern forts were, in order to maximize the defensive structure's angles of fire. The fort itself was 300 meters by 300 meters from hexagonal face to hexagonal face, making it the largest and most powerful fort in the Verdun area. The structure was also built on a hill that stood 1200 feet higher than the town of Verdun and the other forts. The entire village had been built up before the war to act as a defensive stopgap in case of a German offensive. And it had withstood all the Reich had sent at it in the fall, as everywhere else the Entente retreated.

Its defenses were as multiple as they were impressive. In addition to its 1,000-soldier garrison, it had a powerful and protected 155 mm Galopin turret with two armored observation posts. There were two 75 mm guns in the "casemate de Borge," a strong and fortified gun battery. There was another turret with a 75 mm gun, reinforced with two meters of added concrete to make the structure sustain the heavy damage from modern guns. For close-in protection, the fort had a plethora of firing ports for the soldiers and also two armored machine gun turrets, each with two Hotchkiss machine gun nests. The setup was crowned by two armored command turrets and two armored lookout posts.

It was where Generals Louis Franchet D'Espèrey (5th Army), recently reinstated General Charles Lanzerac (9th Army), and General John French (British Expeditionary Force) had established their forward headquarters to lead the offensive the overall Allied commander General Ferdinand Foch had ordered them to execute.

When planned and launched, the entire affair had been one desperate gamble, first, to surprise the Germans with a sudden attack and impede them from continuing to send troops East, and second, to try and turn things in their favor here.

But, as unexpected as it was, it was met with a resounding success. Many in the French Army had lost faith in the fabled "offensive à outrance" military dogma (the spirit of the offensive), and thus, both Lanzerac and d'Espèrey had been skeptical about the entire affair.

But they obeyed and tried to make the best out of it, and now they were through the German trenches. The enemy was counterattacking with some mobile forces and was pouring reinforcements forward by the hour, but the offensive had already achieved great success. The French forces had advanced over 20 miles and liberated the French villages of Etain and Damvillers, and were poised to advance to Luxembourg, one of the German headquarters and important rail nodes.

"An amazing job so far, Generals," said visiting Commander-in-Chief General Ferdinand Foch to the three other men meeting with him that day. He moved to one of the room's gun embrasures, giving way to the outside. He noticed that it was scarred, probably from the fight in the fall. *"I might even add, it's a stellar job."*

The two other generals basked in the moment, happy to have pleased their commander. Only French harbored a mildly more neutral face. He was, after all, British. *"Thank you, Sir,"* said Lanzerac. The French officer had been reinstated to command after being sacked by Joffre in the fall for advocating defense, while the former Commander-in-Chief had wanted to attack at all costs.

Foch turned back and walked the short distance to the dusty table in the middle of the room, leaning over the maps and putting both his closed fists on the table. *"But the real question is, can we reach Luxembourg and beyond?"*

British General French spoke up. *"Sir, it is a given that the enemy will send reinforcements, and that resistance is already stiffening. The reports from the frontline are clear. The German Army is digging in further back while troops are fighting in the front to give more time to their brothers to prepare the trenches."*

Foch made an understanding face. *"And our artillery ordnance is almost dry after six days of continuous fighting...."* He answered, putting his fingers on his chin as he was thinking hard. While the Allies were in a great position to break through, the Germans were hardly going to step aside, and their limited supplies of ammo (accumulated for weeks for the Verdun attack) were dwindling rapidly.

It was time to make a decision for the Entente. Go for broke, or play it safe and dig in with the gains already won to try again down the line? If Joseph Joffre had still been in command everyone around the table knew what the choice would have been. But this type of attitude and go-for-broke attack was why they were in deep trouble with Paris and Northern France occupied.

"Thoughts, gentlemen," said Foch. The man was looking for other people's opinions, as his command style was quite different than his predecessor. D'Espèrey spoke up. *"Sir, I think you have pretty much summed up our situation, and General French is also right. The enemy resistance is stiffening, and we are still in a precarious position. We don't want to be caught off-guard by an enemy counteroffensive."*

Foch nodded silently and then looked at French and Lanzerac. They also nodded. And then it was what it was. *"Send orders to stop attacking and to dig in, gentlemen. Let's keep what we have gained."*

The entire affair ended up being a great decision by the Allies since they didn't risk more and had already attained their strategic objectives of distracting Germany from its Eastern successes.

Troisvierges railway station (Bahnhof Ulflingen) Luxembourg
Infanterie-Regiment Graf Schwerin, February 11th, 1915

The Great War's first action was in Luxembourg at a small railway station called Troisvierges, and it happened quite by error. At 7 PM on the evening of the 1st of August, the German 69th Infantry Regiment moved into Northern Luxembourg, but without being aware that the Kaiser was trying to keep Britain's neutrality by delaying the invasion of Luxembourg and Belgium.

It was quickly realized that the unit had blundered into Luxembourg before the planned operation (because of the Kaiser's meddling), and an hour and a half later, the troops were withdrawn, but not before destroying the telegraph station and some parts of the railway.

Then, the next day, the full invasion was launched, and the entire event was forgotten, except for the stories between soldiers who made fun of the event. The rumor mill was strong in any army, and that funny event was something the German grunts liked to talk about.

Thus, both Oskar Dantz and Florian Storch smiled when the wagon they were in entered the Troisvierges Station. *"So... this is where this damned war started,"* said Florian as he stretched his head out to look at the long white building beside the dock. *"Appears so, buddy,"* answered Oskar. They'd heard the story so many times they looked forward to seeing the train station.

The train screeched to a loud, steel-wrenching halt; they stood up and were instructed to exit the railcar. They moved through the white billowing smoke and stepped down the stairs and onto the docks. Immediately, they noticed the fay away thunder, proof that battle was near. *"Well, Dantz, new place, same old fight,"* said Florian as he put his arm on Oskar's shoulder.

And indeed, they had moved to a new part of the front. Following the surprising and destabilizing enemy offensive in Verdun, the German High Command scrambled troops from everywhere to try and desperately plug the gap. The Infanterie-Regiment Graf Schwerin was thus detached from the 4th Division (2nd Army) and earmarked for redeployment in the area between Luxembourg and Verdun. Their instructions were simple. Move to the Troivierges Station, march to the frontline, and dig.

"Indeed, my friend," answered Oskar, smiling back at Florian. Sergeant Wilhelm soon dispelled any smiles they had, however, and they were told to get in line since the Regiment was going to march right away to the frontline.

Apulia Enclave
Anglo-French forces, February 10th, 1915

Private Soldier Armand Bonnier sat on the trench board facing the trench's rear revetement. He always stayed near the so-called *"bolt hole,"* a small side tunnel dug into the trench wall to hide in when and if the enemy lobbed artillery shells at them. The idea was to try and avoid any direct hit and also protect oneself from shrapnel. There were more elaborate bunkers at regular intervals in the trench, but one didn't always have time to go there when the artillery started falling.

Looking behind him, he saw the sandbag wall that they used when they fought an enemy assault and that they had to step over with ladders when they themselves charged the enemy line. Further down, facing the front of the trench, was the beginning of the no man's land (the area between the two frontlines). Then, about ten to twenty feet from their own trench began the line upon line of barbed wire. Behind him towered a machine gun nest protected by its own small little hole circled by barbed wire and sandbags. Below his feet was about three inches of water, thanks to the last rainfall a couple of days ago. Armand shook his head about the insanity of it all. The entire concept of trench warfare was fast becoming a well-organized tactic, and he wasn't certain he liked it since it meant being stuck in this rat and disease-infested hole for a long time.

A plane flew above and, from its perspective, saw things differently from its position of height. All the elements that Bonnier saw were there, but the French pilot could see the intricate design of the defensive positions as if he was looking at geometrical patterns and designs carved into the earth.

Starting from the rear position, he first flew over the artillery line; there was a bunch of lined-up guns in shallow box-like trenches crisscrossed by side tunnels for the soldiers and the gunners to move about even during an enemy artillery barrage.

Right after that was the first support line trench, where some of the ordnance and support people were located. There again, an intricate pattern of tunnels ran to and from it. The next batch of tunnels and trenches was called the frontline support, and finally, the pilot saw the frontline trench where Armand was. Following that was no man's land and the tangle of barbed wire.

The pilot shook his head, thinking that he was incredibly lucky to be in a plane and not stuck in the blackened, pockmarked, and waterlogged hellhole below him.

Armand saw the plane fly above and longed to be with the man looking down on him, scarf in the wind. He took a deep breath, trying to will himself back to reality when his friend and comrade Philipe Cren walked by his feet into the ankle-deep water, sloshing his way toward him. *"Dreaming about the sky again, Bonnier,"* said Philippe, laughing out loud. *"You know that isn't for us. We're born to be in this shit!*

"I know, buddy, but I can't help it. If there had been no war, I would have flown a plane like that. Do you think I could apply to be a pilot in the Air Corps?" Cren laughed even louder. "Don't be ridiculous, Armand; you are stuck with me and this beautiful vacation resort," he continued, gesturing largely with his arms.

Armand skulked as he turned back to the rapidly disappearing biplane in the sky and decided he would continue to dream. Armand had flown a plane before the war with his friend Roland Garros. He hadn't been with him in the Morane-Saulnier aircraft when the now famous man had gained his fame by making the first flight (non-stop) across the Mediterranean Sea from Frejus to Bizerte in Tunisia. Nevertheless, Roland had shown him the ropes on how to fly them. Once in the air, it was relatively easy; the problem was when one had to land or take off. And he didn't worry too much about it since Roland had told him that he would be fine as he was a natural pilot.

The fight in the Apulia enclave was sort of stalemated as nothing was moving either south or north. The Italians couldn't break through, and the Entente forces were in the same boat. Armand and Philippe didn't know it, but there were talks in high places in London and Bordeaux about potentially evacuating the troops since the main strategic objective was reached. The Italian fleet was destroyed.

On the ground, the action was pretty much stale as none of the two sides bothered to attack the other anymore. The Italians seemed to be pretty shy on artillery and they rarely fired any significant barrages at them, while the Entente forces were doing a good job of plastering the Italian side every night.

From Armand's point of view, things could stay the same for a while. The only problem he had with the status quo was the squalor he had to live in, the rats, and the general discomfort of it all.

Castellammare shipyard, Naples
Dreadnought battleship launch, February 11th, 1915

The sinking of the entire Italian battle fleet was a traumatic moment for Italy, and almost toppled it out of the war right from the start. The government of Italian Prime Minister Antonio Salandra was seriously challenged in Parliament, as the King and many others in Italian leadership circles knew that the reason the Entente had attacked was because the man had been about to have the country join the Central Powers. In the end, the coalition held, and Salandra was able to hold on to power, but it was by a hairbreadth's margin.

In 1913, a new class of huge battleships was started. The goal was to build four of them, intended to match the super-dreadnought battleship class the British had come up with (Queen Elizabeth Class). The ships were armed with eight 381 mm guns and a plethora of secondary 152 mm guns with top-of-the-line armor. By 1914, however, things had looked like the ships, including the two that already had their keel laid down would be canceled for budgetary reasons.

Following the destruction of the fleet, things changed radically. The Francesco Caracciolo class went from being a nice "long-term" project to being a national emergency. Italy didn't have one major warship left because of the Franco-British's dastardly attack, and that was unacceptable for Rome. The building program went into overdrive and the four intended ships were confirmed and being built at an accelerated pace.

The first of those ships was the Francesco Caracciolo, built in the Castellammare shipyard located in Naples. It was one of the oldest shipyards in all of Italy, going back to the Kingdom of the Two Sicilie's during the Napoleonic Wars. The place was well-suited for the development of new prototype ships and was thus chosen to build the first two of the new super-dreadnought class (the second one under construction, further down to the left of where the group of visitors was standing and encased in girders, was called Marcantonio Colonna).

The ship before the Prime Minister looked pretty powerful, with its imposing shape and height. *"Watch this big crane, Mr. Prime Minister,"* said one of the shipyard bosses in charge of Salandra's visit. The Italian leader had wanted to see the new ships and the hopes of his country for himself. He was flanked by Leone Viale, the Minister of the Italian Navy, and Hans von Flotow, the German Ambassador to Italy.

"I thank you again for the funds and resources your country is providing, Ambassador Flotow," said Salandra, as he smiled at the shipyard boss to look at the huge crane moving one of the big 381 mm barrels from the dock to the deck of the battleship under construction. Indeed, the German Empire was footing the bill for these constructions, as there had been no available funds and not enough steel before the war, and now that Italy was at war with the Entente, even less. The Reich, having an interest in Italy fielding ships, had thus again saved the day. *"The Kaiser wanted me to convey to you the unflagging support of all of Germany,"* answered von Flotow, a career diplomat who had been in Italy for the last five years.

ITALY
Regina Marina, Admiral Amedeo di Savoia-Aosta

BB Francesco Caracciolo in construction	BB Cristoforo Colombo in construction
BB Marcantonio Colonna in construction	BB Francesco Morosini in construction

The powerful class of new dreadnoughts was going to be Italy's comeback in naval affairs. The 32,000-ton Francesco Caracciolo was going to be ready at some point in 1915, and Salandra looked forward to it. With the powerful Austro-Hungarian fleet and the Ottoman fleet, soon to be joined with the Greek one, he believed they had a chance to reclaim control of the Central Mediterranean and re-establish contact with their overseas empire in Tripolitania and Cyrenaica in North Africa.

Things were not fixed, however, as the enemy had proven their willingness to attack harbors, even the most protected ones like Taranto. In order to make sure this didn't happen again, two full Italian divisions were stationed in each of the shipyards building the ships (two in Castellammare and two in the Ansaldo Shipyards, located in Genoa). Also, several heavy guns and mortars were brought forward, with trench and bunker defenses constructed around them, making the two critical ship-building towns impregnable even from a large enemy fleet.

"When will the first one be ready, Minister Viale," asked Salandra, now keenly watching how the workers were putting the gun in place. The entire affair seemed like tough precision work. *"I would think that the Francesco Caracciolo should be ready to launch in June of this year, Mr. Prime Minister." "Very well."*

"Mr. Prime Minister," then said the shipyard boss. *"Would you like to see the machine shops where the parts are being made..."* Salandra smiled. *"Of course..."* and the tour continued.

Shipbuilding of the Great Powers
Battleships and battlecruisers in progress, February 1915

The naval arms race that was in force before the Great War had produced many warship projects. While construction was slowed down in most countries because of a lack of funds and a better allocation of resources, the Entente and Central Powers did not stop building ships altogether. The goal was, of course, to either keep control of the seas (Entente) or else take it (Central Powers).

The Entente thus started the war with a ship superiority that was hard to challenge, and the British intended to keep it that way with the most robust naval building program of all the Great Powers.

United Kingdom

BB Canada (1915)	BB Royal Sovereign (1916)
BC Renown (1916)	BB Ramillies (1917)
BC Resolution (1916)	BB Royal Oak (1916)
BC Courageous (1917)	56 Cruisers (from 1915 to 1918)
BC Furious (1917)	236 Destroyers (From 1915 to 1918)
BB Revenge (1916)	156 Submarine (from 1915 to 1918)
BB Resolution (1916)	

First and foremost, it canceled an order from Chili in order to keep the Almirante Latorre, buying the ship back to rename it Canada. The transaction was completed at the end of January 1915 and the battleship, ready to sail, was thus about to be incorporated into the Grand Fleet. The ship was of the super-dreadnought type, sporting 32,000 tons and 13.5-inch guns.

Then came the Renown Class of battlecruisers (Renown, Resolution, Furious, Courageous), with their 27,000 tons of displacement and 15-inch guns. Not to be undone, the Revenge Class of battleships (Revenge, Royal Sovereign, Ramillies, and Royal Oak) was yet another set of powerful warships, clocking in at 32,000 tons and armed with 15-inch guns. Finally, a plethora of support ships were in the works as well, with 56 cruisers, 256 Destroyers, and 156 submarines. With this building program, there was no chance for Germany to catch up on the already overwhelmingly superior Royal Navy.

The next Entente power in terms of fleet size was the French Republic. While it had avoided the destruction of its pre-war battlefleet by sailing away in time before the German Army had arrived to occupy its northern military harbors, such was not the case of the ship projects underway. The "Marine Nationale" had the Normandie Class battleships underway when war broke out in August 1914. Right off the bat, both the Normandie and the Gascogne were lost to the approaching German troops (scuttled by the construction crews). The class was supposed to be France's next generation of super-dreadnought (28,000 tons and 13.4-inch guns). The ones left were being built either in Bordeaux or Toulon (Bearn, Flandre). Several other ship types were destroyed (5 cruisers and 10 destroyers), and it remained to be seen if France would have any resources left to finish the ships it had started. Without the industrial north and the revenue lost to the German occupation, there were better things to build than capital ships. The French Army needed the steel to build artillery shells, bayonets, steel helmets, and, most importantly, bullets.

France	
~~BB Normandie (1916)~~	~~BB Gascogne (1917)~~
BB Bearn (1916)	5 heavy cruisers (From 1915 to 1918) ~~5 destroyed because in German occupied ports~~
BB Flandre (1917)	15 Destroyers (From 1915 to 1918) ~~10 destroyed because in German occupied ports~~

Imperial Russia started the Great War without any dreadnought battleships, but that didn't mean they weren't building any. It was a good thing because they lost their entire Black Sea battle fleet at the Battle of Cape Sarych in the Fall of 1914, and the Baltic Fleet had not yet recovered from the terrible Battle of Tsushima nine years before.

The country was building three Imperatritsa Mariya battleships. Two of them were being built in the Black Sea (Mariya and Ekaterina Velikaya) and one in the Baltic (Imperator Nikolai I). These ships were state-of-the-art super battleships (24,000 tons and 12-inch guns), and it was hoped they would help to tip the scales currently in the Central Powers' favor in both Seas.

The Russians were also building (in the Baltic) the battlecruisers of the truly impressive Borodino Class (32,500 tons and 15-inch guns), with the names Borodino, Izmail, Kinburn, and Navarin and the battleship Gangut (24,000 tons and 12-inch guns). A small number of support ships were also being built in the Baltic (five cruisers and 12 destroyers).

Russia	
BB Imperatritsa Mariya (May 1915)	BC Kinburn (1918)
BB Imperatritsa Ekaterina Velikaya (May 1915)	BC Navarin (1917)
BB Imperator Nokolai I (1916)	BB Gangut (1917)
BC Borodino (1916)	5 heavy cruisers (From 1915 to 1918)
BC Izmail (1916)	12 Destroyers (From 1915 to 1918)

Russia was a land power, and while it had been the second-largest navy in the world before the Russo-Japanese War of 1905, it was now reduced to a secondary role in the Great War.

If there was one power that could challenge British supremacy, it was Germany. The Kaiserliche Marine was second only to the Royal Navy in terms of dreadnoughts and number of ships. A true naval power, the Kaiser's fleet was also busy building more ships to try and keep pace with the madly gearing-up English.

Germany	
BB Bayern (May 1915)	BC York (1917)
BB Baden (June 1915)	BC Mackensen (1916)
BB Sachsen (1917)	14 Heavy cruisers (From 1915 to 1918)
BB Wurttenberg (1917)	60 Destroyers (From 1915 to 1918)
BC Hindenburg (April 1915)	370 Uboats (From 1915 to 1918)
BC Ersatz (1917)	

Germany's newest class of dreadnoughts, the Bayern, were true monsters that would be able to challenge the biggest Royal Navy's super-dreadnoughts like the Queen Elizabeth. They came at 31,000 tons and were armed with eight 15-inch guns. The shipyards were building four of them: Bayern, Baden, Sachsen, and Wurttemberg. Then came the last of the Derfflinger class of battlecruisers, the Hindenburg (31,000 tons and eight 12-inch guns). The Germans were also building a new class of battlecruisers, the Ersatz Yorck class, which promised to be some of the most powerful ships afloat at 33,500 tons and eight 15-inch guns.

But the true effort for the Germans was put in to support ships, with 14 cruisers, 60 destroyers, and a staggering 370 planned U-boats. The submarines were the only way the Kaiserliche Marine saw they could challenge the British on the sea and effectively cut their supply lines.

The last power building warships in any important way was Austria Hungary. It was very limited because of the very nature of the country's limited naval presence and capabilities. The K.u.K. fleet was based in Pola, and there was also just one other shipyard (Trieste).

Austria-Hungary	
BB Szent Istvan (1915)	2 Destroyers (1917)

Many ships were in the design stages, but after the resounding defeats of the fall of 1914 and the resource shortages, it was decided to only finish the last of the Tegethoff Class battleships, the Szent Istvan, a ship with 22,000 tons of displacement and four 12-inch guns.

The Austrians, while they were about to try and break it, were blockaded in the Adriatic, and thus, the powerful fleet didn't have much of an impact to date in the war. This was because if it wanted to sortie into the Mediterranean, it would have to force the so-called Otranto Barrage, the Allied naval blockade of the Strait of Otranto between Brindisi in Italy and Corfu on the Greek side of the Adriatic Sea.

The occupation of Crete
Operation Kronos, February 13th, 1915

The problem of the powerful Germano-Ottoman fleet based in the Bosphorus, which could sail out into the Aegean and then into the Mediterranean, was an acute one for the British. They had enough ships to challenge the Eastern Mediterranean Squadron based in Alexandria. Now that Greece had also joined the Central Powers, adding two pre-dreadnought battleships and two heavy cruisers to the roster, it was a given that trouble was on the horizon.

While the British had no real fear of the enemy ships and believed themselves superior in seamanship and power, the possibility of Admiral Souchon's sailing out of the Dardanelles and into the Aegean to raid Allied convoys was very real.

Eastern Mediterranean Squadron		
Vice-Admiral Sackville Hamilton Carden		
BB Dreadnought	Pre-dread BB Almermale (6th battle squ.)	CA Amethyst
BC Indefatigable	Pre-dread BB Duncan (6th battle squ.)	CL Falmouth and Diamond
BB Superb	CA Aboukir	9 DD

The British economy relied heavily on trade with its Empire. All the critical goods coming out of India and its Eastern possessions transited through the Suez Canal and into the Mediterranean. It was the same for the French, who possessed important holdings in Asia (Indochina, Thailand, and more). These ships represented a very juicy target for the burgeoning Central Powers fleet, and the British couldn't guard against a quick move from where the East Med Squadron was currently based (Alexandria, in Egypt).

While Churchill had been of the mind to execute a repeat of Operation Ares (the sinking of the Italian Fleet and the invasion of Taranto), the entire endeavor represented more of a stretch for the already overtaxed Royal Navy. To succeed in this type of attack (like attacking the Greek harbor or forcing the Dardanelles Strait open) required a number of ships and troops that weren't readily available.

Admiral John Jellicoe, the commander of the Grand Fleet and top Admiral in the Royal Navy had thus proposed an alternative to the First Lord of the Admiralty because the ships that the British used for Operation Ares were now dearly needed in the Atlantic following the breakout of the German High Seas Fleet and its rebasing in St-Nazaire and Brest.

The invasion and occupation of Crete represented a good middle-ground solution to their problems. It was located at the crossroads between the Aegean and the Eastern Mediterranean and possessed a pretty good harbor. The port of Heraklion wasn't the biggest, but it was large enough to house the ships of the Eastern Med Squadron. From there, it would be able to rapidly intervene against any Central Powers attempt at a breakout and an attack against Allied shipping.

For the invasion, the British didn't have a lot of troops available as all hands were on deck to defend France, but it did have the so-called "Force in Egypt," established in the fall of 1914. The force totaled about 30,000 men, split into several units.

Crete wasn't really garrisoned by the Greeks, who entertained a small 200,000-man army on the continent. About a half-battalion was thus scattered around the island but was in no position to stop any attack.

The British, keenly aware of Ottoman troop movements toward the Suez Canal (an Army was approaching through the Sinai), couldn't spare much, but they did have enough to master the small Greek force. Hence, the troops that landed on that fog-laden morning of the 13th of February were the British 2nd Battalion (a part of the Devonshire Regiment), the 2nd Field Company, Royal Engineers (to get the harbor up to speed and ready to receive the Royal Navy), and for artillery support, the 7th Mountain Battery of the Royal Field Artillery (RFA).

As it happened, there wasn't much resistance from the Greeks, and within a couple of hours, the city and harbor of Heraklion were in

British hands. By dusk on the same day, the Greek commander on the island offered his official surrender.

Two days later, the British Eastern Mediterranean Squadron arrived in the harbor, and soon after that, the Royal Navy started to aggressively patrol the Southern Aegean, landing troops on some of the islands. The hour was grave for the Greeks, and worries were great that a full Entente invasion was coming in Epirus. It would not materialize, but the event was the final straw in convincing King Constantine to send his ships to join Admiral Souchon in the Dardanelles.

CHAPTER 4
The war in the East

Truk Lagoon
Caroline Islands, dusk, February 3rd, 1915

(...) Dreadnought battleship Westfalen (...)

"Admiral," said Chief of Staff Vice-Admiral Max von Krenk, *"The flag signaler reports that the enemy has split its force in two, and both are sailing around the island."* Von Spee made a sour face. *"Togo wants a battle for sure,"* he said in response. While that was a given, the path he'd chosen would not bring him under the Japanese guns until he was almost out of the lagoon, and he then had a surprise for the man.

German Pacific Squadron	
Admival von Graf Spee	
BB Westfalen stern damage	CL Emden
BB Kaiserin stern and boiler damage	CL Nurnberg
CA Kaiserin Elisabeth (Austria-Hungary)	CL Leipzing

"The Fleet is ready for battle, Sir," continued Krenk. The German ships, all six of them, were as ready as they could get, fully repaired, full of coal, and determined to survive. Von Spee wondered if Togo's men and ships felt the same and were as ready as his people were. They certainly weren't engaged in a fight for their lives, and he hoped it would show in the battle.

Japanese Imperial Fleet Battle Squadron 1	Admiral Heihachiro Togo	
BB Setsu	Pre-dreadnought BB HIZEN	Pre-dreadnought BB MIKASA
BB Kawachi armor belt damage	Pre-dreadnought BB IKI	CA X25
	Pre-dreadnought BB IWAMI	CL X 6
Pre-dreadnought BC Tsukuma,	Pre-dreadnought BB SAGAMI	DD X30
Pre-Dreadnought BC Ikoma I	Pre-dreadnought BB SUWO	-

(…) Dreadnought battleship Setsu (…)

"Admiral," said Captain Nagata, the Commander of the battleship Setsu. *"It appears the enemy is coming up on our side just as you predicted."* Togo smiled. *"And as we expected, I guess the enemy fleet is keeping the islands in the line of sight?"* "Indeed, Sir," answered Captain Nagata. *"Send a couple of volleys anyway in the general areas of the smoke columns."* "Yes, Admiral. Visibility is starting to be very low, its hard to distinguish the smoke from the surroundings and growing darkness." Togo nodded. *"Just tell the gunners on every ship to do their best. I just want to rattle the bastards."* "Yes, Sir."

A minute later, the Japanese guns on battleships Setsu, Tsukuma, Ikoma, Hizen, and Iki traversed upward to gain some elevation and fired above the islands, blocking their direct line of sight to the enemy fleet. Their salvos blossomed in the growing night in large fireballs. From a distance, it looked like distant but very powerful lightning, reverberating like a huge summer storm.

(…) German Fleet (…)

The Japanese shells started to land in front of the German fleet, startling Admiral Maximilian von Spee. *"Admiral,"* said one of his men on the bridge, but he lifted his arm to silence him. *"I see it. Don't worry about it, people. The Japanese are firing blind. They are shooting above the islands but have no direct bearing on our position."* Togo's opening salvo was to rattle him and his men, but he was determined to keep his plan together. *"Captain Ritter,"* he continued. *"Have your people relay the same message to the fleet. We steam out as fast as possible. Also, are the Kaiserin Elisabeth and the Emden ready to implement the last phase of the plan when we exit the atoll?"* Ritter nodded. *"Yes, Sir, relaying the message."* He gestured to his communications officer to execute. *"And the two cruisers are indeed ready to implement and trailing behind as planned."*

Von Spee looked left, seeing battleship Kaiserin's two rear turrets (it had another one in the front and two in the middle between the funnels and the bridge traversing to face the enemy ships behind them). This was going to be an interesting battle.

(...) The fight (...)

The night was relatively clear with a full moon, and it was thus possible for the two opposing fleets to see their silhouettes gliding over the water. Togo's ships eventually rounded the island, coming into range and with a direct line of sight to the German ships.

"Fire star shells," said Togo, as Setsu's bow finally turned toward the anticipated location of the German fleet. The forward gun fired them almost as the Admiral said it. Star shells were explosive devices meant to illuminate the battlefield, either on land or on the water.

The shells contained a fuse, bursting at a pre-arranged height, igniting a magnesium core that burned while the ordinance fell down slowly under the guise of a parachute. Burning magnesium was as bright as the sun, and it did a good job of illuminating the German ships.

"The bastards are almost at the exit," said Captain Nagata, as surprised as anyone else at the speed of the German ships. Togo pretended not to hear what his Captain had just said. *"Order everyone to fire at will."*

The flurry of Japanese fireballs was seen from the German fleet, as it was pretty obvious. Then, the star shells exploded above them, illuminating the entire area. *"Admiral,"* said Krenk in a calm voice. *"The enemy is in sight and firing."* Von Spee couldn't see the enemy as his ship, the Westfalen, steamed at full speed toward the atoll exit. The bridge thus faced forward. He thus walked across and exited the bridge on the other side to watch from the observation deck's rear windows. *"Well, I hope we shoot back,"* he said with a smile, hoping to relax the tense atmosphere.

As if on cue, the six backward-facing main gun turrets blossomed with fire, and von Spee crossed his arms behind his back. "Let's give some pain to the enemy, gentlemen." Across the German fleet, the main guns blasted back in a cacophony of fire and sound.

The range at the start of the battle was 10,000 yards. This was far enough to avoid getting hit at the start of the battle, and it ensured the gunners would take some time to process the correct firing solutions.

The first Japanese salvo was scattered, as not all of its ships rounded the atoll, blocking the line of sight, and the German one was the same. A couple of weird hits slammed on the island in powerful blasts of fire. But by and large, both fleets missed each other in the first ten minutes of the fight, firing above, to the side, and too short. Several straddling shots landed around the German battleship Kaiserin, but the Japanese Admiral should have paid more attention to the two trailing ships, the Kaiserin Elisabeth and the Emden.

(…) Austro-Hungarian ship Kaiserin Elisabeth (…)

Both the Kaiserin Elisabeth's and the Emden's sailors were busy throwing large objects overboard from the rear of their ships. The large things splashed into the water and started floating. The objects had chains and anchors to keep them in place.

The Elektriche Minen A (E-Mine) was a Kaiserliche Marine contact mine using the Horn firing system. The Hertz horns (spark plug in German) were shaped as brass and steel objects and reminiscent of horns. They enclosed a visible tube containing brown-colored liquid sulfuric acid. The horns were fragile enough to break on contact with a ship hull, and that liquid was then designed to pour into the mine to chemically react with the exploding charge, detonating it.

This was how the explosion was created, and it was a very cheap way to take out capital ships without firing a shot. One of the sailors smiled as one of the mines fell into the water. The Japanese would soon have a surprise. He turned, seeing that the fleet's main body had already crossed the channel exiting the atoll and was in the open ocean. "That's the last one," said the man behind him. *"Good; tell the Captain we're done, and we can speed up to catch up with the fleet."*

Beside them, the Emden was already picking up speed and speeding away from the Kaiserin Elisabeth, having had fewer mines and thus finishing earlier.

The entire operation was too far away for the Japanese to have any idea of their presence, and thus was the full brilliance of von Spee's plan. Steam out through the exit and deny the Japanese the ability to follow them, forcing Togo to take another one, losing precious time that the German Pacific Squadron would use to sail into the horizon.

(...) The fight (...)

Fifteen minutes into the fight, the second half of Togo's fleet rounded the island and came into view, soon figuring out a firing solution on the Germans. More fireballs blossomed from another direction, startling von Spee. *"Ah, Krenk, this is where the other Japanese ships are!"* "Indeed, sir," answered Krenk. He leaned to pick up a message from one of the flag officer orderlies running from their position on the deck to the bridge. *"Admiral, the Kaiserin Elisabeth and the Emden both report they are done laying their mines. "*

Von Spee was about to answer when a bright flash appeared, temporarily blinding him. He turned to the left to see that battleship Kaiserin had just been hit by an enemy salvo. His view was soon obscured by a towering column of water as tall as his own ship, the Westfalen, that rose high above the bridge. *"Sir, Kaiserin has been hit! The Nurnberg is also hit!"*

The German Admiral didn't answer anything, as there was nothing to say. They needed to escape and increase the distance as quickly as possible. Until the Japanese pursuers hit the minefield, his ships would just have to run the gauntlet.

A minute later, and with several more salvos fired on both sides, the Japanese pre-dreadnought battleship Iki was slammed dead in the middle, seriously damaging a funnel and igniting an explosion in the boiler room. More straddling shots were scored, but no more major hits happened until the Japanese were about to approach the Truk atoll exit where von Spee's ship had exited. By that time, the range was 9,000 yards, still a pretty hard distance to shoot from.

(...) Dreadnought battleship Setsu's bridge (...)

Things were going well for Togo. He had the enemy on the ropes, over three times his numbers, and it was in the range of his guns. The Germans had been good at keeping the distance, but he was confident in his two dreadnought battleships and the supporting cruisers, who appeared to be faster than their Kaiserliche Marine opponents.

As it was, he was trying to concentrate on the cruisers about to engage into the channel at the atoll's exit. It was hard for him to see through the darkness, with the flashes and explosions. Then, he thought he saw something weird. He shook his head, rubbed his eyes, and again put the binoculars to his face.

And then, the same thing happened. An explosion in the midst of his cruisers in the channel. *"Admiral..."* Started Captain Nagata in an uncertain tone. And then, Togo blanched, knowing what he was seeing.

(...) Atoll channel (...)

The five Japanese cruisers that engaged in the channel started to hit mines almost all at the same time and never got the chance to understand what was happening. One of them opened up like a ripe egg, another was split in two by the force of the explosion, and a third one was holed from bow to stern and sank below the waves almost instantly. The last almost survived. The first one stopped his engines and almost made it, but even at the slower speed ended up hitting a mine that obliterated its bow in a catastrophic explosion. The other turned hard to port, and that did it; the ship was hit near the middle, and the mine detonation ignited its own ammunition store. The ship disappeared in a blinding light.

(...) An hour later, dreadnought battleship Westfalen (...)

"The enemy is nowhere to be seen, Sir," said Krenk, the Fleet's Chief of Staff. "Very well, Vice-Admiral. I will retire to my cabin. Let me know when we approach New Ireland," answered Maximilian von Spee. "Yes, Admiral."

The Battle of Truk had ended in a blinding explosion, with no less than five enemy heavy cruisers slamming into the minefield that von Spee's men had laid in the atoll channel, giving way from the lagoon to the ocean. The Japanese had thus not been able to follow him and his ships into the open Pacific and had lost the scent. His squadron was now free and again on its way toward the Atlantic and the Reich.

(...) An hour later, dreadnought battleship Setsu (...)

Admiral Togo was looking at empty air while he strolled the bridge and walked amongst the stricken cruiser's survivors. The German Admiral had outsmarted him, and he was mad as hell. He tried to be comforting to the shaken and injured men who had just been rescued, but his insides were boiling with frustration. He'd cornered the enemy Admiral, and the bastard had escaped.

He felt powerless, as he knew von Spee was speeding away while he had to take on the survivors of the minefield disaster he'd witnessed. Also, his fleet was now very far from Japan, and he didn't know if he had the operational leeway to continue deeper into the Pacific to chase the enemy squadron. It was entirely possible the chase was over, and he didn't like it one bit. He wondered if he could continue to sail or if he needed to report. As he comforted yet another burned sailor, he decided that the decision would just have to wait a little more.

Battle of Rafajlowa
Night of the 11th and 12th of February, the town of Rafailowa

The extensive fight for Galicia produced an ebb and flow of advances and retreats across the land, and it had ended with the 2nd Brigade of the Polish Legion in control of one of the most important passes in the Carpathians near the town of Rafajlowa. The Polish troops were fighting for the Austro-Hungarian Army, just like their brothers were for Russia, because they were on the other side of the border. Poland was not a country in 1915, as it was completely occupied by the Russians, the Austrians, and the Germans.

Dimitri Fedorov, a Private Soldier in the 16th Moscow Regiment, was walking in the night toward the small village that was their objective. He cursed as it was a high hill, and the entire affair was winding and difficult. His breath fumed in the cold, and his feet crunched in the knee-deep snow. Beside him, his comrades were walking as well, and they were about two hundred yards from the enemy trenches. Things had been quiet for a blissful ten days following their conquest of Przemysl, but they were now back in action following a quick train ride up north. They all had their guns ready and were as quiet as possible to try and surprise the enemy.

The idea was to launch a surprise attack on the Austro-Hungarian trenches and try to take control of the mountain pass. Russian High Command wanted to have it for the planned restart of the offensive when the good weather appeared again in March or April.

They advanced another fifty yards, and Dimitri started to see the outlines of the barbed wire defenses. Then, loud thumps were heard, and several shells were fired from the Austro-Hungarian side. Dimitri followed them climbing and climbing, and then they exploded high in the sky. *"Flares,"* yelled grumpy Sergeant Radetzki. *"We've been detected by the enemy, everybody down!"*

The next moment, bullets started to blaze around Dimitri and bury themselves in the snow all around him. Men started to be hit, and blood flew in every direction. Dimitri plunged into the snow and was lucky enough to slam his head on a large rock that the snow had covered. This saved his life because the rock protected him from the Polish bullets killing his comrades. *"Bozhe moi!"* (my God), he eventually blurted out, as a taste of iron flooded his mouth. He was stunned because he fell on the rock, and he then noticed his nose was bleeding. He rolled on his back, looking at the vast, illuminated sky, and saw so many bullets crisscrossing it that he closed his eyes for a moment. Since he was stunned, he didn't realize that being on his back while his nose bled wasn't ideal, and he choked. Turning again, he vomited.

It was rough, he thought while taking a deep breath to calm himself. Just as he thought he was mastering his inner panic, the enemy shells started falling in big fireballs, dirtied by the scattering snow and mud. The ground started to shake, and a fog installed itself because of the plethora of explosions, melting snow directly into vapor. And then his experience and resilience kicked in; it was time to move, and he lifted himself up from the snow, wiping his nose and picking up his fallen rifle. He ran right behind a knot of soldiers who seemed to know what they were doing. He noticed that the Russian artillery was also now in action, and the shells were exploding about sixty yards ahead, trying to smash the barbed wire lines for the infantry to stream through.

"Go, Go, Go!" yelled the men ahead, giving Dimitri heart to run even harder, even if it was difficult in the snow. Soldiers fell left and right; he was slammed to the ground by a nearby artillery shell, but lifted himself up, yelling out of his lungs, rifle held by his left hip.

The group of soldiers he ran with eventually made it to the barbed wire line and were able to cross it because it had been mangled by the Russian guns. The level of enemy bullets increased to a crescendo since they were charging right in front of a machine gun nest. One of them grazed Dimitri's shoulder, and he felt it as if someone had slapped his shoulder. Almost losing his balance again, he wobbled for a couple of steps but kept going.

He was now in a frenzy and stopped to fire his rifle, snapping off a couple of shots. He kneeled to reload his weapon and then followed a new group of men rushing in the flashing darkness with him.

By then, he'd completely lost sight of his section and squad and fought with a hodgepodge of soldiers that also seemed lost. Fighting in the darkness, even if flares partially illuminated the land, was a difficult and confusing affair. When he stood up again with a reloaded weapon, he noticed that Russian soldiers were fighting in the enemy trench or near it. Looking back, he didn't see many more coming to fight, and he hesitated, understanding that there weren't enough additional forces charging toward the enemy positions. The attack was obviously going to fail.

And then he decided. He wanted to live, and to charge stupidly in a losing battle was not the best of ideas. He dropped flat on his belly and stopped moving.

The battle lasted for another hour, but it was obvious he had made the right decision since there was no more fighting in front of him. He decided to wait it out and to crawl back when things got quiet again. He was cold as hell in the show, but that was better than being dead.

The Battle of Rafajlowa was thus a short affair where the Polish Legion was able to easily repulse the Russian surprise attack attempt. The surprise attack failed, and the two opposing sides just went back to their trenches. The battle was over by the next morning, the attackers leaving a little over two thousand dead in the snowy field of battle.

Dimitri crawled the distance between the no man's land, the hill, and the Russian lines down below, making it back by mid-morning. He fell into the trench, exhausted, and no one bothered to ask questions, as he was covered in blood from his nosebleed and his superficial injury on the shoulder. His look thus helped him go unnoticed in terms of not having charged right at the enemy and being considered a coward. Not many made it back, and if he'd been unscathed, it would have been suspicious.

Defense in the Carpathians
February 1st, Austro-Hungarian 4th Army field headquarters, February 8th, 1915

Conrad von Hotzendorf, the Commander-in-Chief of the Austro-Hungarian forces, crossed his arms behind his back and walked the distance from the map on the table to the door, giving way to another room where there was a set of chairs and a small stool where hot teas were steaming, deposited by one of his staff people moments earlier.

The man was again at the K.u.K. 4th Army's field HQ in the Carpathian Mountains. Right now, the area formed a high barrier about sixty-five miles wide with an average elevation of 3000-some feet and was a great defensive position for the Empire. The entire area was very limited in roads, and most communications went through the few rail lines built in the mountain passes by the Austrians over the years.

The commander of the Austrian 4th Army, General Moritz von Auffenberg, followed suit, as well as the German General in charge of the much-weakened (recently) German 11th Army.

Conrad sat down and stayed silent for a moment. The Germans would not help him in launching his new offensive, and he needed to decide what to do. The Reich had its own problems, with the French having launched a powerful attack in the Verdun sector. The Germans, of course, needed to reinforce it since the front was pierced 30 miles deep on a broad line of 45 miles. This meant the troops needed to come from somewhere, and the German 11th Army, which the OHL wanted to stay on defense for now, had been one of the logical places to find the much-needed soldiers.

Thus, Max von Gallwitz, its commander, was ordered to send 50% of his forces, most of his big guns, and even some of his supplies back to the Western Front, where he'd recently come from.

Conrad didn't like it one bit since, without the German 11th Army, his offensive could not go forward.

"The Kaiser and our Commander-in-Chief General von Moltke convey their apologies for the move, General Hotzendorf," said Gallwitz. The entire affair did not please him as well. After all, which commander liked to have 50% of his men removed from his command?

"It cannot be helped, General," answered Hotzendorf bitterly as he picked up his teacup to take a sip. The other two men did the same. An uncomfortable silence hung between the three men, and then von Auffenberg broke it. *"At the very least, gentlemen, things are looking a lot better in Transylvania with the breakdown of the Romanian offensive. By spring, we'll be able to do something about the Russians."*

The situation in the Carpathians was pretty much a stalemate as it was the dead of winter, and the Russians were not attacking. The Central Powers were firmly on the defensive in the mountains, but it remained to be seen what each side would do when the good weather came back.

In Transylvania, things were indeed better, as the three Romanian armies that had invaded were either in full retreat or trying to, following the Turko-Bulgarian offensive on its southern border that resulted in the stunning victory of Turtucaia.

"And in the good news category, the offensive on Bucharest is progressing nicely. Things are looking good for a complete Romanian defeat soon," continued von Auffenberg. Hotzendorf took some heart at his subordinate's comment. *"Indeed, this should clear our extreme right flank and free up the necessary troops for the offensive I had planned. By that time, the German Army will have also re-established the situation in France, and we should get more reinforcements".*

The German 11th Army commander was a little more prudent in his predictions. *"Well, Sir, I do hope that the troops in Transylvania can be put to good use in the Carpathians, but we don't know what the Russians will do. After all, they have a great numerical superiority over us and should attack again in the spring or early summer."*

"That is the entire reason why I wanted to make a jump on them and attack before they did to disrupt their plans," answered von Hotzendorf. *"We'll just have to see since we do not have a choice in the matter now. Our troops are on the defensive."* He paused to take another sip, grimacing because it was still scalding hot. *"General von Auffenberg, please send the orders for everyone to go back to a defensive stance. The offensive is canceled for now." "Yes, Sir."*

21st Landwer Division, 8th Austro-Hungarian Regiment (Prague)
Somewhere on the Transylvanian frontline, February 13th, 1915

Private Soldier Helmut Gottenburg advanced cautiously through the cold-fogged morning. The town they were in (the 21st Landwehr Division) was in a shambles as the Romanians had conquered – and destroyed- it sometime before. His foot crushed the small pebbles and glass pieces on the ground, creating a noise he didn't want to make. The debris came from the blasted-out houses and buildings on each side of the street. He had his rifle on his shoulder, finger on the trigger, while his comrade (and now friend) Radno Karacivs did the same beside him.

The 21st Division was in the broken town of Hermannstadt in southeastern Transylvania, where it had just arrived from the Balkans, originally earmarked for the Carpathian Front in preparation for the planned Hotzendorf offensive now postponed indefinitely.

The Division had been doing garrison duties in Southern Serbia in a region called Macedonia following the Central Powers victory and overrunning of the small Balkan country, and things had been pretty sweet for both men. However, the realities of the war eventually bubbled back to the surface, and the 21st Landwehr Division was called to the front as Austro-Hungary scraped the bottom of the barrel for troops to bolster its frontlines against the Russian juggernaut.

They were thus put on trains and railed through Southern Hungary, but just as they neared the Carpathians, they were stopped and re-directed to Transylvania to help the beleaguered Austrian 1st Army that was reeling under the Romanian assault of three full armies in Transylvania.

"See something, Radno?" said Helmut to his friend, who mumbled something back. The damned Slovene was now speaking some German after being around Helmut and others. *"No, Herr Helmut,"*

said Radno, who had an annoying tendency to always call him Herr Helmut. He'd tried to explain that the Herr wasn't necessary when they were speaking between comrades and close friends, but Radno seemed to struggle with the concept.

Ahead of them was a swirling, billowing fog that seemed menacing and imposing. A lone shot rang out in the air. *"That wasn't far,"* said one of the men near Helmut. *"Far enough for you not to worry about it, Soldier,"* said one of the lieutenants flanking them on the side.

"Sir," said another of the men further out in front. *"Building coming up." "Spread out,"* said the sergeants, knowing that it wouldn't be good if there was a Romanian machine gun in the place. The town was still occupied by scattered remnant pickets of the Romanian division they'd beaten the day before in a battle north of Hermannstadt. They had been tasked with clearing out the rabble.

In a more general sense, the entire Romanian offensive was broken, and now its units tried to retreat as fast as they could to their border, as the Bulgarians and Ottoman forces were advancing in the south and now threatening Bucharest, Romania's capital city. And it didn't look like they would arrive in time to face both the vengeful Bulgarians (there was a lot of hate between Bulgaria and Romania because of the Second Balkan War) and the resurging Ottomans.

Radno and Helmut ran to the side of the street and hugged the wall of a half-demolished house. The town had been heavily shelled by Austro-Hungarian artillery for hours before they entered to execute their assault.

It was at that moment that all hell broke loose. The sergeants had been right; the Romanians had installed a French Hotchkiss machine gun in the building located at an intersection. They'd done so in the town's bank and, thus, the building was well protected with thick concrete walls and a vault. They put the machine gun into the vault and opened the door. Hence, they were in a great position to fire without being fired at.

Bullets started to blaze down across the fog, scattering it. They slammed onto the paved ground, the buildings, and, unfortunately for the Austro-Hungarian soldiers, onto bodies. Men started to fall, but since Radno and Helmut had been the smart ones to spread out as far as possible to the flanks, they were untouched. "In here," said the Slovene to Helmut, and they both, along with four more soldiers, slipped into a broken door.

The rest of the Austrian soldiers either dropped to the ground, were killed, injured, or did the same and stepped into buildings when it was possible.

Shots crisscrossed from both sides, the street, the bank; the entire area became a mighty killing ground. Radno and Helmut, for their part, went through the house and exited on the other side of the alley and made their way toward the enemy machine gun position. They held their guns at the ready, either aiming upward or in front, as it was possible the enemy had troops in the side streets as well.

As they advanced, the eerie silence in the alley contrasted heavily with the mayhem on the main street just a building across from them. Helmut was startled when Radno fired a shot from his rifle, hitting an enemy soldier on a roof fifty feet down from where they were. The man fell on his belly and rolled on the stone tiles to fall with a heavy thud on the paved stone alley. "Damn Radno, great shooting and great eye," said one of the other guys in their group. Helmut just smiled at his friend and nodded. The next moment, shots rang from where the alley seemed to curb back to the main street and toward the bank. Two of the soldiers in their group were hit and fell backward in yelps of pain. Helmut fired three rounds in rapid succession, hitting a couple of Romanian soldiers who had appeared in view. Radno did the same and killed one. The rest of the soldiers with them eliminated the rest.

They continued to advance cautiously at the bend in the alley and made it to the edge. Radno was the first in front. *"I can see the building they are firing from,"* he said, leaning forward and then back to tell them. Helmut leaned to watch and saw that, indeed, they were just beside the bank, as he saw the bullet stream exiting the front broken window coming from the inside of the bank. *"Does anyone have a grenade?"* asked Helmut. By now, all of them were experienced fighters, having fought the damnable and as tough as nails Serbs for months on end before defeating them. One of the guys fished a couple of Rohr Stielhandgranate (Rohr hand grenades) from his pouch, showing a blackened tooth smile. *"Like these, Gottenburg?"*

Helmut smiled back and gestured for the soldier to come to his spot with a hand signal. *"Indeed, Behring"* (it was the soldier's name). The Rohrs were cast-iron cylinders packed with explosive materials attached to a wooden handle.

The soldier advanced to the front of the group, lit the fuse on one of his two Rohr Grenades, and threw it into one of the broken window openings. And then they all charged. The grenade exploded with a loud thump. Smoke and debris immediately filled the bank, and Gottenburg jumped inside, landing hard on the debris-strewn ground. More shots rang out, and for a moment, he thought he was dead, but a second later, he realized he wasn't hit. He leveled his rifle and fired right into the face of a charging Romanian wielding a bayonet. The poor man's head disappeared in a spray of blood as he somersaulted backward and crumpled to the floor. Radno did the same, firing into the belly of another enemy, and two of the soldiers with them hit both of the Romanians with the butts of their rifles.

Within a moment, they were masters of the room they'd entered and could peer outside into the rapidly dissipating fog where the Austrian soldiers were pinned down. *"The bastards are in the vault,"* said Behring, pointing to the still-firing machine gun and the bullet stream it spewed out in a line. He showed the rest of his group his grenade and again smiled. He walked to the side of the opening, lit the fuse, and threw the Rohr inside. A second later, a cry of surprise was heard, followed by the muffled thump and shaking of the grenade's blast. Moments later, the machine gun was silenced, and the soldiers in the street started to advance again. *"All clear in the bank,"* yelled Helmut to the officers and men advancing toward them with leveled guns.

The building was theirs.

A day later, the town of Hermannstadt was declared liberated, and the men of the 21st Landwehr Division assembled back at the railyards to be moved to yet another hot spot where Romanians were in need of being rooted out and killed.

Vardar region of Macedonia
The Greek 1st Army occupies Macedonia, February 9th to 17th, 1915

Macedonia was under the yoke of the Ottoman Empire for centuries, and its population thought they had seen everything in terms of exactions, killings, and tragedies. Then, the two Balkan Wars were fought, and they were liberated from the Turks. The area was divided between Serbia, Grece, and Bulgaria, who each had ancestral claims and ethnic populations.

Just as things were finally settling down for the poor people of the Vardar region, the Great War was unleashed. At first, things were okay as the fighting between the Austro-Hungarians and the Serbs was limited to the north. But then the conflict expanded with the Bulgarian intervention, and soon, the Serbian armies were defeated.

It didn't take long for the entirety of Serbia to be occupied, and a mix of Austrian and Bulgarian soldiers were soon assigned to garrison the area.

But by the middle of January, these troops (K.u.K. troops) were needed elsewhere to try and relieve the beleaguered forces of the Austro-Hungarian 1st Army, reeling back in disarray from the Romanian offensive in Transylvania. The Bulgarian corps occupying the area was also needed as Sofia was preparing an offensive of their own on the Romanians while the bulk of their armies were occupied invading Transylvania.

Since Serbia was a conquered country, something had to be done to garrison the area, and the Greeks were called in for help. Having recently joined the Central Powers but not possessing a gigantic army, their untrained and badly equipped forces were ideal to fill the void left by the departing Austro-Bulgarian forces.

It was why the 7th, 11th, 13th, and 14th Greek Divisions crossed the border over to the Vardar Region of Macedonia on the 9th of

February. Then, they started to systematically occupy the land while more troops (4th, 9th, and 2nd Divisions) moved up north. The demoralized and impoverished people of Macedonia didn't even shrug their shoulders in reaction. They were so used to war and its disasters that they took the event as stoically as people in the Balkans could: resigned to their fate.

The Greek soldiers were, however, sort of a nice change from the Bulgarians and the Austro-Hungarians since, during their short tenure, they committed a lot of exactions on the poor civilians and defeated population. The Greeks, on the other hand, had not fought the bitter battle against the Serbian Army and thus didn't feel angry.

By February 17th, the entirety of Serbia was in the hands of the Greeks, and they controlled the land with an iron fist worthy of the best hate-fueled Balkan rivalries. Serbia entered the long night of occupation and defeat that would last until the end of the war.

The Greek fleet breakout Part 1
Aegean Sea, February 18th, 1915

(...) Heavy cruiser Giorgios Averof, Greek Fleet flagship (...)

"Admiral," said one of the bridge officers to the commander of the Greek Fleet executing its sortie out of Piraeus, its home harbor near Athens. *"Yes, Commander Konstantopoulos,"* answered Admiral Pavlos Kountouriotis. *"The lookouts are reporting a host of dark smoke columns to our south. Something big and numerous is coming toward us at full speed."*

GREECE

Admiral Pavlos Kountouriotis

CA Giorgios Averof (flagship)	CA Helle
Pre-Dreadnought BB Kilkis former Idaho	7 old DD
Pre-Dreadnought BB Lemnos former Mississippi	

"It can only be the British. After all, they are now based in Crete and only hours away from us. They must have known we were sailing out," continued the Admiral. The British had spies everywhere, ships working for them as lookouts, and it wasn't impossible that they even had a clandestine telegraph station somewhere in Epirus to watch for the fleet. Kountouriotis had worked with the Royal Navy on joint exercises and knew from experience that the British could not tolerate anything but their own ships. He'd had enough discussions with many of their fleet's officers to know that.

The recent Greek entry into the war on the side of the Central Powers had already triggered the invasion of Crete a week before, and the reason for the English to do so was because of the fleet he was commanding. Greece had the most powerful fleet of all the Balkan nations because of the naval arms race with the Ottoman Empire. In the process of building up its fleet, it had acquired two American pre-dreadnought battleships, while one of the country's millionaires had bought the nation a cruiser with his own money from Italy that now bore his name, the Giorgios Averof. The warship was the very same one he was standing on. The Greek government had found the finances for another modern cruiser to be built right after the Averof, bought seven old destroyers from France, and there it was: A powerful fleet capable of challenging anything that wanted to sail in the Aegean. Well, anything but the British East Mediterranean Squadron, sporting three modern dreadnoughts, two pre-dreadnoughts, three cruisers, and nine destroyers.

"Well, this was to be expected, I suppose," continued the Admiral. *"Tell every ship to steam full ahead toward our objective and to push their stokers."* Stokers were the men shoveling the coal into a ship's furnace, feeding the boilers. The more they put in, the faster they could go. *"Yes, Admiral,"* answered the nervous Commander Kostantopoulos.

(…) Battleship Dreadnought, thirty miles to the south (…)

"We have got the bastards," said Vice Admiral Sackville Hamilton Carden as he slammed his closed fist into his left palm. *"Our dreadnoughts are for sure faster than their old American tubs; let's catch them and sink the impudent Greeks,"* he continued.

Eastern Mediterranean Squadron		
Vice-Admiral Sackville Hamilton Carden		
BB Dreadnought	Pre-dread BB Almermale (6th battle squ.)	CA Amethyst
BC Indefatigable	Pre-dread BB Duncan (6th battle squ.)	CL Falmouth and Diamond
BB Superb	CA Aboukir	9 DD

The ship he was on was an iconic warship since Dreadnought was the first of the new breed of battleships that sparked an intense naval race between the European Powers from 1908 onward. It had even given its name to the new class of battleships. Dreadnought was faster, better armed, and tougher to kill than anything fielded before its launch, hence the designation of pre-dreadnoughts and dreadnoughts. What the Greeks had were ships that even the Americans had decided were too old to field in their fleet, and they were consequently a lot weaker than the three modern warships

Carden had. (battleship Dreadnought, Superb, and battlecruiser Indefatigable). *"Admiral, our ships are steaming at full speed, and we should be within range within a few hours at this rate."* "Very well," answered the Eastern Mediterranean Squadron Commander with a wolfish smile.

There was only one problem with the easy victory Carden anticipated that day. The Greeks and the Ottomans, putting aside their centuries-old rivalry, had communicated with each other and coordinated the operation to get the Greek fleet to safety. This meant that another player was steaming hard toward the Greek fleet that day. However, it was not to destroy it; it was to help it.

(…) Battlecruiser Sultan Yavuz (Goeben) (…)

Ottoman Navy- Admiral Souchon	
BB Sultân Osmân-ı Evvel,	CA Hamidiye
BB Reşadiye	CA Mecidiye
BC Yavuz Sultan Selim (HMS Goeben)	6 DD ~~(2DD)~~
Pre Dreadnought BB Barbaros Hayreddin	
Pre Dreadnought BB Turgut Reis, destroyed funnel and gun damage	

Admiral Wilhelm Souchon still harbored the scars of his last battle in the form of a blue-brown bruise on the side of his face. He also had to face recurring headaches, like the one he was having that day as his fleet sailed yet again toward battle. Only this time, they weren't going to fight old, outdated, and badly trained Russian ships and crews. They were going against the powerful Royal Navy, and the day promised to be eventful.

The Admiral and his fleet still had the damage from the last fight when they tried to raid the Nikolayev shipyards in the Black Sea, where the two newest Russian dreadnought battleships were being built. The entire affair had ended in a miserable failure. The only thing they'd achieved was the smashing of some unimportant and outdated coastal fortifications in exchange for important damage on their ships. He hoped that this time, it would be worth it.

The level of risk was certainly higher, and he wasn't certain it was the greatest of ideas to try and save the Greek Fleet. Two aging pre-dreadnoughts the U.S. Navy didn't even want anymore and two okay heavy cruisers were not necessarily worth the risk of losing one of his pristine ships. But then again, he'd agreed with Enver Pasha, the Minister of War, and Cemal Pasha, the Minister of the Navy, to try and save them.

It was risky, but if he could get them safely into the Dardanelles without a glitch, then it was worth the risk, and the diplomatic-strategic advantages were great. It would be another naval humiliation for the Brits and solidify the Greek's resolve in the conflict.

His fleet was just sailing out of the Bosphorus (having started from the Golden Horn, the main Constantinople harbor) and was entering the Dardanelles. The ships were sailing quite slowly as there was a minefield that they needed to thread around, but he was confident he could be at the mouth of the Dardanelles in a few hours.

Kaunas Fortress, Northeast Front Sector Army
General Rennenkampf's headquarters, February 19th, 1915

The Kaunas Fortress was the largest land defensive complex in the entire Russian Empire and was designed to defend against a major German offensive. Covering a staggering twenty-five square miles, it was built from 1882 to the end of 1914. The setup included no less than nine forts and nine-gun batteries. It was mostly modernized with the latest defensive technologies designed to withstand modern shells and contained nineteen miles of internal railways, a power plant, water supply system, mill, bakery, brewery, food bank, and telegraph. It was a fully functional, independent fortress. The frontline was about fifty miles away from the fortress by the middle of February 1915.

At the start of the war and then at the height of the Russian offensive in Eastern Prussia, General Rennenkampf had never thought it possible that the Germans would one day threaten the Kaunas fortress, but things looked quite different now that he'd evacuated his forces from the German Empire and into Lithuania. He was just back from Baranovichi, where he met with Grand Duke Nikolai, the Commander-in-Chief of the Russian Army (the Tsar's uncle). The discussions had been a little on the rough side because the man was not happy with the retreat. But at the same time, it had been decided not to go for broke for Koenigsberg since there had been a risk his forces could be annihilated. Anyway, that was that, and Rennenkampf had indeed received a drubbing but also had been allocated a lot of new, fresh troops.

The Northwest and Southwest Armies had finally been moved toward the front. They included the men and military equipment from the Moscow area but also from beyond, like the western Ural region (of cities like Ekaterinburg, Nizhnii Tagil, Chelyabinsk, and Perm), and also from Siberia, and the southern reaches of the Empire (Central Asia). These formations had to be railed through an already overtaxed logistical system, and thus, priority had been given to the units that were needed in the offensive in Galicia and Eastern Prussia in the fall. Now that the armies were at the front, they had finally been moved forward and put in Kaunas and neighboring cities.

Northwestern Front (Lithuania and Baltic States)			
1,490,000 soldiers	Commander	Soldiers	Area of operation
1st Army	General Paul von Rennenkampf	350,000 soldiers	Baltic States
10th Army	General Vasily Flug	400,000 soldiers	Baltic States
Northwest Army	General Yakov Zhilinskiy	333,000 soldiers	Baltic States
Southwest Army	General of Infantry Nikolai Ivanov	410,000 soldiers	Baltic States

Rennenkampf felt good about the impressive numbers he had since they were probably triple the size of Hindenburg's forces now fifty miles away. His army group had been renamed the Northwestern Front and he was coming back from Baranovichi with a defensive mission until the spring.

He was in the main building at the center of the fortress, which was supposed to act as the official residence of the Kaunas Commander. The man was there, but he had given his quarters to General Rennenkampf to establish his command staff and organization. Managing an army as large as the Northwestern Front needed a lot of staff paperwork and, thus, space.

He sat down in the chair by the hearth where a fierce fire burned and extended his arm to pick up the vodka bottle on the low table beside his plush chair. It was well into the evening, and he was done for the day. He poured himself a drink and then gulped it in one quick motion. He was alone in his quarters, surrounded by darkness and the eerie glow of the fire trying to dispel it.

He was pondering on what was next in store for his forces. One thing was certain, his comeback into Russia had fixed a lot of his supply issues, which was nice. He wondered what the problem with the logistics in the Empire was. He had no way of knowing that the factories didn't produce enough for the troops and that the corruption of the elites took too much as it was delivered to the front. The only thing he was certain of was that Russia didn't have enough rail lines to match its war ambitions. He'd experienced it firsthand when he entered enemy territory. The rail gauge in Germany wasn't even the same width as the Russian one, meaning that none of the trains from Russia could simply roll into East Prussia. The goods had to be transferred to a different train and set of wagons of the right width. It was exceedingly complicated, explaining the difficulties he'd had. He'd brought some proposals to the Grand Duke about having people widen the tracks (since it was the only sensible solution), but the Commander-in-Chief had seemed uninterested. It was weird how some problems and issues never got solved in the Russian Army. Or else maybe the Grand Duke himself was part of the problem; he didn't know.

His days were being spent trying to organize the major influx of troops he'd received that doubled his forces. He was also trying to figure out what Hindenburg's next move would be. He was certain that the Germans, emboldened with their Koenigsberg victory, would try and exploit it when the good weather came. He thus intended to be ready when the enemy assault came and also prepared his counteroffensive once he'd neutralized the enemy attack.

As it happened, his German counterpart would attack earlier than that and do something unexpected.

The Greek Fleet Breakout Part 2
The Battle of the Dardanelles, February 18th, 1915

The distance between the port of Piraeus in Athens and the two fortresses guarding the entrance of the strait (Fort of Kum Kale on the European side and Fort of Seddul-Bahr on the Asian shore) was 620 miles. This explained why the Greek fleet of Admiral Pavlos Kountouriotis was approaching it without yet having been intercepted by the British Eastern Mediterranean Squadron. The chase was on, and the British were now in range. They were about to fire their first gun salvos.

The Greek fleet was trying to reach the safety of the Dardanelles Strait. It was one of the world's narrowest straits, connecting the Aegean Sea with the Sea of Marmara and beyond to the Black Sea. At 39 miles long and not even a mile wide, it was a critical area for ships and also easy to interdict any shipping they didn't want transiting for the Turks, who controlled it with a series of forts and minefields. In clear terms, any Entente fleet venturing into the Dardanelles was promised a world of trouble, with fixed naval fortifications bristling with guns on both shores and mines to slam their waterlines. This was why the Greek fleet was sailing there, since once inside, the British would not be able to touch them or repeat an operation like Ares against the Italian Fleet in the late fall of 1914.

However, the whole affair was an unforeseen and extraordinary development. The Kingdom of Greece and the Ottoman Empire were sworn enemies, and that was the exact reason why both had sizeable fleets. The Turks occupied the Greeks for almost four long centuries, and they had only recently freed themselves in the mid-19th Century.

The two countries had then fought two wars against each other in the Balkans just before the Great War, and there certainly was no love lost between them. But common enemies had a way of fixing unfixable issues, and the Greek hate for the Turks was supplanted by the fear of losing their fleet to the aggressive British.

Also, in purely military terms, the prospect of joining the Germano-Ottoman fleet was something interesting, as it would make the combined fleet the equal of the British Eastern Mediterranean Squadron. What they had to do, however, was to reach the safety of the straits before the British intercepted them.

(...) Bridge of heavy cruiser Giorgios Averof (...)

Yet another set of large water geysers rose just ahead of the ship, and the Averof sailed right into them moments later. The water splashed hard and wide on the deck of the ship. *"Admiral,"* said commander Iani Kostantopoulos, the captain of Averof and his second in command. *"Another straddling shot. The next one will be on target, I am afraid."* Admiral Kountouriotis looked to the ship on the right, the pre-dreadnought Kilkis (former Idaho) that was on fire. The battleship was hit a minute earlier by shells from the Superb, one of the British enemy dreadnoughts. This was going to be tight. One destroyer had already been sunk, and his other heavy cruiser, the Helle, was damaged and losing speed because of a serious hit on her engines and boilers. His vessels were firing back, but there was a reason dreadnoughts were considered better than pre-dreadnoughts. The ships Admiral Kountouriotis had didn't have the sophisticated targeting systems that the newer Royal Navy ships had, maneuverability was not as good, and their speed was a lot slower. That's not even counting the guns themselves or the armor protection.

"Can we reach the safety of the Turkish forts we see in the distance," asked the Greek Commander. The fleet was about 2,000 yards from the entrance to the strait, and he could see the outlines of the large but old and outdated Turkish forts supposed to guard the entrance. If his ships could make it there, they would be sort of protected by the fixed naval defenses. And also, Admiral Souchon was surely near and about to intervene. Commander Kostantopoulos didn't have the opportunity to answer as a powerful explosion rocked the Averof,

sending everyone not strapped in (thus, everyone on the bridge) flying or to the steel deck. The hit was produced by a couple of shells from the battleship Dreadnought, Admiral Carden's flagship. For a moment, the Greek Admiral was stunned, and he struggled to get back to his feet and senses. *"Report…"*

(…) Bridge of battleship Dreadnought (…)

"Another hit, Admiral," said the lookout officer to Vice-Admiral Sackville Hamilton Carden, the commander of the British Eastern Mediterranean Squadron. *"Yes, I can see Lieutenant, thank you,"* answered the man with a smile.

The British fleet had caught up with the Greek fleet and had it under the sight of its guns. The battle was going rather well so far, with the sinking of an enemy destroyer and three hits on the enemy ships. The opposing fleet had yet to score even a straddling shot. Having ships was fine and well, but the Greek sailors were not trained to the level the British ones were, and Carden's sailors had battle experience while Admiral Kountouriotis men didn't. The fight hadn't been forecasted to be long and appeared to be developing into a one-sided affair. But another player was about to join.

"A….," started the lookout officer. *"What,"* answered Carden, understanding that the man's hesitation didn't bode well. *"Flashes have been spotted from inside the Dardanelles Strait, sir."* The British Admiral was hopeful for one thing and dreaded the other. *"Please tell me it's the Turkish forts firing." "Arhhhh… No Sir. An enemy fleet is entering the battle. "*

(…) Battlecruiser Yavuz Sultan (Goeben) (…)

"Admiral," said Vice-Admiral Hubert von Rebeur-Paschwitz, his Chief of Staff. *"The Greek fleet appears to be in difficulty; Several of their ships are on fire. They are about to enter the strait and should pass by the Turkish naval fortification in the next half minute."* German

Admiral Souchon crossed his arms behind his back as he looked in the distance at the flashes and the many smoke columns that were represented by the two fleet's funnels of smoke as well as from battle damage. *"Have they received their instructions with the flag signals on how to navigate entry into the minefield?"* "Yes, sir." Souchon moved closer to the observation window, hopeful. *"Well, then, let's support our new friends with our guns and hope they make it to safety inside."*

A new (horrible) way to make war
The Battle of Raseiniai, February 20th, 1915

Raseiniai was a small town in Western Lithuania, near a famous place called Tilsit, where Napoleon and Tsar Alexander the 1st met to discuss peace following the War of the Fourth Coalition (1806-1807). The place had nothing special, however, apart from the Russian trench lines and defensive positions running in the middle of it.

That was why it was going to be on the stage for the Great War and would soon be known for more ominous reasons. *"Fire,"* said the field artillery officer to his men, and the order was repeated across the entire gunline. The German shelling of Russian positions by artillery chemical shells was thus going to be the first use of poison gas in the conflict. It would, sadly, not be the last, but only the first instance in a long list of horrible attacks and results.

The German guns blasted in a majestic display of firepower, one after the other. From a distance, it looked like a bunch of fireballs blossoming into a line in a beautifully coordinated fashion, like a firework display. But what spewed out of it was anything but majestic and beautiful.

A total of 18,000 shells were fired as a preparatory bombardment for the German attack that was about to be launched, which amounted to eighty tons of the twin xylyl bromide and xylylene bromide gas. The concept was that they were both tear gases.

Tear gas worked by irritating mucous membranes in the eyes, nose, mouth, and lungs. It caused crying, sneezing, coughing, difficulty breathing, pain in the eyes, and temporary blindness.

The German command was waiting with interest for the results of the use of chemical projectiles, as, from their point of view, it would give their soldiers the time they needed to approach the Russian lines while the enemy was incapacitated.

The shells started to land on the Russian trenches and bunkers. For the soldiers crouching on the ground and expecting explosions, blasts of fire, and ground shaking, the moment was anticlimactic. The shells landed and spewed a grey-white vapor, making a weird thumping sound instead of an explosion. The men watched with attention, first thinking that the German shells were defective. However, it didn't take long for a thick fog to envelop the area as the billowing white-grey gas spread into the cold air and the slight wind. The gas didn't spread like it was intended to do because of the cold weather and low temperature, impeding it from expanding.

Nevertheless, the soldiers near the falling shells fell terribly ill and were incapacitated, vomiting, blinded, and yelling horribly. They started to yell and move in spasms. Panic soon spread like wildfire across the ranks.

Others clutched their throats as they couldn't breathe properly, and the Russian defenses disintegrated in place. However, the cold weather stopped the gas in place, and it didn't spread. Thus, the effects were rather localized and would soon prove disappointing to the German generals having planned the attack.

The German line started its attack moments later and advanced across the field. Within minutes, they crossed the no man's land without many casualties since their Russian counterparts were busy struggling against the gas effects. But without masks, the poor grunts also fell ill as the wind shifted and drifted the poisonous gas in their direction. It was the turn of the Germans to wiggle and spasm on the ground, clutching their throats and covering their burning eyes. Again, the cold February weather dampened the effects, but the attack soon became ragged and disorganized. Not many of the Kaiser's soldiers reached the Russian line as they had more important things to do than kill. The tear gas effect was terrible on the human body, and they were going through the worst of it.

General August von Mackensen, the commander of the German 9th Army attacking in the Raiseinai sector, climbed the hill overlooking the distant battlefield and expected to see a routed enemy. The gas was outlawed by the 1899 Hague Convention on War, but the Reich had decided to use it regardless. After all, it was locked in a two-front war of survival, and all hands were needed on deck.

But he was instead greeted by the long faces of his staff officers. He was given a pair of binoculars by one of his men and overlooked the scene. He didn't say anything at first. *"General,"* started the officer who had given him the binoculars, *"it appears the mix of tear gas we have fired at the enemy did not have the effects we had hoped for."* The man had a low voice, riddled with disappointment. The Germans had hoped to equalize the playing field (the Russians were three times superior in troop numbers) by using poison gas, but the first try was obviously a failure. *"It appears the gas has not disseminated enough, and our troops have also been gravely affected by a sudden and unexpected shift of the wind."*

Mackensen dropped the binoculars and readjusted his cap and winter jacket (it was a cold, windy day). His troops were far from achieving anything on that day, and he could hardly afford to lose more men as the damned Russians had triple his numbers.

"Well, that's that. Recall the men; we're going back to our starting lines," he said in a grumpy but resigned voice. *"Yes, Sir,"* answered the staff officer.

Regardless of the result of the Battle of Raseiniai, the cat was now out of the bag, and poison gas was out there as a weapon of war. There would be only so much the Entente Powers would accept thrown at them before they retaliated.

The development of poison gas was something that every nation had been able to do before the war. Each and every one of the fighting nations had healthy stocks of them and the means to produce a relatively unlimited amount of them.

This was not going to be pretty.

The Greek Fleet Breakout Part 3
The Battle of the Dardanelles, February 18th, 1915

The Greek fleet sailed across the narrow spot between the forts of Kum Kale (Asia) and Seddul Bahr (Europe) while being fired upon by the British ships. Both works were from the 17th Century (1656-1659) and thus had not been modernized in the years before the war. Apart from a few 152 mm modern guns, the rest of the defenses were equipped with old field guns, hopelessly outmatched by the modern British ships approaching.

If this had been a one-on-one fight, the Royal Navy could have just sailed out of range from the old cannons and shelled the two buildings and other small fortresses around (Ertugrul and Orhaniye Tepe) to raze them to the ground.

But as it was, Vice-Admiral Sackville Hamilton Carden's purpose was to sink the fleet trying to escape his clutches. Because of this, the British ships had to sail as close as possible to the Greeks, enabling the outdated guns in the forts to join in the battle. While that didn't mean it would change the outcome of the battle, all those antiquated guns firing at the incoming enemy vessels made for an impressive display. The brave Turkish gunners started to score hits on the smaller of the approaching Eastern Med Squadron vessels.

All the while, Souchon's ships were not even five thousand yards away, and soon, the entire affair became one gigantic naval brawl. The first Turkish salvo from the arriving Germano-Ottoman dreadnoughts overshot the Royal Navy squadron by a lot, landing in a spectacular but ineffective bunch of splashes further away.

Seeing the incoming ships, Carden then hesitated, not certain he wanted his fleet to continue the fight, but let his men do their job and kept silent, calculating what his next move should be. The fortresses on both sides of the strait's entrance soon started to blossom into fire and exploding debris as the British support ships (heavy cruisers

Aboukir and Amethyst and nine destroyers) advanced even closer to shell the old Turkish forts. Meanwhile, Carden's bigger units concentrated on trying to smash the Greeks and keep the Germano-Ottoman newcomers suppressed. Superb scored another hit on Kilkis, this time splashing the stern with fire and destroying one of the ship's main guns. Both cruisers, Giorgios Averof, and Helle, were brightly burning, and dark smoke enveloped them as Albermale and Duncan kept them under steady gunfire, hitting each again a couple of times.

Carden's other big boys (battleship Dreadnought and battlecruiser Indefatigable) retrained their cannons on the modern Ottoman battleships Sultan Osman i Evvel, Resadiye, and Yavuz Sultan, and they did the same. The Turkish pre-dreadnoughts Barbaros Hayrredin and Turgut Reis (along with both cruisers Hamidiye and Mecidiye) moved closer to support the Kum Kale and Seddul Bahr fortresses being pummelled by the British cruisers and destroyers.

From a bird's eye view, the scene was extremely destructive and bright. Shells crisscrossed the sky while towering columns of water rose all around the fighting ships. Once in a while, a ship scored a hit against the other side, and then a new, brief fireball blossomed. Smoke prevailed all around, with the funnels gushing some of it out generously, the damages of the battle adding, and the explosions and resulting fires completing the dark and fiery picture.

Aboard battleship Dreadnought, however, Vice-Admiral Carden had seen the writing on the wall after cruiser Amethyst slammed into a mine and exploded catastrophically. He ordered his ships to turn around as he decided that he'd battered the Greeks enough and that his mission was accomplished.

And he wasn't wrong in his assessment. Pre-dreadnought battleship Kilkis was sinking just offshore from Seddul Bahr Fortress, making for a fantastic view, with the ship sliding below the waves while in the background a bright fire that was the destroyed and burning fortress dominated the skyline. Cruiser Helle had just exploded in a million bright and fiery shrapnel pieces under the relentless fire of pre-dreadnought battleship Duncan, and a few hits were scored on the Yavuz Sultan (Goeben) and the pre-dreadnought battleship Turgut Reis, killing its speed to zero, making it drift in the current. The ship would eventually beach on the Asian shore and would later have to be salvaged.

The Turkish strait fortresses were gutted, having no modern defenses whatsoever, their walls being built to withstand cannon balls from the age of sail. Their garrisons fought bravely, but in the end, the ten-minute battle was enough to raze most of the forts to the ground or to half-standing, smoking piles of rubble.

The British Eastern Mediterranean Squadron turned away from the battle surprisingly unscathed. Apart from Amethyst lost to a naval mine, the rest of his ships had damage yes, but nothing serious.

Dreadnought had light damage across its superstructure, a few blown windows on the bridge observation deck, and a fire on the forward deck. Battlecruiser Indefatigable had a boiler explosion caused by a shell hit from Resadiye, plus deck and forecastle damage. Superb only received two hits that didn't penetrate its deck armor, while Albermale and Duncan were lightly hit as well.

Souchon did not get away with the same amount of damage. Besides the soon-to-be-beached Turgut Reis, Sultan Osman i Evvel had serious deck and gun damage, Resadiye a serious hit on the waterline and was taking on water by the hundreds of gallons, and his own Goeben had a destroyed funnel and some serious stern and bow damage.

Within an hour, the fight was over, and the British sailed away back to their new base in Crete while the Greek-Ottoman-German fleet licked its wounds and tried to salvage its burning ships.

(...) Aftermath, Golden Horn (...)

"Watch your step, Admiral Kountouriotis," said one of the young Ottoman officers on the docks in the Golden Horn who spoke Greek, a common occurrence in Turkey. The Greek fleet commander needed help to cross from his stricken and still-burning ship to firm ground. In the background, heavy cruiser Giorgios Averof showed the extent of the terrible fight it had been in just a few hours earlier. Further out, pre-dreadnought Lemnos was moored near the harbor, smoking like a dirty oil fire because of the heavy damage it had sustained during the fight.

The rest of the Central Powers' ships were also near, with the three Ottoman dreadnoughts gushing dark smoke and showing the dreadful signs of the damage they had received.

"Welcome to Constantinople," said Admiral Wilhelm Souchon to the still seemingly stunned man, who harbored a bandage on his bloody head. The Battle of the Dardanelles, as it would soon come to be called, was a terrible defeat for the combined fleets and a dire lesson that the Royal Navy was no pushover. *"Than... Thank you, Admiral,"* answered the poor confused Kountouriotis. They moved further away from the ship and toward the buildings while the wounded were being evacuated on stretchers behind them. The Giorgios Averof was seriously damaged, and the casualties were very high. *"Let's move you to the field hospital and let you rest, Admiral,"* continued Souchon. *"We will talk later."* The Greek officer just nodded with a weary and tired move of the head before being put on a stretcher and sent off on his way.

Souchon then turned toward his ships, his damaged ships. All of them harbored some kind of damage, and many sailors were either dead or gravely wounded. He had not expected such a casualty rate but then he was not necessarily surprised. The Ottoman sailors and ships had performed well against the old Russian ships and shore fortifications in the Black Sea, but now he knew that against real opposition and a powerful opponent like the Royal Navy's superbly trained men, they were not ready. That set of facts would need a lot of thinking on his part.

(...) Aftermath, Heraklion Harbor, Crete (...)

Souchon's opposing commander, Vice-Admiral Sackville Hamilton Carden, touched the dock on the harbor a few hours later with a very different state of mind, that of a victorious naval officer. Finally, some good news to report to the First Lord of the Admiralty. The morale of the nation would be boosted by this resounding success.

His ships had done very well, inflicting ten times their own casualties and battle damage. Only the Turkish mines had stopped them from finishing the job. Without them, Carden knew that he would have sunk every damned ship the bastards had fielded against him in the Dardanelles.

The Greek fleet wasn't entirely sunk, but the strategic objective he set out to achieve was now a reality. The Central Powers fleet was bottled up in their own little Bosphorus and Dardanelles Straits, or else they could sail into the Black Sea. But the warning he'd given them was strikingly clear. Sail into the Aegean Sea or try to face me, and I will destroy you.

He turned toward the slowly setting sun and smiled. It was a grand day to be British.

The Romanian and Transylvanian fronts
Balkan and Southern situation, February 4th to February 25th

Following the fall of the Turtucaia Fortress on the Dobruja and the complete collapse (destruction of their 3rd Army) of the defense on their border with Bulgaria, things went downhill for the Romanians. The King had made a truly bad decision in joining the Entente while his country was bordered by many enemies (Turks, Bulgars, Greeks, and Austro-Hungarians) and an ally that couldn't really help him (Russia).

First and foremost, the 1st, 2nd, and 4th Armies stopped their attacks in Transylvania against the Austro-Hungarian 1st Army and began retreating southward back to the border to try and save the country from complete disaster.

Battles were fought at Craiova (February 10th) and Cernavoda (February 14th), both ending in a complete rout for the Romanians facing the Bulgar-Ottoman forces. All the while, the three invading armies, moving out of Austria-Hungary, were attacked by the K.u.K. forces in the rear, producing two more defeats, one at Campolung and at the Battle of the Vulcan Pass in the western part of the country, again resulting in resounding defeats for the Romanian Army.

Then, on the 19th of February, as some elements of the 1st Army made it back to Bucharest to at least make a show of defending the capital, another battle produced yet one more defeat, resulting in the fall of the capital, the flight of King Ferdinand toward the eastern parts of the country, and a general withdrawal movement toward Bessarabia and Moldavia, in an attempt to salvage what was left of the country's military forces by joining them with the Russian Imperial troops and hoping for the Tsar to be able to supply them properly.

Two more battles were fought by the retreating Romanians as they tried to salvage what was left at Ploesti and Focsani, and they succeeded in extricating their forces from the clutches of the by-then combined forces of the Austrians, Bulgars, Germans (the Reich had about a division fighting in the theater), Greeks, and the Ottomans.

Ferdinand the 1st should have listened to the men supporting the late King's (Carol the 1st) diplomatic stance of neutrality or of honoring the alliance with the Central Powers. But the man was young and full of ideas of glory. After all, Austria-Hungary had been on the ropes, and Transylvania was ripe for the taking.

The front eventually stabilized by the end of February on the Dniester River, more because both sides were exhausted than anything else. Romania was also falling into the long night and darkness of enemy occupation.

FINAL STRATEGIC SITUATION BY FEBRUARY 28TH IN THE BALKANS AND SOUTHERN EUROPE:

ROMANIA			
400,000 soldiers	Commander	Soldiers	Area of operation
1st Army	General Ioan Culcer	350,000 soldiers (-400,000)	Moldavia
2nd Army	General Alexandru Averescu	70,000 soldiers (-50,000)	Moldavia
~~3rd Army~~	~~General Mihail Aslan~~	~~25,000 (-50,000)~~	~~Drobudja, Bulgaro-Romanian border~~
4th Army	General Constantin Prezan	80,000 soldiers (-70,000)	Moldavia
BULGARIA			
176,000 soldiers	Commander	Soldiers	Area of operation
1st Army	General Kliment Boyadzhiev	75,000 soldiers (-17,000)	Bessarabia
2nd Army	General Georgi Todorov	31,000 soldiers (-13,000)	Bessarabia
3rd Army	General Toshev	33,000 soldiers (-10,000)	Bessarabia
GREECE			
125,000 soldiers	Commander	Soldiers	Area of operation
Army of Thessaly	Crown Prince Constantine	100,000 soldiers	Northern Grece and Serbia Macedonia
Army of Epirus	General Konstantinos Sapountzakis	25,000 soldiers	Epirus (Southern Greece)
Ottoman Empire			
3rd Army	Hafiz Hakki Pasha	15,000 soldiers (-6,000)	Bessarabia

By February 28th, the Central Powers reigned supreme in the Balkans and were in complete control of the entire area. Greece was an ally and occupied Serbia, while a mix of Bulgarian, Turkish, and Austro-Hungarian troops occupied Romania. The Central Powers veil of steel had fallen over the region, and for now, there wasn't much the Entente nations could do about it.

The Naval Battle of German Samoa
Von Spee vs Cradock, February 28th-29th

In order to sail clear through the Magellan Strait or Cape Horn and into the Atlantic Ocean to continue their epic adventure, Admiral Maximilian von Spee and his men had one last major obstacle in front of them. While having distanced themselves from the Japanese fleet of Admiral Heihachiro Togo following the Battle of Truk and a brilliant maneuver at the beginning of the month, another fleet was hunting for the unsuspecting but resourceful German Admiral.

German Pacific Squadron	
Admival von Graf Spee	
BB Westfalen stern damage	CL Emden
BB Kaiserin stern and boiler damage, 1 rear turret destroyed	CL Nurnberg
CA Kaiserin Elisabeth (Austria-Hungary)	CL Leipzing
Collier ship Oldenwald	Collier ship Brukenheim

His fleet was approaching the colony of German Western Samoa (Island of Opulu), another territory of the Reich in the Pacific. No news had been heard from the place since the start of the war, but that didn't necessarily mean it had fallen to the enemy. There was a telegraph station on the island, but von Spee correctly surmised that it had been destroyed by an enemy raid. And it had been, right off the bat, when the cruiser Good Hope sailed from New Zealand and bombarded the station to destroy it in September 1914.

"We will soon be in sight of the Apia harbor, Admiral. We are about an hour and a half out," said Krenk, his second in command. *"Very well. I will be in my cabin,"* answered von Spee as he stood up from his command chair to go to his place for a quick nap. If something was to happen, it would be in an hour and thus, there was no harm in getting refreshed before the fight.

Apia was located on the island of Opulu and had been, before the war, a coaling station for the German Navy. The German Admiral's gamble was that it was still under the control of Reich officials. The idea was to fill up with coal. He figured he had enough to get to the Atlantic, but the meeting he'd organized with Hugo von Pohl, the commander of the German High Seas Fleet, was anything but a certainty. The idea was thus to maximize his chances.

The chain of Islands known as Samoa had a rich history of being wanted by the world's powers. By the end of the 19th century, it was in the middle of intense international tensions between Britain, Germany, and the USA. In the end, Germany got the western part of Samoa and the United States the eastern part and the island with the biggest potential for a harbor. It didn't take a genius to see the strategic importance of Samoa. It had a great location halfway between the Hawaiian Islands and Australia. The power that controlled it also controlled the sea lanes going to the Sub-Continent.

Following the conquest, the U.S. Navy built a base on the small Island (Tutuila) that housed Pago-Pago. The Americans thus had a fleet near the German territory, and von Spee even toyed with the idea of trying to hail the neutral Americans and buy coal from them if he didn't find what he wanted in Apia.

As it happened, von Spee's gamble would soon pay off, as the islands of Opulu and Savaii, both German colonies, were still under the control of the Reich. There had been plans for a rapid occupation by a 1,500-soldier force in September-October of 1914, but the German Pacific Squadron's breakout into the Pacific following the Siege of Tsingtao had postponed the operation for fear that von Spee sailed to Samoa right off the bat and sank the attackers.

(...)

On the lookout mast of battleship Westfalen, Seamen Theodor Black scanned the horizon as best he could for enemy smokestacks and or ship silhouettes. On every German ship and, for that matter, in every other navy, one or more ratings (another name for seamen) were placed at the mastheads or at the top of a ship to keep a lookout and report to the Officer of the Watch. Each lookout kept watch for a pre-determined period of time before being relieved by another man. Staying on top of a mast in the wind, rain, and sun wasn't an easy job. It was the responsibility of the lookout to make sure the Officer of the Watch was notified of anything unusual. In return, that officer would relay the message to the bridge for the higher-ups to decide what to do with the information.

Theodor was a young man from Bremen, a German city near the North Sea, and had always been fascinated with the sea and the burgeoning German Navy. He was truly proud to serve as a sailor on one of the best battleships of the Fleet, the Westfalen. His adventure in Asia had been, to say the least, interesting so far. He'd joined the Kaiserliche Marine in 1912 and was assigned to the ship as a lookout because of his exceptional eyesight. During his time in Tsingtao, he managed to get a beautiful Chinese girlfriend and make a ton of friends there. The departure from the city and its subsequent fall was a true bummer, but he hoped that if Germany won the war, it would get it back from the dastardly Japanese.

Seeing something from the corner of his eye, he turned toward the black dot and leveled his binoculars. What he saw made him have a cold chill run down his back. He quickly relayed the information to the OOW (Officer of the Watch) below. *"Sir, about a dozen large smokestacks near the northwestern side of Opulu."* The officer below, Lieutenant Heilmein, yelled back. *"Do you see anything else, like high masts?"* *"Too far to sell, Sir, but I'll keep looking."* By then, the other lookouts of the masts and the central island structure of the battleship had all eyes trained on what he'd spotted. *"And Sir, the smokestacks appear to be getting closer. This is a fleet or a bunch of ships, and they are coming toward us."*

(...) British battlecruiser Furious (...)

The British Pacific Squadron was originally planned to be very small, as there were no real enemies, and the Germans didn't have a powerful fleet in Tsingtao. Then, the arrival of dreadnought battleships Westfalen and Kaiserin changed all of that. When the Siege of Tsingtao began, there were people, amongst others, the First Lord of the Admiralty Winston Churchill, who had hoped for the Japanese fleet to bottle up the Germans in the Chinese colony and be done with the pesky Admiral Maximilian von Spee. But things had not ended up that way, and the man had broken loose into the Pacific, dodging or successfully fighting off the larger fleet of legendary Japanese Admiral Heihachiro Togo.

After the fight and the subsequent escape of the Germans into the Pacific Ocean's immensity, a powerful squadron was hastily assembled to deal with the threat. While the British entertained a very large fleet in Europe, not many ships were available in the Pacific, with only a few units to help with the defense of Hong Kong, Australia, and New Zealand.

Thus, two powerful battlecruisers (under the overall command of Rear-Admiral Sir Christopher Cradock) were detached from the Grand Fleet and sailed to the Southern Atlantic. There, they were joined (in the Falkland Islands) by two aging, outdated Majestic Class pre-dreadnought battleships, the Majestic and the Caesar. They sailed around Cape Horn and then moved to Australia to pick up the few ships in the theater in the form of heavy cruisers Good Hope, Monmouth, and Australia, with two light cruisers, the Otranto and the Glasgow.

PACIFIC SQUADRON

Rear-Admiral Sir Christopher Cradock

BC Furious	
BC Incomparable	CA Monmouth
Pre-Dread BB Majestic	CA Australia
Pre-Dread BB Caesar	CL Otranto
CA Good Hope	CL Glasgow

The ships searched for von Spee in the Caroline Islands then waited for him in New Britain, but in the end, they never caught up with him until now. Craddock had been escorting the New Zealander attack forces and had just landed them in Apia when reports reached him that a fleet was approaching. Knowing the whereabouts of the Japanese Pacific Fleet (nowhere near Samoa, but still scouring the Caroline Islands to find von Spee), he ordered his ships to steam at full speed around the island to attempt an interception of the incoming fleet.

(...)

Lieutenant John Pawley, an officer on the battlecruiser Furious, was in forward gun turret No.1 (15-inch guns), and he was making certain his men were getting everything ready to fire. The man at the firing solution was trying to figure out an angle of attack, but they were still too far away for that at the moment, while the rest of the men were busy turning the cranks to bring the big shells up from the magazine below. Others were doing the same but with the powder charges.

All the while, the British fleet soon formed into a battle line with both the Furious and the Incomparable in front. The smoke on the horizon grew larger and larger as the minutes went by, and eventually, the order to fire was given. *"These bastards are Germans if the Admiral has given the order to fire,"* said Pawly to his men.

Soon, the battle started, and the No.1 turret fired its first salvo at 12,000 yards. The entire chamber was filled with smoke and the heavy smell of cordite mixed with the sweaty odors of hard-working men. Lieutenant Pawley did his best to keep his people in line, but once the battle started, they knew the drill, as they'd practiced so many times that it was second nature to them. The first few shots were ranging shots, and they fell short. The next one shot over. The rest of the fleet fired as well, and Pawley saw with pride that a deluge of shells were being fired at the enemy. Targeting solutions and precise naval gunnery in 1915 was in its infancy, and it was a miracle if battleships hit in their first salvos. The concept was to fire many and then eventually hope that it would work based on the volume of fire.

The ship was reverberating with the thundering of the guns firing in anger, while the sea was very rough under a leaden sky. As the battle progressed and the two fleets fired at each other, some of the giant waves came clean overboard, splashing large gushes of water and vapor over ships on both sides, increasing the difficulty in hitting anything worthwhile because of the pitch and roll of the sea.

The Lieutenant thought the battle was going well when the ship was hit fifteen minutes into the fight. The large clanging and steel bending noise shook the entirety of Furious, and for a moment, the lights in their turret blinked, and everyone inside stopped what they were doing. Then, a second, even stronger blast rocked them, and they barely kept their balance. Furious was taking a beating, and the only thing they could do about it was to keep firing and to try to do the same to the Germans.

(...) German dreadnought battleship Westfalen (...)

From his position of height, Theodor Black could see the battle unfolding, and he felt naked. He wasn't protected by anything, and just one little piece of shrapnel could kill him. He almost panicked and went down but remembered his training instructions. *"The lookout is as safe as any other place in the ship. Do you think the enemy is aiming for the top of the masts? No, they are trying to sink the ship, not kill a lookout seaman and a bunch of gulls!"*

His view of the battle was unbeatable. He could even figure out the shells arcing from both fleets. Warship fire was not horizontal. Instead, the shells were fired with some elevation to reach further away. They thus fired high, and the trick was to calculate where they would land to try and hit a ship. From where he was, he cheered as two powerful blasts blossomed on one of the enemy's largest ships, either a battleship or a very large battlecruiser. Indeed, Black didn't know it, but the Furious was one of the biggest ships afloat in 1915, displacing close to 30,000 tons and sporting 15-inch guns.

One British cruiser (namely, the Good Hope) blew up spectacularly from a distance, and again he cheered. It was to be known after the battle that one of battleship Kaiserin's shells slammed into the shell magazine, causing a catastrophic explosion. Another enemy cruiser (the Monmouth) soon afterward also blew up. He'd been amazed that until the last moment, its British handlers had fired their guns even if it was obvious the ship was tilting hard forward and taking on a lot of water. The entire sky above the British fleet was darkening with gushing dark smoke and it looked quite good for the German Fleet if you only looked in that direction.

But when he took the time to look at the damage to his own fleet, his smile vanished. The Kaiserin Elisabeth, the Austro-Hungarian ship that had joined them not so long ago (during their stay at Yap Island), was sinking rapidly and raked with a plethora of secondary explosions. Light cruisers Leipzig and Nurnberg were already gone, having blown up some time before. The only thing left of them were large patches of floating, fiery debris.

(...)

All the while, and regardless of the brave individual sailors on both sides fighting as best they could, the battle raged on, with a mighty duel developing between the four dreadnought titans of the fight, Westfalen, Kaiserin on the German side against Incomparable and Furious on the Royal Navy's, supported by the two aging battleships; Majestic and Caesar. One thing was certain, however. The German Admiral tried to disengage and sailed on an oblique heading away from the British, who, in the best of the Royal Navy's aggressive tradition, closed in for the kill regardless of the odds. Twenty minutes into the battle, hits started to blossom on all four ships, hitting each other in succession with their guns. By then, the range was 8,000 yards, and it was close enough for regular hits.

(...)

Being a fireman was the hardest job in the entire Royal Navy, and it was the same in every navy in the world. The job was shoveling coal into a burning furnace, which in turn produced heat and steam to make the ship's engine work. The Royal Navy and others were starting to experiment with fuel-burning ships (the Furious and the Incomparable burned fuel, for that matter). But that didn't apply to the old pre-dreadnoughts Majestic and the Caesar.

Michael Bunting was one such man as he toiled to shove coal into the fiercely burning furnace in front of him. He was sweaty all over as the heat was almost unbearable. Like all the others beside him (there were many furnaces in the large boiler room) who did the same, they were all dirty, and their skins were blackened with dark soot. But they worked feverishly to get the coal in as the engineers around pushed them to their limit. Speed and power were critical during a battle, and since Majestic was currently fighting, they were all operating themselves at peak levels. It was a very hard job, and some of the men fainted because of the accumulated fatigue and ambient heat. When that happened, another man was put in front of the furnace, and that was that, he started shoveling like the others.

Firemen were highly skilled laborers, as it was a very hard thing to make sure the furnaces burned in a coordinated fashion and to the needs of the ship. Engineers dictated the pace in order to optimize the ship's performance and also used a Kilroy stocking regulator in order to optimize efficiency. The regulator gave the firemen the pace and the rhythm they needed to have to get the ship working properly, and their loud ticking noise could be heard over the racket of the boiler room.

Michael staggered to the side as a powerful explosion raked Majestic, and he had to crouch to keep his balance. Several of the men around him fell on their coal piles. *"Keep at it, you buggers,"* yelled one of the engineers. *"The guys up there need every ounce of speed we can give them if we want to survive,"* yelled the engineer near Michael, and he heard the others down the line do the same. Then the ship perceptibly tilted to port, and it was obvious Majestic was not faring well above. "Damn," said the fireman right beside Michael, as all the coal drifted away from him just as he'd tried to take another shove to feed his fire.

Then, another gigantic hit slammed the ship, and by then, it was impossible to stand, with everyone falling on the deck. Two of the German battleship Westfalen's shells had slammed into the hull of Majestic, and that was one hell of a crippling hit. From the outside, a gigantic explosion blossomed, with smoke, debris, and fiery shrapnel flying everywhere.

Inside the ship, the scene was even more horrifying, with a wall of fire rolling across the hull, instantly burning sailors and officers alike. For Michael, who was already stunned like the rest of the guys in Boiler Room Three, the next instants were filled with dread and the certainty of death. Smoke and dust had completely invaded the room, and he couldn't see anything. Then, for one fleeting instant, a light broke through the dark gloom, and then it flashed, zapping him out of existence.

(…) Lookout on battleship Westfalen (…)

"Oh wow," exhaled Theodor in a short yelp as he saw the volcanic explosion marking battleship Majestic's death. First, it was raked by two large explosions from shells on the port side, followed by two large horizontal bursts of smoke and debris, and a bunch of secondary detonations rolling across the hull of the ship like bursting bubbles. For a moment, it seemed like the world stood still, and then Majestic exploded in one hell of a blast.

The old pre-dreadnought was right beside Furious, the enemy flagship, and the large expanding fireball enveloped the battlecruiser into a maelstrom of fire, smoke, dust, and debris.

(...) Battlecruiser Furious (...)

Moments later, No.1 gun turret Lieutenant John Pawley struggled to his elbows as he tried to lift himself from the steel deck following the catastrophic blast Furious had been subjected to. His mind was groggy, and he tried to register what had happened. He then realized he could see the sky and a bunch of smoke billowing in the fiery wind above him. That wasn't normal, and then he registered that there was no turret anymore. The entire top of it was sheared away by the explosion. The next moment a rain of shells both from Kaiserin and Westfalen slammed on the ship, and then it was over.

(...) Battleship Westfalen (...)

Theodor could see that the battle was ending following the incredible explosion of the enemy battlecruiser. The ship was still there, but a large glowing fire burned where its boilers and funnels had been. The British were throwing up a large smoke screen. He smiled as they didn't need to do that much; their ships were burning, and they had had enough smoke already.

(...) The final tally (...)

The battle, a German victory, was one hell of a destructive fight. On the British side, the Furious was gone, burning fiercely and sinking. The Majestic was now just a patch of debris on the ocean. Both cruisers, Good Hope and Monmouth, were destroyed. The root of the problem and why the British had taken such a drubbing was because of the design of the Furious Class battlecruisers, gifted with great guns (15-inch) but not enough armor compared to their two German counterparts.

The Germans didn't sail away unscathed, however. The Kaiserin Elizabeth, their Austro-Hungarian heavy cruiser, was sunk, and the light cruisers Nurnberg and Leipzig as well. Collier Brukenheim was also sunk, hit by a shell from the heavy cruiser Australia.

Both Kaiserin and Westfalen sustained damage but were still operational. The German sailors, gunners, and officers were the deciding factor in the battle. Their experience was starting to be impressive, as they had fought many battles since the start of the war, while the Battle of Western Samoa had been the first battle for their British opponents. The Royal Navy would need to do a lot more to get rid of Maximilian von Spee and his merry band of adventurers.

CHAPTER 5

Assaut on Fort Mont-Agel
Württemberg Mountain Battalion (Württembergische Gebirgs-Bataillon), February 17th, 1915

The next fort for the Germano-Italians to assault on the Séré de Rivières system was called Fort Mont-Agel. Compared to the Fort of Bear Mountain (Fort do Mont-Ours), this was the real deal. The very large fort was originally intended to serve as one of the main points of resistance on the border and also as a large artillery support position with a powerful 145 mm gun battery. The thing was firing every day on the Central Powers' positions, and it was about time that they silenced it.

Captain Erwin Rommel, maverick and officer in the Wurttemberg Mountain Battalion, looked with interest at the big blossoming fireball above him as one of the 145 mm cannons in the battery blasted away once more. The sound was powerful as it reverberated across the high mountain walls and seemed to echo away into the distance. He was well over 3,500 feet in elevation, above Nice and Menton. The air was cold and thin, and it was a little hard to breathe. Every time he exhaled, his breath produced a cloud of vapor. *"Well, Captain, this is going to be a bitch to storm,"* said Private Theo Stark, the man whom Rommel liked because he was as brave and reckless as he was. *"Indeed, Private. And there's no easy way in, like at Bear Mountain,"* he answered. As he finished his phrase, another resounding boom exploded as yet another 145 mm in the battery fired.

The battle for the other fort had ended in them looking pretty sharp to the battalion commander, Major Theodor Strosser, since they outflanked the French defenders and took them prisoners without a shot being fired. The man had said they would get yet another Iron Cross, but both of them didn't care much about getting those trinkets.

"From what we know, Sir," said Lieutenant Stammer beside both men, holding an old map placed on a flat rock (they were on a ledge in the rock wall and further down from the French fort*)*, *"the enemy position*

has eight blocks or buildings, some carved into the rock and others built out of reinforced concrete." Rommel looked up with interest, trying to spot any weak points he could see. *"How many entry points,"* he said. *"Three, Sir, including one with an aerial tram and a road going up from a town called... La Turbie"*. The Lieutenant paused, pointing to a road on his map, and Rommel leaned to look at it. *"The road is unavailable to us, as it is behind enemy lines, as is the town of La Turbie, Sir."* The Germano-Italians had advanced a few kilometers since the storming of the Bear Mountain Fort but not enough to have access to either the aerial tram or the road. Rommel mulled it over as he again looked at the French gun, producing yet another fireball and a large cloud of dark smoke. *"I guess we'll just have to do this the hard way,"* he finally said, thinking that the only solution was to climb off the rockface and get to the fort. Lieutenant Stammer, always the pessimist, spoke up. *"But Captain, climbing this rockface,"* he pointed at the large rock wall in front of them, *"in winter is one hell of a difficulty."* *"I know, Lieutenant,"* answered Rommel, smiling to Stark, who smiled back because he also liked the idea that was obviously forming in his superior's head. "And that is why the enemy won't think us crazy enough to attempt it."

A few hours later, they were back at the Bear Mountain Fort, or more to the point, the destroyed Bear Mountain Fort, and Rommel was attempting to convince Major Strosser of his plan. They were in one of the surviving casemates, and a small table was installed, with the rubble pushed to the side by the walls. This was the new battalion's HQ.

"So, you say you can do this with how many men again?" *"Sir, give me a full company with the climbing gear, and I can make that happen."* Württemberg Battalion was a mountain unit, and even if not all of its men knew how to do rock climbing, enough of them did that Rommel's request was possible. The young Captain continued. *"We would climb here,"* he said, pointing to a spot on the map that represented a large split in the rock. *"The way the rock is, I believe we can climb without being seen."* Strosser looked skeptical. *"And then*

what" "Then, we arrive at block 4, the so-called entry guard block. It's defended by two machine gun ports and one machine gun turret. It's the thing we see over here," he continued. "If we take it, the rest of the unit will be able to come up the track here, as it won't be under enemy fire anymore." "How do you know there is a track there?" Rommel smiled. "There is, Sir; I have spoken to one of the local Italians, and they told me it's a shepherd's track not often used, but it's there." Rommel and Stark had indeed spoken to one of the locals, and the track existed for real.

Strosser leaned back in his makeshift chair, a broken piece of concrete. "Rommel, you are one crazy son of a bitch." He looked at his young Captain in the eyes. *"You are certain you can do this? I don't want to lose an entire company to a fool's errand."*

"*I can, sir,*" answered Rommel, gesturing to Stark and a couple of his NCOs with him in the casemate. "*We can, Sir.*"

Zeppelins yet again
The second raid on London, February 17th, 1915

"The so-called Zeppelins are like a swarm of truly formidable bumblebees..."
Winston Churchill to Parliament, February 12th, 1915

'It was a most thrilling and wonderful sight. I was dead tired but hardly had gotten to bed when I was roused by the sound of an aircraft and the rushing of motors a few minutes after, so I turned out of bed and, looking up, saw just above us 2 Zepps. The searchlights were on them, and they looked as if they were among the stars. They were up very high and like cigar-shaped constellations...The wonderful part of it was that no one seemed frightened ... there were ... a great many people in the streets.

Brown, Malcolm: The Imperial War Museum Book of The First World War: A Great Conflict

Fighter pilot William Leefe Robinson of the Royal Flying Corps was at the helm of his Vickers Gunbus two-seat fighter, a magnificent airplane. It was the first operational fighter plane in the world. The aircraft came equipped with a .303 Lewis gun (a light machine gun), using a round, pan magazine holding 47 rounds on top, placed at the front where the observer (the second man in the two-seat plane) was located.

The British fighter was an open canopy-like all planes of the era, meaning that both men had their heads sticking out in the open. Thus, they were clothed from head to toe in warm garments, including a scarf that was flapping in the wind, a fur shako, and large goggles to protect their eyes from the stinging cold and wind.

Robinson looked around and tried to find the big Zeppelins that had been spotted south of London. He looked at the observer and his friend, David Slaumbaum, who shook his head in the negative. Both men were flying above London. The air was cold, and even with their thick, warm clothing, they both could feel the sting. Their breaths fumed and it was very hard to stay fully concentrated. Not one part of their skin was exposed, their scarves covering their face, their goggles covering the rest.

The last raid on the capital had created quite an impression on the British. The lone Zeppelin that raided the city had dropped bombs. It was a tiny amount, but the population's morale was affected in a big way. For the first time in the war and in British history, an enemy country had been able to attack them without landing a soldier on the island. The bombing had damaged some buildings and killed a couple of people, which was no big thing in the grand scheme of things; however, it was a big deal for the British and a matter of pride for the military.

Thus, the Royal Air Corps had been called forth to station several of the Vickers Gunbus two-seat fighters near the capital (in a bunch of farm fields north and south of London) to be called upon when the next enemy attack came. Also, machine gun positions were set up on the city's highest roofs. Powerful searchlights were installed at different spots in the city to try and spot the damned things since they always attacked at night.

From his position, Robinson saw the beams of lights climbing in the sky and reflecting on the clouds. And then he saw the big enemy bastards. Three of them exited a large cloud, gliding silently above the city. Almost immediately, he started to see the climbing bullets reflecting in the searchlight's glow. Slaumbaum, his observer, had also seen them, and he gestured toward the area. Robinson nodded and pushed the stick down and to the right, and the plane plunged toward the big airships lumbering silently below.

The three-Zeppelin raid was the German's third attempt in the same week as twice before, the group was blown off course by strong headwinds that veered them away from London. Airships were a good way to bring the war to the British, but they were too light to fight against strong winds and sometimes could not go where they wanted to.

Zeppelin L12 (the lead airship) and its two brothers were propelled by four powerful Maybach engines below the nacelle. They each carried (again) three tons of bombs. They were gigantic beasts of war, with a length of 479 feet, two machine guns in the cabin below the nacelle, and one on top of it. As Robinson approached, he found the sight of the reflecting lights on them was eerie and daunting at the same time.

Slaumbaum prepared his gun and then started shooting from a distance since he tried to get his aim. Robinson saw the bullets arcing in the cold air, going wild and losing themselves in the darkness.

Then, the fighter was flying just above one of the German beasts, and he let loose a long burst from his 47-bullet chamber, emptying it in a flurry of arcing shells that slammed into the cover of the enemy Zeppelin. The German machine gun on the top of the thing also fired at Robinson's fighter but missed. It was very hard to hit a moving object when you were also moving. Although scary for the two British aviators, the German bullets streamed past without even coming close to the plane.

And then they were past the airship; Robinson turned his plane to look at the damage. He took a risk, as both the top and the bottom machine gunners let loose at him. But again, the bullets streaked harmlessly into the white clouds and the darkness.

He cursed, and Slaumbaum looked at him with a shrug of the shoulders. No fire, no explosion. He was baffled as they'd riddled the Zeppelin with most of the Lewis gun's ammo. He estimated that over forty .303 bullets had slammed home.

He wondered for one moment why there was no fire or explosion. Weren't the damned things made of highly flammable hydrogen? Robinson was to know eventually that regular ammunition just ripped through the (surprisingly tough) outer cover. The holes Slaumbaum had made weren't going to let out much of that monstrous amount of gas even over the course of a day or two of flight, nor ignite it. Zeppelins were not like regular balloons that could be shot down with the slightest puncture. They had multiple redundancies, with dozens upon dozens of hydrogen bags inside their structure.

As it appeared, some bullets were deflected by the outer skin, and the ones that went through did make holes, but most simply passed through without causing significant damage.

He gestured for Slaumbaum to reload and that they would try another pass.

Every round Lewis' ammo magazine held 47 shots, and they had emptied one on their first pass. They had one more magazine, and then they would be dry. To reload, Slaumbaum had to stand up in his open cockpit to load another heavy magazine. All the while, Robinson tried to stay away from the streams of bullets from the three Zeppelins trying to shoot the fighter down. Bullets were normally difficult to see, but in the cold air, they were obvious, and since there were many beams from searchlights, he could see them arcing across the sky.

When his observer was done reloading the Lewis, he climbed above the Zeppelin they'd attacked before and then dove. The air resistance increased, and it was very hard to keep the plane level. Slaumbaum's aim was affected by this, and half of his .303s streaked past the airship. But about twenty more slammed home, again without igniting the thing or doing any apparent damage.

The Zeppelins, apparently not bothered in the least by the lone British fighter, dropped their bombs and then turned south and disappeared into a large cloud. Robinson cursed loudly as he saw the bombs explode below. From his perspective, the blasts were only flashes of light and fire, but he knew that below, people died, and buildings were being demolished.

He followed the large airships from a distance for a while. But since he was out of ammo, he eventually let them go and turned back toward his airfield. He sulked all the while, wondering how they would kill those big bastards.

Assault on Fort Mont-Agel
Württemberg Mountain Battalion (Württembergische Gebirgs-Bataillon), February 18th, 1915

The going was treacherous. Rommel put his metal pin into the rock, trying to be as silent as possible. He then attached his rope and signaled the men below him to keep going up. The goal was to jam them in place so he could put a rope for the others to climb more safely.

The wind and the snow were slashing his face as the cold bit at his skin. He, along with a group of 250 men (a company), were climbing the rockface along a fault in the rock in order to reach the French fortress of Mont-Agel up on the top of the mountain. The road and all the approaches were controlled by the enemy, and thus, this was the only *"unprotected"* route because it was not something the French thought of as an angle of approach because it was crazy to think that you could.

But Captain Erwin Rommel and his enterprising soldier Theo Stark had decided that they could and that they would attempt the climb to surprise the cozy enemy soldiers in the high fort. Mont-Agel was not on the frontline, and thus, no one expected it to be attacked in any way.

The fort was a gun platform to support the defensive positions below. This was reminded to the climbing Germans every other ten minutes or so when the big 145 mm gun battery of the fort fired at the Germano-Italian positions. They climbed directly below it, and Rommel, looking up once in a while, even saw the trail of fire and smoke from the weapon's blast.

The climbing was harder than Rommel had expected because of the wind, the snow, and the ice. Already, two men had fallen to their terrible deaths below, with two more injured by falling rocks from the men above them. But, overall, things were not going so bad. Private

Stark was ahead of his Captain, being the first in line and the one responsible for installing the first metal pins for Rommel to follow.

As he went through the motions of climbing, installing ropes, and making sure he didn't fall, the young maverick Captain thought about what awaited him at the top. He knew that the fortress had eight different areas called blocks and that they would end their climbing at the most difficult spot to take, block four, what the plan he had had called the *"entry guard block,"* which supposedly had a couple of Hotchkiss machine guns. He figured that if they could take it, it would facilitate the rest of the battalion's approach, as an assault was planned on the slopes of the mountain.

Mont Agel had a rock face (where Rommel and his company were climbing) and a *"gentler"* slope that the Württemberg Mountain Battalion could use to approach the fortress. In any normal circumstances, no assault would have been attempted as the Guard block possessed a plunging view of the entire area, and the men would have been easily mowed down as they climbed. The slope was climbable, but only through great effort and deliberate slowness to avoid falling down. This was the perfect formula for the men to be killed on their way up.

The idea was thus to storm the guardhouse and control it while Major Strosser made his way up with the rest of the battalion. Since it was estimated the enemy probably had a maximum of four to five hundred men up there, the 1200-strong Württemberg Mountain Battalion could storm the place easily if it was able to get up there without being destroyed while climbing.

(...)

Three hours later, a winded Rommel finally made it over the last ledge, just below the concrete wall of the guardhouse. The company had managed, so far, to remain undetected. Stark had been the first up and Rommel second. The Private signaled him that all was well, and then he relayed the info below for the rest of the men to climb. Looking down, he almost felt dizzy, as the rock face was a sheer drop of about eight hundred feet going down into a deep ravine. No wonder the French didn't expect them to climb there.

The rest of the company took about an hour to get up by which time both Stark and his superior officers had gotten the men to spread out into the jagged rocks and holes around the guardhouse. They remained on the side of the rockface to avoid being spotted, as on the other side was the road and the machine guns facing toward the road. Having found no entrance on their side, they made a quick plan to attack the front in a rush involving all of his men to overwhelm the French without giving them time to realize what was happening or to organize themselves.

The door to the guard house was open, as the enemy didn't expect any attack. After all, none were underway, and they were well above the frontline defensive positions below. The steep slope facing them could be used by the Germano-Italians to make their approach, but none of the French in the guardhouse were worried since they would see the enemy soldiers climbing from very far and would be able to kill them before they got anywhere near. It would take them hours to climb, and machine guns only needed seconds to kill.

(...) The assault (...)

Rommel stumbled upward as small rocks and dust fell on the sides, making his footing precarious. All the while, the damned French fired at them from their concrete blockhouse. Right beside him, one of his men was hit in the head by the enemy. It exploded in bloody gore, splattering Peters all over. "*Up! Up! Up!*" yelled a couple of his sergeants, flanked by a now worked-up Stark.

The man had his blood up, Rommel could tell. All around them, several bullets zipped by, and an explosion rocked the area. One of his men had thrown a grenade to the side of the fortress, making more noise than damage. The yelling of the men all around and reverberating sounds of rifle fire across the mountainside seemed overbearing for a moment as he ran toward the guard block entrance. A few of his men were already inside, and a couple lay in pools of blood beside it. Bullets ricocheted noisily around him, creating bright sparks and dust.

"Chaaarrrggge!" he yelled, and the rush pushed the Germans inside the guard block. Some of the French had picked up their rifles and hit four more men but then got overwhelmed by Rommel's superior numbers. They were quickly dispatched with knives, bayonets, and point-blank firing.

He then saw the back of a British soldier running down some tunnel going deeper into the structure. The French, had, of course, built connecting tunnels below the surface. The gallery the soldier was fleeing into was sloping downward. *"Quick, men,"* he gestured stiffy. *"Follow the bastards and seal than tunnel."* *"Yes, sir,"* answered Stark and the five soldiers around him. They started running in pursuit of the fleeing enemy.

By then, the quick, deadly fight for the guard block was over, and the Germans were in control. He quickly stepped out of the concrete fortification and fished out his Hebel Leuchtpistole Model 1894, a flare gun that was the signal for Major Strosser to get the men to start climbing the steep slope. The flare arced high in the sky and exploded brightly. The commander of the Württemberg Mountain Battalion saw it and sent the men up.

"And now, the difficult part, gentlemen," said Rommel, as his soldiers spread out into the structure, removing the machine guns from their emplacements and re-installing them to face toward the likely direction of a French counterattack.

Another explosion shook their world, and Rommel smiled again. It was Stark who had blown up the charge to block the tunnel where the enemy could come and attack them. Now, he just needed to defend the place until Major Strosser came up with the rest of the men, and the fortress would be theirs for the taking.

Infanterie-Regiment Graf Schwerin
Verdun frontline, February 20th, 1915

The chattering and steel-clanging sound of the Maxim machine guns was overbearing to Private soldier Oskar Dantz, and he watched as his comrades mowed down yet another batch of brave, blue-uniformed Frenchmen assaulting their position. All the while, he also fired his Gewehr rifle, emptying five-round stripper clip after five-round stripper clip into the withering mass of enemies.

Bullets whizzed around his ears, and he felt the urge to slide back down into the trench, but it was not to be, as the NCOs near him would soon kill that idea and send him back up. Dantz was right on the trench's wooden-planking parapet, with his torso sticking out as he fired round after round. Beside him to his right, his friend Florian Storch was doing the same. On the left, another soldier went through the same motions. They were also flanked by comrades. The entire affair looked like a firing line reminiscent of the Napoleonic Wars.

A large shell explosion blasted earth and debris on his head, and for a moment, he staggered down on the parapet. The smoke from the blow filled the trench, and he soon got back up to fire some more as he was uninjured.

As he watched, more and more Frenchmen fell while others started to fall on their bellies to avoid the terrible firepower facing them. It was like the Entente soldiers had hit a wall of lead and fire. Oskar wondered why the enemy commanders kept sending men to the German lines. From his standpoint, it was obvious the French advance was over and that now, their defenses were strong enough to withstand anything the Verdun-based attack could throw at them. But no one seemed to have told the French commanders yet. The number of accumulating bodies in no man's land was truly appalling, and Oskar wondered for a moment what the hell these officers were doing. He didn't have a clue, nor did the generals sending these men to the attack and certain death. Such was the absurdity of the Great War and its trench warfare.

"Good shooting, lads," said Sergeant Wilhelm, walking by Oskar and Florian, tapping both of them on the shoulders. "Maybe the bastards will understand that there is nowhere to go now," he continued before moving on to the other knot of men on the wooden-planked parapet. Although the stout Sergeant kept a calm tone and attitude, Oskar thought that the Frenchmen were getting awfully close to their position. No matter how many they killed, more always appeared, and that wasn't good in his experience. While he was pretty certain the enemy wouldn't break their entire line as other trenches were backing his own, he didn't like that it looked like he would soon be at close quarters with the enemy.

The Allied attack, which had started ten days before, advanced well at first because the Reich didn't have enough troops in the area, but was now stalled. In the last few days, the poor French and British sods clambered out of their trenches and crossed no man's land under a withering barrage of German bullets and artillery shells. The entire affair was deteriorating into disaster, and at one point, Franco-British morale was bound to break, thought Oskar, between two shots, with one hitting home on a big brute of a Frenchman's shoulder, sending him falling sideways in the slushy, wintery and muddy ground.

"Steady, lads," yelled Sergeant Wilhelm once more. Oskar admired the man's calm demeanor, even in the face of imminent danger. A flurry of their own artillery shells landed in succession about fifty yards ahead of them, blasting the earth, soldiers, and everything else, slamming it into a million directions. They all knew that the artillery barrage was the last hope of avoiding yet another hand-to-hand fight. The explosions continued for some time and then stopped, followed by a deathly silence, only broken by the whistles of the French artillery, flying over them and falling in the German rear. Oskar thought he heard voices. Was he the only one? *"Sergeant, did you hear that,"* said one of the men as he thought he heard the clicking

sounds of walking men laden with a burden. "Shut up, Private," answered Wilhelm in a roar.

The smoke and the dust lifted up by the barrage billowed in large clouds, but the wind pushed it away quickly. Out of the drifting, artificial grey fog came the ominous silhouettes of the enemy soldiers, rifles at their waists. It was an eerie sight, and for a moment, Oskar was almost overwhelmed with fear. But the Sergeant was there to keep them steady. *"Lads, fix bayonets!"* And he did, along with his friend Florian and the rest of his comrades.

The Maxim machine guns continued to fire away, chattering as they did. More enemy soldiers fell, mowed down by the terrible weapons. But again, it wasn't enough. The Frenchmen walked where the barbed wire had been before being destroyed by the night-long shelling the day before. *"Get ready!"*

Another minute went by while Oskar killed or injured four more French (and British soldiers) then the battle was joined, the enemy jumping into their trench. He almost immediately came face-to-face with a dirty, black-faced enemy soldier. Both clutched their rifle-tipped bayonets in dread of what must happen next while fighting, and mayhem erupted around them.

For a moment, Oskar felt the fear of death mount in him, and in a fraction of a second, he realized he was out of his funk because his opponent lunged at him. After all, the bastard was after his life exactly as he was after his own.

Oskar was quicker than he was. He parried his rifle away with a large swing and then slammed his blade through the enemy's chest. The man fell, put both his hands where the blade had penetrated, and then... he fell on the ground in one great gasp of air. With no time to think, he turned as yet another soldier lunged at him as he jumped into the trench. The man was British this time, and he swung his blade like a bat, just as if he was playing cricket when he was younger. The blade at the tip of his bayonet slashed a deep gouge into the other man's chest, and he fell down on his back with a great yelp of pain. Not wasting a second, Oskar moved over him and planted his blade into his chest with all his strength.

He almost lost consciousness in the next instant, with a French rifle firing right beside his left ear. The man had jumped into the trench while firing at the same time but missed Oskar by an inch. Staggering backward with his head spinning, the German soldier wondered where he was for a moment. He slammed his back on another German and turned in surprise. *"It's me, you bugger,"* yelled Sergeant Wilhelm, seeing the crazy look in Oskar's eyes. His blood was up, and he was worked into a frenzy.

Coming back to his senses, he turned again to face his attacker and, having enough distance from the man, leveled his rifle to fire. The round slammed right between the soldier's eyes, killing him instantly. Yelling out of his lungs in rage, he looked for another opponent but didn't find any. The ones left were already fighting with someone. Seeing the back of a blue uniform, he decided to lunge at him, piercing the poor soldier's back. The man fell in a spray of blood, and the grateful German soldier who was about to get killed stared at him with a thankful look.

The battle continued for a while and ended in the Anglo-French either being all dead or having surrendered. They were assembled back on the trench ledge and parapet, ready to repel yet another attack, but none came that day, or the next day, or the day after that. Finally, the Entente generals had enough casualties to pay attention to the fact that their offensive was clearly over.

Let's try once, but not too hard
The Austro-Hungarian Navy attempts a breakout, February 21st, 1915

(...) Deck of battleship Tegethoff (...)

Admiral Anton Haue, the newest commander of the Austro-Hungarian Navy, took a deep breath as he walked the deck of the dreadnought battleship Tegethoff.

AUSTRIA-HUNGARY
Austrian Battle Fleet, Admiral Admiral Anton Haue

BB Prinz Eugen,	BB Viribus Unitis	Pre-Dread BB Radetzky
BB Tegethoff	Pre-Dread BB Franz Ferdinand	Pre-Dread BB Babenberg
Pre-Dread BB Zrynjy	Pre-Dread BB Arpad	Pre-Dread BB Habsburg
Pre-Dread BB Ferdinand Mac	Pre-Dread BB Friedrich	Pre-Dread BB Karl
3 CA	4 CL	12 DD

His entire fleet was slowly making its way out of the main K.u.K. Navy naval base of Pola. Haue was clearly disgruntled and unhappy about the move, but the Emperor had decided that he was to do it.

He had taken command of the Navy in 1913, following Admiral Count Rudolf Montecuccoli's retirement. His policy had been to keep the fleet safe and use it as a deterrent to fix the enemy navies in the Mediterranean. As long as his battle fleet existed, the Entente would have to keep a sizeable force in the Central Mediterranean.

Now, he was to risk it all in a breakout attempt against the co-called Otranto Barrage, the blockade by the Franco-British ships in the strait of Otranto at the mouth of the Adriatic Sea. The idea was to make a break for the Dardanelles and join the Greco-Germano-Ottoman fleet, there to make one powerful Central Powers fleet to rival the Entente.

It was not the first time the Admiral had faced the idea of sending the Imperial and Royal fleet into the Dardanelles. On August 5, 1914, the Austrian foreign office, through the Austrian Army High Command, had asked him to sail the K.u.K. fleet into the Bosphorus, where it would be safe from harm.

Count Aehrenthal, the Austrian Minister of Foreign Affairs, had succeeded in getting the go-ahead from the Ottomans for the Austro-Hungarian ships to sail through the Dardanelles.

Aehrenthal's idea was influenced by the desire of the German High Command to strengthen Turkey and create a super fleet in the Aegean Sea. Admiral Haue had, however, opposed the idea. From his point of view, the very reason for the existence of his warships was to protect the Empire, not play into Germany's grand strategy games. General von Hotzendorf had agreed with him and in the end, the diplomats were denied, the aged Emperor confirming this decision. But that was 1914 and before the many disasters that befell the Empire. Now surviving mostly because the Reich supported it with troops and supplies, it had less of a say in what was being decided in the grand scheme of things, and the next demand from Berlin was accepted, giving Haue no choice.

The idea was interesting, but the entire concept remained difficult to achieve from his point of view. The fleets he was about to face were not only numerically superior to his own; their sailors were more experienced, and there was a real danger he could be annihilated.

Austria-Hungary had amassed a powerful fleet worthy of a great European Power, with three dreadnought battleships (Prinz Eugen, Tegethoff, and Viribus Unitis), nine pre-dreadnought battleships (Zrynyi, Ferdinand Mac, Franz Ferdinand, Arpad, Freidrich, Radetzky, Babenberg, Habsburg and Karl), plus three heavy cruisers, four light ones and twelve destroyers.

While this was the type of force that many countries would shy away from and avoid a fight, that was not the case for the Entente, who could count on two powerful fleets to watch the Otranto Strait.

FRANCE
Apulia(Taranto) and Otranto Strait

Battleships		
BB Courbet [Fleet Flagship]	BB France	1 CA
BB Jean-Bart	BB Paris	3 CL
1st Battle Squadron, 1st Division		
Pre-Dread BB Diderot	Pre-Dread BB Vergniaud	2 DD
Pre-Dread BB Danton	2 CL	
1st Battle Squadron, 2nd Division		
Pre-Dread BB Voltaire	Pre-Dread BB Mirabeau	1 DD
Pre-Dread BB Condorcet	1 CL	
2nd Battle Squadron, 1st Division		
Pre-Dread BB Verite	Pre-Dread BB Republique	1 DD
Pre-Dread BB Patrie	1 CL	
2nd Battle Squadron, 2nd Division		
Pre-Dread BB Justice [CA]	1 CL	2 DD
Pre-Dread BB Democratie		

The French fleet, under the command of Admiral Augustin Boue de Lapeyrere, rivaled the Austrian Fleet in strength and was responsible for a permanent presence in the strait, while the British Mediterranean Squadron remained based in Malta and Gibraltar and was responsible for escorting the precious convoys from the Central to the Western Med and then beyond to the Atlantic. The French fleet had four dreadnought battleships (Courbet, Jean-Bart, France, and Paris) and eleven pre-dreadnought battleships (Diderot, Danton, Vergniaud, Voltaire, Condorcet, Mirabeau, Justice, Democratie and Republique), with many heavy cruisers, light cruisers, and destroyers.

The idea was that if battle was joined between the French and the Austrians, the British would sail to the rescue and help smash the K.u.K. Fleet.

"Admiral," said a staff lieutenant who walked near him on the Tegethoff's deck. *"Yes, Lieutenant,"* answered the commander-in-chief, turning to face him. *"The entire fleet is underway, sir. Only*

waiting for your final go-ahead to exit the harbor." "Very well, give the order. I will be on the bridge shortly." "Yes, sir."

He turned back to see his ships, their steam up. Their funnels burned coal and started the dark smoke going along with the act. The ships of the Austro-Hungarian Empire were ready for the fight.

(...) Bridge of dreadnought battleship Courbet, half a day later (...)

The Courbet was a brand-new warship launched in August 1914. First of the four-strong Courbet Class, it was the first dreadnought built by the French. The ships were armed with twelve 305 mm guns and were very decently armored. Capable of going head-to-head with anything the Central Powers could throw at France, Courbet was, along with its sisters, the backbone of Admiral Augustin Boue de Lapeyrere's battle fleet.

Having just heard the news of the incoming Austro-Hungarian fleet, the Admiral felt some nervousness in the form of a tingle racing up and down his spine. He had felt the same before the battle of Taranto during Operation Ares.

"This is it," he told himself as he looked one more time at the report of the incoming enemy fleet. The French fleet had been built for this very reason. Not to fight the British, the allies of France. Not the Germans, as this was the job of the Grand Fleet. The target had always been the Austrians and the Mediterranean. The exact reason the French had built dreadnoughts was because Vienna (and Rome, but that wasn't a problem anymore) had decided to build them first.

The fight was now. The British ships were on their way, but the first clash was going to be between the French and the Austro-Hungarian ships only.

(...)

The battleships from both sides plowed the waves like giant behemoths in a churning sea, side by side and bearing down on each other. The weather was very foul, and the sea was a boiling mess of foaming water, the sky pouring heavy rainfall. The epic wind made it difficult to even stand on deck. But the situation was simply perfect for the Austrian breakout attempt and also to attenuate Haue's fear of losing his precious ships. Thick clouds prevented good visibility from long range, further comforting the Austro-Hungarian Admiral.

(...) The battleship brawl (...

As the first shells landed amidst his fleet, Admiral Anton Haue ordered his ships to keep full steam south. His lookouts had not been able to detect the enemy as efficiently as the French had been. The result of the first few agonizing minutes of the battle, in which only the French fired shots at the K.U.K. fleet, were straddling shots, soaking the decks of the Austro-Hungarian fleet and announcing death was near. Eventually, the range diminished to 9,000 yards, and Haue's ships fired back. However, the Prinz Eugen was hit by a 303 mm shell from Paris. The great ship rocked from the hit but remained otherwise unharmed. Tegethoff suffered the same fate as it was fired upon by a combination of guns from pre-dreadnoughts Democratie, Voltaire, and Verite. Again, Tegethoff's strong armor shrugged off the hits. The blasts were, however, quite impressive, covering the ship with a rolling wall of fire and killing fifteen sailors.

The churning sea continued slashing the decks of both fleets with tall waves and soaking rain. The weather was thus too foul to actually have anything close to accurate shooting. The meant it took another ten minutes and a range of 6,000 yards to see the first significant hits across both enemies.

The first significant one was made by dreadnought battleship Jean Bart's guns on pre-dreadnought Ferdinand Mac's superstructure. The hit reverberated loudly in the ship's hull, producing tremors reminiscent of a small earthquake. A second or two later, another volley bracketed the older Austrian warship on one of its forward turrets. When the smoke cleared above the conning tower, three of its gun turrets were half-mangled and inoperable.

A few additional hits were scored by the French across the Austro-Hungarian fleet. In quick successions, Freidrich, Radetzky, Bebenberg, and Habsburg received damage ranging from critical to light.

Admiral Anton Haue's vessels were not to be undone. By then, the range had closed to 5,000 yards, an effective range for the under-trained Austro-Hungarian gunners. A plethora of shells started to land amongst the French fleet, with several fireballs and debris clouds scattering all around.

Jean Bart lost a turret to a direct hit and Paris got serious waterline damage. Diderot (stern), Danton (funnel), and Vergniaud (bridge) all suffered damage. The most serious hit was on the Concordet, a hit in the boiler room that resulted in a catastrophic explosion.

The Coubert class and the Tegethoff class, the most powerfully gunned ships afloat in the battle, struck each other in succession with multiple volleys. The Austro-Hungarians were (sadly for their crews) the sore losers in the exchange, not being able to score significant hits while receiving important damage to their own selves. The most serious hit of the day so far was on Prinz Eugen, which was slammed hard right down the middle of the ship. The resulting blast destroyed the control tower and the gun control; it killed most of its command crew, including its captain. The battlewagon, smoking, burning, and severely wounded, was not to fire a shot again that day. It started drifting, and the French redirected their fire on the other Austrian ships.

Then, everyone in the battle was startled by multiple fireballs exploding across the French pre-dreadnought battleship Mirabeau, with one of Tegethoff's shells plunging into its deck and igniting its ammo magazine. The entire ship exploded outward in a catastrophic display of fire and death, its debris plunging down in a star-like fashion everywhere around the surrounding Austro-Hungarian ships and in the water.

All the while, the *"smaller"* pre-dreadnoughts also fired madly at each other. While the Austro-Hungarians achieved several hits on their French counterparts, the Entente ships got the best of the exchange, their crews being better trained. Seeing the Prinz Eugen crippled and most of his ships on fire, Admiral Haue's worst fears were realized, and he lost his nerve, ordering his fleet to turn back toward the Northern Adriatic.

(...) Bridge of dreadnought battleship Tegethoff (...)

The ship was groaning from the recent hits, and Admiral Haue could see raging fire just in front of him as the No.1 forward turret had been hit, and the deck was holed in several places. To his left, the Prinz Eugen was almost out, enveloped in a deep and dirty cloud of black smoke, and he could see a bright fire burning inside the cloud. A few secondary explosions raked the ship as well. To his right, battleships Zryniy and Fredrich didn't seem to be faring any better, with multiple fires across their hulls.

Haue watched with nervousness while his ships turned, and his destroyer screen in front was laying a large smoke screen to try and mask his ship's escape. He'd given the order to retreat back to Pola sometime earlier, as it was obvious his fleet wouldn't pass the Otranto Barrage. *"Hell,"* he thought to himself, *"and to think the British fleet isn't even here yet."*

He watched the arcing enemy shells landing amongst his precious fleet and sighed. If only the Emperor and the stupid diplomats had listened to him.

(...) Dreadnought battleship Courbet (...)

"Let them go," said Admiral Augustin Boue de Lapeyrere to his Chief of Staff, asking for orders following the Austro-Hungarian turn. *"But sir," we have them on the run,"* answered the younger officer. *"I know, Vice-Admiral. But we have achieved our objective; the enemy fleet is turning back and remains bottled up in the Adriatic."*

De Lapeyrere had a victory, but it had come at a heavy cost. His ships were battered, and he wasn't interested in pursuing the Austro-Hungarians into their lair. He was also pretty certain the K.u.K. fleet would not come back for a long time.

His decision was not aggressive and there was one part of him that wanted to pursue the enemy. But his ships were seriously damaged, and the British were still a long way away. Thus, if he pursued hard, he would lose more men and ships, and he decided that his strategic purpose was achieved. After all, his orders were quite clear: keep the Austro-Hungarians in the Adriatic and try to avoid heavy damage. He'd succeeded in the first part, while the second goal was not achieved.

"Vide-Admiral, I know we could pursue the bastards, but I am not ready to pay the price. Let's keep it at that for now." "Yes, Sir," answered the disgruntled officer.

And thus ended the Battle of Otranto. The Austro-Hungarians lost the dreadnought battleship Prinz Eugen, while the French lost the pre-dreadnought Mirabeau. Both fleets were raked with heavy damage and would need long months of repairs in the shipyards.

But the end result was that the Central Powers remained stuck in their bases along the Adriatic Coast and could not have any impact whatsoever in the Central Mediterranean nor join the Germano-Ottoman-Greeks in the Bosphorus.

The defeat created yet another major morale crisis for the already shaky Austro-Hungarian Empire, and from there, it wouldn't take much for the country to crumble on itself and call for peace and an end to the war.

EPILOGUE

Strategic situation at the end of February 1915
From France to Romania via Russia

As the white mantle of winter settled hard on the land, war raged across Europe. The frontline was stalemated in France, as the French offensive in Verdun petered out with the arrival of strong German reinforcements in the Verdun area.

The situation was the same in Prussia-Poland, with both the Germans and the Russians settling on the defensive. The Reich had to stop its offensive because of the much-needed reinforcements in France, and the Tsarist forces needed to lick their wounds after the defeat of Koenigsberg. Things were sort of left in limbo until the good weather returned (in the case of the Russians) or when the situation was stabilized (for the Germans).

The situation was a disaster for the Romanians as the Central Powers offensive was now in control of most of the country, even occupying Bucharest, the capital. All remaining Romanian troops had retreated to Moldavia in Imperial Russia to continue the fight. Transylvania was now safe from harm, and the Austro-Hungarian 1st Army was advancing along with the Bulgarian, Ottoman, and German forces against the leftover Romanians.

In Galicia and the Carpathians, the situation was also stabilized, with line upon line of trenches from Poland to the Northern Romanian border. The Austrians were in no position to launch any offensive and could only maintain themselves in the field because of the German troops of General Max von Gallwitz. The Russian forces of General Brusilov were experiencing some supply difficulties and were preparing for an offensive in the Spring or early Summer.

The Balkans were completely under the control of the Central Powers, with Greece, Bulgaria and Turkey part of the alliance and Serbia-Romania occupied. The theater was done, for the moment.

Things had not moved either way in the Ottoman Empire, with a stalemate in the Caucasus and the Turks preparing an offensive on the Suez Canal for the middle of 1915.

The naval war was in full swing, with the German High Seas Fleet poised to sortie to the rescue of beleaguered and adventurous Admiral Maximilian von Spee, trying to escape the clutches of the Japanese and British fleets in the Pacific.

In strategic terms, the war was definitely swinging in favor of the Central Powers for the moment; since Paris was occupied and the Russian offensive was stalled. Greece and Italy were now members of the alliance, and the United States, prone to support the Entente, was staying resolutely neutral.

The summer of 1915 would see much action and decide the fate of entire nations, but for the moment, the snow of February put an end to military operations in Europe.

THE STORY WILL CONTINUE IN BOOK 4 OF THE WW1 ALTERNATE SERIES:

WELTKRIEG 1915

Thank you very much for reading my work.

I HAVE A NEW FACEBOOK PAGE! PLEASE GO AND VISIT:
https://www.facebook.com/profile.php?id=61558770082344

*** Please review my book(s) on Amazon and Goodreads.com and try not to be a troll.
.

*** Send me an email at souvorov@hotmail.com if you feel like chatting with me. I respond to every email.

Some of the books that I have published will soon be for sale on:

www.maxlamirande.com

THE BLITZKRIEG ALTERNATE SERIES
BY MAX LAMIRANDE

Book 1: Blitzkrieg Europa – 2nd Edition – 15 December 2024
Book 2: Battle Europa 2nd Edition – Winter 2025
Book 3: Struggle Europa 2nd Edition – winter 2025
Book 4: Fortress Europa 2nd Edition – winter 2025
Book 5: Stalemate Europa 2nd Edition – TBD
Book 6: Staggering Europa 2nd Edition – TBD
Book 7: Faltering Europa 2nd Edition – TBD
Book 8: Crumbling Europa 2nd Edition – TBD
Book 9: Falling Europa 2nd Edition – TBD
Book 10: Soviet Europa 2nd Edition – TBD
Book 11: Red Europa 2nd Edition – TBD
Book 12: Climax Europa 2nd Edition – TBD
Book 13: The Walder Chronicles Part 1
Book 14: The Walder Chronicles Part 2
Book 15: The Walder Chronicles Part 3

THE PACIFIC ALTERNATE SERIES
BY MAX LAMIRANDE

Book 1: Blitzkrieg Pacific
Book 2: Battle Pacific
Book 3: Struggle Pacific
Book 4: Staggering Pacific
Book 5: Burning Pacific
Book 6: Sallying Pacific
Book 7: Siege Pacific
Book 8: Faltering Pacific
Book 9: Crumbling Pacific
Book 10: Collapsing Pacific
Book 11: Shattering Pacific

THE NAPOLEONIC ALTERNATE SERIES
BY MAX LAMIRANDE

Book 1: *Austerlitz Alternate*
Book 2: *Friedland Alternate*
Book 3: *1809 Alternate – Winter 2025*

THE AXIS ALTERNATE SERIES
BY MAX LAMIRANDE

Book 1: *The Bear and the Swastika*
Book 2: *World War*
Book 3: *Axis Triumphant*
Book 4: *Axis Victorious*
Book 5: *Axis Overwhelming*
Book 6: *Stalemate*
Book 7: *Axis Resurging*
Book 8: *Axis Siege*

THE GREAT WAR ALTERNATE SERIES
BY MAX LAMIRANDE

Book 1: *Schlieffen Alternate*
Book 2: *Great War Alternate (Summer-Fall 2024)*
Book 3: *1915 Alternate*
Book 4:
Book 5:
Book 6:

Also, from the same author:

BLITZKRIEG PACIFIC

The year is 1942.

The world is at war. Almost every major nation has declared for the Allies or the Axis. Europe is occupied by the Third Reich, and the British Islands have been invaded and conquered by the Germans. Metropolitan France has fallen, along with its North African colonies. Spain and Turkey have joined the Axis. The Middle East is Axis. The USA and Soviet Russia are also at war with the Third Reich.

Only one major power is still on the sidelines. Imperial Japan, already busy in its war of conquest in China, dawns on the idea of conquering the Pacific and Southeast Asia following German successes in Europe and the subsequent weakening of the resource-rich Franco-British and Dutch colonies.

The United States, following Japan's occupation of the French colony of French Indochina in 1940, froze all of Tokyo's assets, stopped scrap metal deliveries, and is just about to stop delivering oil to the hungry Japanese military machine, a move certain to trigger a reaction from the warmongers in Tokyo.

President Roosevelt's decision to do so is about to have dire consequences for America. The Imperial Navy has set its sights on the main US base in the Pacific, Pearl Harbor. And all across the Japanese-held islands of the Pacific, the forces of the Rising Sun prepare for a full-scale invasion that they hope will give them control over the resources the country needs to continue on its expansion.

This is the story of the War in the Pacific.

Also, from the same author:

AUSTERLITZ ALTERNATE

DECEMBER 2ND, 1805

The War of the Third Coalition rages in Europe. Battles have been fought, and Napoleon Bonaparte's Grande Armée sweeps everything before it. After a big victory over an Austrian Army in Ulm, the French occupied Vienna, the capital of the Austrian Empire.

The Russians entered Austria to come to the help of their Allies and under pressure from the British. The Austro-Russians and the French are about to clash in a small, unknown town called Austerlitz.

And then everything changes. The French stop trying to retake the Pratzen Heights, and the day's battle ends in a stalemate for both armies. Kutusov, the allied army's leader in the absence of young Tsar Alexander (who fell ill and is still somewhere in Galicia), decides to retire the army northward with the Austrian Emperor's approval. The news galvanizes the Revolution's enemies and of the Empire, jealous of Napoleon's success and wanting him gone. The Prussians decide to join the war and move their troops into Austria to link their forces with the two other powers. The German states and other countries like Naples rethink their stances in the conflict. And the French Emperor's internal enemies, ever wishing the old regime's return, start plotting to overthrow the government in Paris.

All the while, the Ottoman Empire, convinced by the French several months earlier to enter the war, has decided to intervene in favor of Bonaparte and invade southern Hungary with an Army. Austria is on the brink of annihilation, but Napoleon's Grande Armée also has a big challenge ahead since it now needs to defeat three major powers simultaneously.

Everything will come down to either Napoleon's genius to overcome the odds and win regardless of the troops arrayed against him or his defeat and the end of the French Empire.

This is the story of the Napoleonic Wars.

Also, from the same author:

SCHLIEFFEN ALTERNATE

Europe, August 1914.

The world explodes into war as Austro-Hungary declares war on Serbia following the assassination of the heir to the throne, Archduke Franz Ferdinand. Russia follows suit and mobilizes, while Germany supports its ally and declares war on Russia. France then joins the conflict, as it is Russia's ally.

The British intervene when the Germans execute their Schlieffen Plan and attack through Belgium to outflank the French defenses. And then pandemonium explodes everywhere. The Austro-Hungarians attack in Serbia and Galicia, the Russians invade Prussia, and the Germans smash into France. In the Middle East, the Ottoman Empire declares for the Central Powers, while Italy stays neutral.

The German Army is unstoppable and closes in on Paris as the Allies retreat in disarray all along the front. The fate of the world hangs in the balance as a big battle looms for Paris. However, no gains come without giving something away. While the German Army is busy conquering the French and beating the British Expeditionary Force around, the Russians storm Prussia and roll over the German 8th Army. The Reich has all of its remaining troops fighting in the West and nothing fresh to put in front of the Russian steamroller. Koenigsberg falls and the Austro-Hungarians fail before Belgrade and in Galicia. Something will have to be done, or else Berlin will fall to the Russian Imperial forces.

This is the story of a war that might have been.

Also, from the same author:

THE BEAR AND THE SWASTIKA

The year is 1939.

The World rocks with the news of the signing of the Germano-Soviet pact. A dark veil soon falls on Europe as Poland is invaded and destroyed by the overwhelming forces of the Wehrmacht and the Red Army.

France and the United Kingdom can only sit by and watch the two military juggernauts obliterate the Polish state. No one believes the two totalitarian regimes can agree in the long term as their ideologies completely contradict each other.

Russia wants influence in the Balkans, has eyes on Finland, and wants an opening to the Mediterranean. Germany needs Romanian oil to keep its war machine operational, and Hitler is adamant about not letting the Bolsheviks gain another inch of ground in Europe. At least not more than he has already given out in the treaty of non-aggression signed before the Polish campaign.

The year is 1940.

The French campaign then unfolds with a disaster for the Allies, and the Germans win an incredible victory over the combined forces of the United Kingdom and France. British forces narrowly escape to their island with the remnants of their armies, and France surrenders. Half of the country is occupied by the Germans. It seems that the swastika will conquer the world, especially with the Russian bear watching its back.

Germano-Soviet Axis talks were organized in October 1940 concerning the Soviet Union's potential entry as a fourth Axis Power during World War II. The negotiations include a two-day conference in Berlin between Soviet Foreign Minister Vyacheslav Molotov, Adolf Hitler, and German Foreign Minister Joachim von Ribbentrop. The two powers will try to agree on a formal alliance to divide the world.

The fate of liberty hangs in the balance.

Also, from the same Author:

BLITZKRIEG EUROPA – 2nd EDITION

September 1st, 1939.

Germany invades Poland, igniting a major European war. A few months later, the French are also invaded, and the Allied armies are utterly defeated. Then the Dunkirk disaster happens, and the United Kingdom loses most of its land army. Soon, the British Isles are also attacked, and the British are hard-pressed with a serious German invasion. The French struggle to resist the Axis forces bent on conquering all of their mainland home country and West African colonies. Watching from its safe shores, America cannot stay still while Western Europe and all of the Mediterranean fall to the forces of the Axis. And when the Afrika Korps plunges over the Suez and invades the Middle East, the Soviet Union finally decides to join.

And through it all, a hero emerges. Erich Walder, tank commander, will have to fight on all fronts and attempt to survive what the enemy will throw at him.

This is the story of the Second World War.

Also, from the same author:

SPACE WAR, An Empire Divided

The Empire built by Haakon the Great is no more. It's 4124, and the Human race has spread to the stars in four different star clusters by discovering light speed and wormholes. A civil war has broken out between the different human enclaves to see who the next Emperor of humanity will be.

The Ptolemy and Hadesian Star Nations are invading Elysium, allied with New America from the Alpha Perseis Cluster. Large battles are being fought in star systems between former comrades of the Imperial Fleet. In space, battleships unload their powerful weapons at each other while giant battle mechas fight for control of the ground.

The opportunity is too great for the evil Cybernetic forces in the Caldwell 14 Star Cluster. Having fought – and lost – a terrible war against the Empire two hundred years ago, they are gathering for a return engagement against humanity.

A thousand years before, Haakon had dreamed and foreseen a terrible time for humanity. The Black Death is coming to consume all, and his Empire will not be there to fight it.